Sex
Stereotyping
in
Advertising

Sex Stereotyping in Advertising

Alice E. Courtney
York University

Thomas W. Whipple
Cleveland State University

LexingtonBooks
D.C. Heath and Company
Lexington, Massachusetts
Toronto

Library of Congress Cataloging in Publication Data

Courtney, Alice E.
  Sex stereotyping in advertising.

  Bibliography: p.
  Includes index.
  1. Sex role in advertising. I. Whipple, Thomas W. II. Title.
HF5827.C672   1983   659.1'042   80–8115
ISBN 0–669–03955–1

Third printing, December 1984

Published simultaneously in Canada

Printed in the United States of America on acid-free paper

International Standard Book Number: 0–669–03955–1

Library of Congress Catalog Card Number: 80–8115

*To the late Raymond A. Bauer.—*A.E.C.

*To daughters Courtney Whiting Whipple
and Erin Whiting Whipple. Their being was
motivation enough to write this book. May
they benefit the most from it.—*T.W.W.

Contents

Tables

Preface and Acknowledgments

It is now more than a decade since research began to document the portrayals of women and men in advertisements and commercials. The first empirical examination of this field was published in 1971 by Alice E. Courtney, who has maintained an active interest and involvement in this area since that time. Thomas W. Whipple became involved in research in this area in 1972. Since then, he has been among those most actively involved in examining the advertising-effectiveness implications of sex stereotyping.

This book includes the authors' previous work in the field, but draws extensively on what is now a large literature on the subject. Over three hundred published sources in the United States, Canada, the United Kingdom, and other countries contribute scholarly work in the area of sex stereotyping in advertising. The literature comes from marketing, advertising, psychiatry, mass communications, psychology, sociology, women's studies, and many other fields. It documents changes in sex roles as they relate to advertising decision making, and describes, analyzes, and comments on the evidence of, and problems with, sex-role stereotyping in advertising. In this book that literature is reviewed, analyzed, and its implications are assessed.

The first part of the book reviews the literature that documents the portrayal of the sexes in advertising and examines its likely effects on children and adults. Chapter 1 reviews the considerable research evidence developed over the last decade, which shows that the portrayal of women and men is stereotyped and reflects traditional sex-role attitudes. Although there have been noticeable changes in recent years, the chapter concludes that advertising's portrayal is still an inaccurate reflection of sex roles in society today. Chapter 2 discusses the studies that have examined attitudes and opinions toward this portrayal. Both critics and the general public are critical of the way the sexes are depicted. In the final chapter available evidence is examined concerning the societal impacts of advertising's portrayal of the sexes. The chapter concludes that it is indisputable that advertising is a major influence affecting the way children and adults view their sex roles in our society.

The second part of the book looks at the new literature concerning sex-role stereotyping and effective advertising strategy. This part begins with a brief review of buyer behavior and attitudinal changes that have important advertising implications. The remaining chapters focus on the communication effectiveness of alternative portrayals of men and women in advertisements. In chapter 5 those studies are reviewed which examine whether, and under what conditions, more progressive, less stereotyped portrayals are preferred to traditional ones. Chapter 6 discusses the use of sex in advertising and reports the research findings on the communication impact of sexual and decorative portrayals. The final chapter in this section reviews research concerning two special aspects of sex stereotyping: the use of humor and the use of female voices. While issues of advertising effectiveness are often complex, the section as a whole concludes that there is ample opportunity to improve advertising's portrayal of the sexes, while at the same time increasing or maintaining communication effectiveness.

The final part discusses ways to change the portrayal of the sexes in advertising. Here, both social change and advertising effectiveness issues are examined. Chapter 8 discusses future research needs concerning sex stereotyping in advertising. The chapter stresses that research can make an important contribution, both in further documentation of the problem and in measuring the effectiveness of alternative role portrayals. Chapter 9 discusses the contribution to change, which has and can be made by regulatory mechanisms. Industry self-regulation is seen as a preferred channel, both for encouragement of improvement and for monitoring industry performance. In chapter 10 the efforts that can be taken to educate and change the attitudes of the advertising industry are discussed. The chapter concludes that the industry can create advertising that is both progressive and communicates effectively. What is required is a more careful examination of market changes, together with a willingness to experiment with and test new strategies and new creative approaches. Thus the material reviewed and discussed in this book will be of interest to scholars and practitioners in a wide variety of fields: marketing, advertising, women's studies, mass communications, psychology, and sociology.

Acknowledgments

We wish to thank a number of people who encouraged our work in this field and who made substantial contributions to its conception and execution. Among them are Sarah Wernick Lockeretz and the members of the Image of Women Task Force, National Organization for Women, Boston, who in the late 1960s first helped to begin this work; Stephen A. Greyser and others at the Marketing Science Institute who have been supportive of it; and to Elizabeth Whiting Whipple who in 1972 suggested that we collaborate on our first research project. What resulted is a program of research, which culminates in this book.

Both authors are indebted to the many others working in this field—feminists, marketing and advertising researchers, observers, and commentors on social change—whose work informs and inspires our own. We are grateful to the many students and research assistants who over the years have aided in bibliographic searches and data analysis. For bibliographic and editing assistance and for their ideas for this volume, special thanks go to Patricia Burton, Grace Corrigan, Nancy Furey, Susan Herbold, Ellen Hexter, and Rebecca Schechter. We also wish to thank Margaret Rothacker for her skill and patience in helping type the manuscript.

**Part I
The Problem**

1

The Portrayal of
Women and Men
in Advertisements

The 1963 publication of Betty Friedan's *The Feminine Mystique* marked the beginning of a new wave of feminism and was followed by a large number of books and articles during the consciousness-raising decade of the sixties.[1] Friedan's work provides an appropriate starting point for this book because of the method she used to investigate and document the status of U.S. women. Friedan herself wrote for *McCall's Magazine* and became interested in the way women's magazines in general portrayed the U.S. female. As a result of her investigation, she concluded that magazines either reflected or actually fostered and perpetuated a limited life-style for U.S. women by portraying motherhood and the care of home and husband as the ultimate goal of woman's life and her greatest creative opportunity.

Friedan, studying the way women were portrayed, their goals, their aspirations, and their lifestyles, researched women's magazines over the decades of the forties and fifties. She found a change over time in the editorial and fiction content of women's magazines. Friedan found that in the late thirties women were more likely to be portrayed in fiction as autonomous heroines seeking to fulfill their own personal goals, but as the forties progressed, the autonomous heroine gave way to the glorified housewife, praised and rewarded for her efforts to run the household and nurture others. Friedan believed that, having sold women on the idea that regardless of education or aspiration their place was in the home, publishers began to believe their own creation and to think of women as intellectually limited. This led Friedan to research the advertising content of these same magazines. She concluded that manufacturers had decided to make women better consumers of home products by reinforcing and rewarding the concept of women's total fulfillment through the role of housewife and mother. This conclusion was corroborated by quotes from advertising strategy reports which Friedan found in the extensive library of a marketing researcher. Samples of reports described how advertisers might make women feel creative while doing household chores at home using the advertised products.

What is striking about Friedan's work is that she looked for the social definition of women's role in the pages of women's magazines; that she saw the portrayals of women there, both in editorial and advertising, as powerful shaping forces in the social fabric; that she saw the medium of print not only as a documentary tool which helped her investigate and research her ideas, but also as a critical moving force in creating for woman a view of her ideal self. While Friedan's work was not strictly scientific, it was solidly researched and carefully reasoned, and it raised questions which have concerned researchers in the twenty-year period that has followed. Because of Friedan, feminists and others working in the sixties and seventies have investigated much more fully the way the sexes are portrayed in the media and their advertising, and they argue that such portrayals can have a cumulative effect on the way women and men perceive themselves.

The academic research that has now accumulated forms a sizable body of data on the existence of stereotyping and its likely consequences. Two recent bibliographies give evidence of the scope of data available: a 1977 bibliography by Friedman includes over one thousand entries concerning sex stereotyping in media content,[2] and a 1980 annotated bibliography by Courtney and Whipple lists 253 scholarly entries on sex stereotyping in advertising.[3] This chapter will begin an exploration of the highlights of that material by examining the evidence for the existence of and nature of stereotyping in print advertising.

Studying the Portrayal of the Sexes in Print Advertising

A large fund of easily accessible data exists for studying the portrayal of the sexes in print media, and it is therefore not surprising that study of these media formed the basis of the earliest examinations of advertising sex stereotyping. However, there are methodological difficulties which must be considered before examining these studies. As Kassarjian has pointed out, a content study is only as good as the categories it defines and the care taken in isolating them.[4] Good content research is exacting, and the material at hand is often difficult to characterize.

In the case of studying the portrayal of the sexes in print advertising, there are numerous problems. The sheer amount of data available creates problems with respect to sampling, analysis of changes over time, and statistical rigor. For example, some magazines are aimed at a general readership, others at more specialized groups. Which should be examined? Examination of general-interest magazines gives insight into the ways the sexes are presented to each other. Examination of men's or women's magazines may show better how the sexes are presented to themselves. Except in extremely obvious cases, the classification of magazines into such groupings may itself be difficult. For example, while *Sports Illustrated* was initially targeted as a men's magazine, there is evidence of growing female interest and readership.

A definition of the categories to be examined also provides difficulties. Testing a stereotype or role means providing some kind of adequate definition for it. The terms *stereotype* and *role* are subject to unconscious or unintended bias even in the most rigorous studies. For example, in many of the early studies of print advertising, the woman's role is characterized as *working* or *nonworking*. Home settings in advertisements are placed in a category with nonworking portrayals, although the characters shown in the home are usually engaging in household chores. To some people this classification scheme could signify that the researchers believe that housewives do not really work within the home—a view that has become the subject of considerable feminist criticism over the last decade.

Another issue is concerned with the relationship between the characters shown in the advertisements and the product categories studied. In the major print-advertising studies examined here, researchers have defined, with some overlap, over twenty advertised product categories for analysis. The researchers seem to have begun with assumptions such as this: if women are shown buying cars or major household appliances, they can be thought of as responsible decision makers; if they are shown buying only cosmetics and housecleaning products, their decision-making capability is applied only to trivialities. While there is some justification to this kind of argument, it should also be noted that the argument abstracts from marketplace realities which indicate that women are the usual buyers and users of cosmetics and cleaning products. In sum, the size of the cosmetic or housecleaning product market is very large; the individual decision may be small, but the mass implications are not.

Perhaps the most serious issue is that of causality. The issue is whether media advertising merely reflects reality or whether it actually influences and shapes reality by providing role models. Some researchers begin with the view that advertising merely reflects reality and then have to admit on the basis of their study that advertising reflects it badly. In addition, there are serious questions of an approach which judges an attitude or stereotype from one advertisement which reflects a moment in time and may not have any historical context.

The following section of this chapter describes several of the most important studies of sexual stereotyping in print advertising and makes comparisons where possible. That different groups of researchers adopted quite different samples and methods indicates the difficulties of approach previously discussed. However, despite the difficulties, these studies in the aggregate overwhelmingly affirm that sexual stereotyping exists in print advertising. It is striking to find that, no matter what the research approach, the conclusions of all major studies are essentially the same.

Content Analysis of Print Advertisements

The first study of the portrayal of men and women in print advertising to appear in the marketing literature was "A Woman's Place: An Analysis of the Roles Portrayed by Women in Print Advertising," a 1971 study by Courtney and Lockeretz.[5] This article gave rise to several major follow-up studies in the marketing literature and has become one of the most frequently cited and replicated studies on the subject. In this section the major related studies reported in the marketing literature will be discussed. All deal with essentially the same sample frame, although later studies extend the time frame of the analysis and apply more formal statistical testing to the data. The studies to be discussed in this section examine the advertisements in eight general-interest magazines (*Life, Look, Newsweek, The New Yorker, Saturday Review, Time, US News & World Report,* and *Reader's Digest.*).

The first replication of "A Woman's Place" was conducted by Wagner and Banos in 1973, who sampled advertisements appearing twenty months later than those initially studied.[6] Belkaoui and Belkaoui added historical analysis to the sample in their 1976 study.[7] The final follow-up to be discussed here is by Wolheter and Lammers in 1980; their study adds 1978 data to the analysis and extends its scope by focusing on the male roles portrayed in print advertising.[8]

Courtney and Lockeretz sampled advertisements appearing in April 1970. They analyzed the number and sexes of the adults appearing in the advertisements, their occupation and activities, and the types of products with which they were shown associated. Emphasis in the analysis was placed on the working roles shown, the kinds of occupations pictured for men and women, and the relative monetary importance of the products advertised. In the 1970 advertisements 45 percent of the males depicted were shown working outside the home. Only 9 percent of the women were so shown; of these, 58 percent were entertainers, and the remainder were depicted in low-status jobs. No woman was portrayed as a high-level business executive or a professional. Nonworking activities of men and women were also analyzed. Among the 90 percent of women who were shown in nonworking roles, 23 percent were shown in family roles, 46 percent in recreational settings, and 31 percent in nonactive or decorative roles. Just over half of the men were shown in nonwork settings; of these, 22 percent were shown with the family, 56 percent in recreational settings, and 22 percent in decorative roles. Product categories also were examined to determine if the preponderance of one sex or another was making the purchase decision or using the advertised product. Courtney and Lockeretz concluded that women were found to be portrayed as buyers of articles like cleaning aids and cosmetics, but men were shown purchasing more important and expensive items like cars, bank services, and industrial goods.

From their analysis Courtney and Lockeretz concluded that four general stereotypes of women were shown in print advertisements: a woman's place is in the home; women do not make important decisions or do important things; women are dependent and need men's protection; and men regard women primarily as sexual objects. These conclusions corroborated the feminist viewpoint, and the authors concluded that more research was warranted to inform advertisers of women's current attitudes toward this kind of advertising portrayal.

Wagner and Banos, who replicated the study almost two years later, found that the percentage of women shown in working roles had grown to 21 percent and that the women shown working outside the home were portrayed in more responsible jobs. In nonworking roles women were shown less in family settings and more often in decorative or nonactive ones. Females, however, were not depicted very often as interacting with each other in the work situation or as independent of men in making major purchases. The authors concluded that the changes observed reflected a cautious response to social change on the part of advertisers, but that a large enough percentage of women in society still worked exclusively in the home to at least partially warrant their depiction there in advertisements.

Belkaoui and Belkaoui were critical of these two initial studies because they did not provide a prior historical context for the findings to show change over time. To remedy the problem Belkaoui and Belkaoui studied a sample of the same general-interest magazines from 1958 (prewomen's movement) and compared this to the previously discussed samples from 1970 and 1972. The authors concluded that print advertising does depict men and women differently in working occupations, in nonworking roles, and in the nature of buying. The 1958 sample showed 13 percent of women in working roles, compared to 9 percent in 1970, and 21 percent in 1972. The predominant female working role in 1958 was secretarial-clerical; in 1970, entertainer; in 1972, once again as secretarial-clerical. Belkaoui and Belkaoui noted that, in nonworking portrayals, women's images changed from predominantly family roles in 1958 to decorative ones in 1972. The sex predominantly shown buying various product categories had changed little from 1958 to 1972. The authors concluded that stereotypes from the prewomen's movement had remained and that advertising was not keeping up with the times in portraying the diversity of women's roles.

Wolheter and Lammers examined these same issues from the male standpoint. Their study, examining advertising in 1958, 1968, and 1978, is closely modeled on that of Belkaoui and Belkaoui. Wolheter and Lammers found that during the twenty year period examined, the male working roles depicted have moved away from the portrayal of big-business leaders and military men and toward entertainment and sports figures. Also, it became more common to see men portrayed in nonworking roles (42 percent in 1958; 57 percent in 1968; 54 percent in 1978). The number of males shown in working settings had decreased from a high of 58 percent in 1958 to 46 percent in 1978. The number of men shown in decorative roles had increased from 27 percent in 1958 to 54 percent in 1978. However, the male and female portrayal in family roles had changed very little. Although in 1978 more women were working outside the home and advertising might therefore be expected to show an increasing percentage of men engaging in family roles, this was not found in the data.

A related study, conducted during the same time period but using a somewhat different sample of magazines, is that of Weinberger, Petroshius, and Westin.[9] They concluded that between 1972 and 1978 there was an actual downturn in the number of occupational roles portrayed by women in print advertisements. However, they discovered that when women were portrayed in working roles, there had been significant gain in portrayals of professional and middle-level-business professions; this gain was at the expense of portrayals in clerical and secretarial roles.

Together, the studies indicate that men and women are indeed shown stereotypically in advertising in general-interest magazines and that over a twenty-year period there have been only minor changes. In particular, the studies confirm that in print advertising woman's place is in the home and that women are primarily concerned with household tasks and personal beauty. Men are more likely to be shown working outside the home and to be involved in the purchase of more expensive goods and services. Both sexes, but particularly the female, are likely to be shown in nonactive, decorative roles in print advertisements.

Advertising in More Specialized Magazines

A number of studies have looked at wider categories of magazines and the advertising in them. This section discusses several of the most important research studies. In 1974 Sexton and Haberman reported their analysis of almost two thousand advertisements appearing in *Good Housekeeping, Look, Newsweek, Sports Illustrated,* and *TV Guide.*[10] The advertisements studied were selected from three time periods: 1950–1951, 1960–1961, and 1970–1971. Advertisements for six product categories used by both sexes were analyzed, and each advertisement was rated on an eleven category system which included examination of such factors as role, relationship to product, and traditional versus nontraditional situations.

Sexton and Haberman found that over the two decades advertisements had not moved very far from a narrow picture of women. Only 16 percent of advertisements presented women in nontraditional situations. The essential selling traits used in the portrayal of women were alluring, decorative, and traditional. Results of the analysis were also reported by product category. In cigarette advertising women were shown primarily as social companions and infrequently or rarely as workers or housewives and mothers. Over the years women became more likely to be shown in their decorative capacity, rather than being portrayed in a wider range of roles and situations. This trend toward increasing use of the female as an allurement or decoration was also found in advertising for beverages, automobiles, and airlines. In advertisements for office equipment and airlines, women were shown as employees or public personalities. However, the authors noted a general impression in such advertisements that women were rarely depicted in a leadership capacity and that their working tasks remained traditional.

Venkatesan and Losco's 1975 study of women in magazine advertisements examined the period 1959–1971.[11] The study compared three time periods: 1959–1963 (prewomen's movement period); 1964–1968 (active civil-rights, equal-rights period); and 1969–1971 (awareness period). Over 14,000 advertisements were selected for study from four general-interest magazines (*Reader's Digest, Time, Saturday Review, Life*); four women's magazines (*Harper's Bazaar, Cosmopolitan, Ladies' Home Journal, Better Homes & Gardens*) and four men's magazines (*Argosy, Esquire, Sports Illustrated, Evergreen Review*). The three most common images found by the authors were woman as sexual object, woman as physically beautiful, and woman as dependent on man. However, the study also showed that the portrayal of women as sex objects had decreased since 1961, although this stereotype was still prevalent in men's magazines and general magazines. The theme of women as dependent on men appeared stable in all three time periods and was found in almost one out of every four magazine advertisements containing at least one woman. The authors concluded that over time there had been a relative decline in those images of women found most obnoxious by women's groups. Nevertheless, like other analysts of the portrayal of women in magazine advertisements, they concluded that advertisers were insensitive to real social conditions and to the characteristics of contemporary women.

A recently published study of U.S. advertising, *Rhetoric and Ideology in Advertising* examined the portrayal of the sexes in the context of a much wider study of advertising content and imagery.[12] The four Scandinavian authors studied 300 advertisements appearing in fourteen U.S. magazines in 1973. The magazines included: *McCall's, Redbook, National Geographic,* and *Playboy*. With respect to the analysis of the roles of women, findings were similar to those of North American investigators. For example, the authors discovered that the number of advertisements in which women only are associated with housework is eleven times greater than the number associating housework with men. Conversely, men are associated three times as often as women with work outside the home. Moreover, women are more likely than men to be shown seeking personal beauty as a goal. The authors were particularly concerned that the advertisements studied implied that women must be strong, tough, independent, and beautiful; this they saw as a prostitution of the values of the women's liberation movement. A similar perspective is found in an article by Warren, who argued that advertising is built around inducing women to fear sexual inadequacy unless they buy advertised products.[13] The portrayal of women as concerned with beauty or as concerned with nurturing of families is viewed by Warren as inducing women to become loved by buying and using products.

Another important approach to measuring the portrayal of the sexes in magazines is that of Pingree, Hawkins, Butler, and Paisley who developed a scale for sexism and tested it against advertisements run during 1973–1974 in *Time, Newsweek, Playboy,* and *Ms.* [14] The sexism scale, developed by the authors, contains five levels. The most stereotypical level, level one, shows women as sex objects. Level two keeps women in their places by showing them in traditional activities. Level three shows professional women whose first place is in the home. Level four shows the sexes as fully equal, and level five shows men and women in individual, nonstereotyped roles. Using this scale for analysis, the authors concluded that the majority of advertisements analyzed portrayed women at the two most stereotyped levels. The findings indicated that even in *Ms.* the most frequently shown role (56 percent) was that of housewife. Of the *Playboy* advertisements, 54 percent were found to be at level one and 34 percent at level two. In *Time,* 73 percent of advertisements were at these two levels; in *Newsweek,* 78 percent. The authors concluded that the print representation of women does not reflect reality and that the image of women in advertisements is significant in influencing women's perception of themselves. They further noted that men are equally stereotyped, but in a reverse of the way women are: men are seen more typically in the work place but are not as responsible for or competent at home care.

Two studies have examined the special issue of the portrayal of women in sports. Slatton's 1971 study traced the role of women in sport as portrayed in advertising in five major magazines from 1900 through 1968.[15] Slatton concluded that advertisements portraying women in sport show only a recreational interest with little acceptance of sport's competitive aspects. Poe, also examining magazine advertisements over a long time period, concluded that sports advertisements were more sexual than athletic in portrayal and that women were shown in recreational rather than competitive situations.[16]

Finally, there is one published study examining trade magazines. McKnight, a female engineering student, investigated 130 engineering and trade magazines in 1974.[17] Her analysis was often subjective, but nevertheless useful. McKnight found that 35 percent of these periodicals contained at least one sexist advertisement during the month studied; 9 percent contained at least two, and many contained more than two. In addition to showing women as passive, silly, or incompetent, some of the advertisements used semiclad or naked female bodies to attract attention to equipment.

In total, the series of studies reported in this section point to a solid body of empirical evidence that magazine advertising presents a stereotyped image of the sexes, particularly in depicting women as decorative, as sexual objects, as working only in the home, and as dependent on men. These results have been derived from a wide variety of studies, employing a wide variety of print media, and examining a fairly extensive time period. While the studies show some improvement in women's portrayal over time, the evidence is that the improvement is minimal and stereotypical portrayals continue to be the norm.

Visual Imagery in Magazine Advertising

A number of important studies approach the identification of sexual stereotyping in print advertising from a radically different standpoint. These studies examine stereotyping primarily from the visual imagery portrayed in magazine advertisements through the use of convenience samples of advertisements. However, they come to conclusions that are startlingly similar to those of the more traditional forms of content analysis reported earlier.

One of the most provocative analyses of visual imagery takes the form of a filmed slide show of print advertisements showing women. Jean Kilbourne has produced this film, *Killing Us Softly: Advertising Images of Women,* to show the portrayal of women from the 1930s to the present.[18] Kilbourne's emphasis is on the sexual portrayals of women. She shows many examples of the representation of women in what other researchers have called the decorative role and analyzes the sexual imagery portrayed in such advertisements. In her view, blatant sexual imagery is used, and many advertisements imply that sexual access to the female is the reward for buying the advertised product. Viewed singly, most advertisements in Kilbourne's film seem acceptable. However, after viewing hundreds of slides showing women's sexual portrayal in advertising, the cumulative impact is extremely powerful. Women viewers of the film typically become shocked and angry at what they perceive as exploitative and degrading sexual imagery.

Kilbourne's film is expressly designed to show the extent of, and problems with, advertising's portrayal of women, and her sample of advertisements is therefore expressly selected for this purpose. However, more scientifically drawn samples of print advertising have illustrated many of the same problems. Trevor Millum examined and analyzed the images of women as portrayed in British magazine advertisements.[19]

Millum developed an analytical scheme for the examination of visual imagery used to portray women in these advertisements. His analysis concluded that the most common images of women portrayed in British magazine advertising were: mannequin, narcissist, hostess, and wife/mother. Millum found that women most often were shown with a mannequinlike expression, devoid of personality; men were more often shown with thoughtful expressions. These categories, developed from a radically different analytic approach and from British advertisements, nevertheless reflect the themes of decorative/alluring portrayals, and in-home/nurturing portrayals that have been reported in the North American content studies.

Dispenza's illustrated anthology of advertising in the United States from 1900–1975 reveals similar themes.[20] Dispenza found six major themes in the advertisements studied: facial beauty, domestic matters, and women's relationship to their homes; the progression from early romance and courtship through engagement and marriage; to motherhood; women's shapes and fashion; the *spare parts* attitude toward women (that is, the focus on their body parts in isolation); and, finally, health and health products.

The most complete study of visual imagery in U.S. advertisements is Erving Goffman's 1976 study, *Gender Advertisements*.[21] Goffman's monograph presented an analysis of approximately five-hundred print advertisements chosen from newspapers and popular magazines. Goffman's perspective is that advertisements do not necessarily depict how men and women actually behave, but that they are a good representation of the way we think they behave. Thus Goffman, in this work, has chosen a series of advertisements to illustrate the details of that stereotyped portrayal. He concentrates on fine details such as the use of hands, facial expressions, and relative sizes of the people in the advertisements. The advertisements Goffman chose for study were reproduced in black and white and were organized into six major areas for analysis: relative size, the feminine touch, function ranking, the family, the ritualization of subordination, and licensed withdrawal. Goffman found that women were almost never shown as taller than men, except in the rare instances where men were shown to be of subordinated social class. Women, more than men, were pictured using their fingers and hands to cradle or caress objects in advertisements. Women were found by Goffman to be portrayed in subordinate occupational roles, and when housework scenes were shown, males were shown in no contributing role at all. In addition, Goffman found that women were more likely to be shown in recumbent positions, including lying on the floor or a bed. Women were often shown in knee-bent or head-cant positions and were often displayed in a childlike guise. Women, more than men, were pictured engaged in involvements which removed them psychologically from the social situation. Goffman concluded that advertisers do not create the ritualized portrayals they employ, but rather conventionalize what already exists in our society.

An interesting analysis of advertising, which uses both visual and verbal content as a basis for examination, is that of Posner.[22] Posner has engaged in a program of research on the sexual messages explicit and implicit in print advertising. She has collected slides of print advertisements and examined the relationship between the verbal and visual content of the advertisements. With respect to verbal content, she looks for instances of ambiguous language and double entendre. In analysis of visual imagery, Posner classifies the content into four major categories: facial expression, setting, body language, and clothing. Then, Posner looks at the advertisement as a whole and examines the relationship between the two kinds of content.

Using this technique, she concludes that the sexual overtones in advertising are pervasive and often demeaning and dangerous. She shows slides to demonstrate that advertising exploits the image of the liberated female by implying that she is sexually available, that advertising often portrays women as seductresses or witches, and that advertising often uses crudely erotic imagery to sell products. She is particularly concerned with sado-masochistic symbolism in advertising, for example, bondage props and poses. One of the interesting features of Posner's work is her analysis of the sexual imagery used to portray men in advertisements; for example, she analyzes the macho image of men in advertising and its sexual implications.

These studies indicate the need for additional content analyses to further document the body language and visual imagery used to portray the sexes in advertising. In particular, sexual imagery requires additional study.

Medical-Journal Advertising

There is a significant body of research which has examined the imagery of women in medical-journal advertising, with particular concern for the image of women in psychotropic-drug advertising to doctors. Studies by Seidenberg,[23] Stimson,[24] Mant and Darroch,[25] Mosher,[26] and Prather and Fidell[27] have all examined this area.

Each of these articles studied advertisements in medical and psychiatric journals; one also examined direct-mail advertisements to doctors. Focusing on advertising of psychotropic drugs, the Seidenberg studies described the results of the author's personal examination of ten years of U.S. medical publications. On the basis of that examination, Seidenberg contended that advertisers, in order to boost sales, widen the indications for these drugs from mental illness to include everyday problems of living. Moreover,

Seidenberg concluded that there is a sexist bias in such advertisements, with women being almost always portrayed unfavorably in drug advertising. He cited advertisements that recommend tranquillizers to alleviate the tedium of everyday tasks like dishwashing or to calm a female patient who is disturbing her family with menstrual symptoms or manifestations of anxiety. The other authors corroborated Seidenberg's findings, noting that in U.S., British, and Australian journals, women are much more likely than men to be portrayed in advertising for psychotropic drugs. The authors all contend that such advertising reinforces doctor's prejudice against women and causes them to prescribe mood-altering drugs, rather than dealing with the cause of women's problems.

Conclusions: The Image of the Sexes in Print Advertising

This section has reported a wide variety of studies describing the portrayal of women and men in print advertising. The evidence of these studies is overwhelming: in print advertising, woman's place is still in the home; women are still dependent on men; women still do not make independent and important decisions; women still view themselves and are viewed by others as sex objects; women are more likely than men to be depressives requiring medical treatment. Men are also stereotyped, but in reverse of the way women are portrayed. In the next section the portrayal of the sexes in television advertising will be reviewed to determine if the picture of the sexes is similar or different on television.

**Studying the Portrayal of the Sexes in
Television Commercials**

In a recent television commercial a young woman smartly dressed in a navy uniform runs toward an aircraft. The voice-over, a woman's carefully modulated tone, says, "I got a last minute call to work the 7:00 a.m. flight, and wouldn't you know it—everything went wrong." Another stewardess, the viewer thinks, but the woman in the commercial enters the airplane cockpit and sits down in the copilot's seat. She is the product representative in a deodorant commercial, and she is one of the few females to be seen in television advertising today in an occupation of some status and responsibility outside the home. She speaks for herself; no male voice-over breaks in to confer authority on what she says. No overt attempt is made to draw attention to her occupation and register that it is exceptional in any way. Among the legion of happy housewives who pass across television screens, the copilot is an exception. Even she, however, is a long way from being the equal in status to the male pilot in the seat beside her.

If the viewer tries to imagine the commercial rerun with a man rushing toward the aircraft, the picture becomes clearer. Would a male pilot use the phrase "wouldn't you know it" and, if he did, what impression would he leave? Would a male airline pilot be shown running toward his aircraft in the course of normal duties, and, if he were, what impression would it convey? Would a male pilot worry about perspiration, and, if he did, would he admit it? The female pilot is exceptional, and she knows it, and it makes her sweat. She is running hard to keep her life organized and to keep her job.

This section will survey many of the studies that have examined the content of television commercials and the roles of the sexes within them. However, as the deodorant commercial illustrates, these content studies often fail to capture important elements of the commercials. A world of complexity can be packed into a thirty-second commercial, as the example indicates. Compared to print advertisements, the television commercial is difficult to capture. Complexities of meaning are not easily categorized; nuances of body language are hard to measure; tones of voice and their effects are difficult to capture; differences in male versus female acting styles defy categorization. At least part of the problem is not matter, but manner, and the studies to be reported here have only superficially examined manner. For example, almost all of the studies to be discussed counted the percentages of male versus female voice-overs. But there is a world of difference between the many commercials where a bewildered female on camera is told what to do by the male voice of authority, and a recent tire commercial where the female voice-over asks advice from the authoritative male product representative on camera. A simple counting of male versus female product representative and voice-overs would fail to register the similarity of sex-role portrayal in the two commercials.

The studies of television commercials to be reported here were developed in much the same way as the studies of print. The earliest work in the area consisted of commentary on the role of women in commercials based on informal observation. This commentary encouraged academic researchers to conduct more scientifically based content-analysis studies. In time, these early studies were replicated to document the changes in portrayal which had taken place. The majority of television studies, like those in print, concentrated on the matter of the portrayal of the sexes; that is, on counting such factors as occupational roles, product-category associations, and sex of voice-over. A recent bibliography on sex stereotyping in advertising contains thirty-four citations dealing with portrayal of the sexes in television commercials.[28] Most of the studies cited use similar sampling and coding procedures and come to similar conclusions. In this section, therefore, only the most significant of those studies have been selected for discussion.

Content Analysis of Television Commercials

One of the earliest examinations of the portrayal of women in commercials, by Bardwick and Schumann, included no formal data analysis but was a disquieting report of the investigators' observations of women's portrayal.[29] The authors noted particularly the contradictory characteristics of the housewife in commercials—the woman who is responsible and expert at home and yet in need of authoritative male advice; the woman who battles dirt, which is never shown in any realistic sense, so that her efforts to clean an already spotless home seem anxiety ridden. As this section will show, data-based studies amply confirm Bardwick and Schumann's informal observations.

The first major content study of television commercials was conducted by the New York City chapter of the National Organization for Women (NOW). The NOW study was reported in 1972 in the *New York Times Magazine* by Hennessee and Nicholson.[30] The study was conducted in New York City over a period of one and one-half years, and 1,241 commercials were examined. Almost all showed women in the home: 42.6 percent of the women were involved in household chores; 37.5 percent as adjuncts to men; 16.7 percent as sex objects. Only 0.3 percent of the women in the commercials were found by the NOW researchers to be shown as autonomous individuals. In 54.4 percent of the sampled food advertisements and 81.2 percent of the cleaning advertisements, men were shown as the beneficiaries of women's services. The authors noted that women in commercials never tell men what to do, but that men are constantly advising women: 89.3 percent of the voice-overs used in commercials were male.

Like the comparable studies of the print advertisements of the period, the NOW study found that commercials rarely showed women as consumers of high-ticket items. For example, car commercials accounted for very little of daytime advertising but were concentrated in evening prime time along with advertisements for banks and insurance. Conversely, men fared badly on the domestic scene, being shown as incompetents when it came to doing household tasks (although expert in advising women how to do them). Men were shown outside the home in a wide range of activities; however, for women, self-betterment seemed to be equated with sex appeal and cleanliness. The authors stressed the force of repetition of these images and their likely cumulative effect upon the self-images and behaviors of men and women.

The first major scholarly study of female stereotyping in television commercials was conducted by Dominick and Rauch.[31] They sampled almost one thousand commercials shown on New York City network stations in prime time during April 1971. Commercials were selected for analysis if a woman appeared for three seconds or more or had one or more lines to speak. Variables analyzed were product advertised, sex of voice-over, sex of prime purchaser, setting, dress, and apparent occupation of female represented, on-camera selling by females, and primary role of the woman in the advertisement. A comparative sample of men appearing in a selection of commercials was taken to measure the differences in the portrayal of the sexes. Dominick and Rauch measured intercoder reliability and applied statistical tests to measure the significance of their findings.

The most striking finding of the study was that 75 percent of all advertisements using females were for products generally found in the kitchen or bathroom. According to the commercials studied, a woman's place was in the home: 38 percent of women were shown inside the home, but only 14 percent of men. The single largest occupation for females was housewife, with over half so portrayed. When women were shown with out-of-home occupations, they were found in a subservient job; women appeared in eighteen different occupations compared to the forty-four shown for men. As found in the NOW study, voice-overs were predominantly male: 87 percent used a male voice, 6 percent a female one, and 7 percent a chorus. In addition, 60 percent of the on-camera product representatives shown were male.

The results also showed that women were overrepresented in commercials for cosmetics and personal-hygiene products. Conversely, they were underrepresented in commercials for cars, gas, and oil. Dominick and Rauch concluded that the typical female in commercials was a young housewife at home, in the kitchen or bathroom, anxiously receiving the advice of an authoritative male, relating to others in a service role, or concerning herself about how to look beautiful.

Another early study was that of McArthur and Resko who examined 199 commercials from the spring of 1971.[32] While their primary findings reflect those of Dominick and Rauch, the interest in this study lies in its examination of authority roles in advertisements. The authors found that 70 percent of men were presented as authorities, but only 30 percent by virtue of product use. Of the 14 percent of women who were authorities, 86 percent were portrayed as product users. Men were also more likely to give an argument for the use of the product; 30 percent of women gave no argument at all compared to 6 percent of men.

Silverstein and Silverstein studied commercials shown in 1973.[33] Findings with respect to occupational roles, voice-overs, product representatives, and product-category associations were similar to those of earlier studies. However, the authors also studied some additional variables of interest. For example, they found that women gave advice in commercials for female and household products, but that more women than men were given advice in every product category. In the sample of commercials studied, there were fifteen explicit directions given, all to women.

Trends during the 1970s. In a 1974 article Courtney and Whipple provide longitudinal and comparative data on the portrayal of women in commercials.[34] Their research compared four studies conducted between April 1971 and February 1973, including the Hennessee and Nicholson and Dominick and Rauch studies reported previously as well as research conducted in Washington, D.C. and Toronto, Canada. Looking at the studies as a group, the authors concluded that: men accounted for 85 percent or more of voice-overs; men dominated as on-camera product representatives in commercials aired during prime-time hours; women predominated as product representatives only in female cosmetic advertising; women were shown predominantly as housewives and mothers, while men where shown in at least twice as many occupations; almost 40 percent of women shown were portrayed within the home, compared to about 15 percent of men; female product representatives were shown most often performing domestic duties, while male product representatives demonstrated product features but did not actually use the product; men were seen as beneficiaries of products used, and of services performed, by women; and older, intelligent males told younger, scatterbrained females what to do and why. The authors noted that over the two-year period covered by the four studies, the number of female product representatives had increased significantly and had become equal to the male. However, while women product representatives predominated in daytime television, men predominated in prime time. The conclusion reached by Courtney and Whipple was that there was little change in the portrayal of the sexes in television advertisements; the typical woman in commercials was still the bewildered young housewife.

Marecek, Piliavin, and others compared trends in sex-role portrayals for the years 1972, 1973, and 1974.[35] Their findings concerning the roles portrayed by the sexes, product representatives, and voice-overs were similar to those of other investigators. However, their work has special interest because they examined male versus female expertise as portrayed in commercials. Experts were defined as characters who delivered authoritative statements about the product, either to viewers or to other characters in the commercial. In commercials which did not contain voice-overs, and these comprised about half of the sample, the proportion of women in the role of expert was 46.8 percent; most of these commercials were for food, household, or feminine-care products. In those commercials where there was a voice-over or both male and female expertise shown, the authors found a highly significant increase between 1973 and 1974 in the proportion of commercials in which the female was the last voice of authority heard. In 1973 a female got the last word in 14 percent of commercials; by 1974 the female percentage had increased to 26 percent. The commercials in which females had the last word were again those for traditionally female products.

A study of television commercials shown during prime time in November 1976 further updated the picture of the portrayal of the sexes.[36] O'Donnell and O'Donnell's study of 367 commercials showed that there had been little change, and some of that negative. Males and females continued to appear in equal numbers as product representatives but women still represented domestic products (86 percent) and appeared in the home (76 percent), while men dominated the nondomestic product categories and settings. The male continued to be the voice of authority; in fact, male voice-overs had increased to 93 percent.

Schneider and Schneider provided another comparative study of the portrayal of sex roles in television commercials.[37] Their sample of approximately three hundred commercials aired in Minneapolis/St. Paul during October 1976 was compared to Dominick and Rauch's 1971 sample. In addition, Schneider and Schneider compared their findings to census data showing changes in population data over the period. Among the major variables studied were age of character portrayed, employment, and employment status.

Schneider and Schneider showed that over time television commercials had become more likely to show older adults. The trend was from portrayal of exclusively young adults to an increasing portrayal of the over-fifty age group. However, women still continued to be shown as relatively younger than men. Female characters were still more frequently portrayed as married in 1976—by 20 percent. Although married men and women were both underrepresented compared to census figures, men were especially so. As regards employment, the authors found a decrease in the percentage of both sexes shown as employed. By 1976 males were still more likely than women to be shown as employed (48 percent males; 18 percent females), but the gap had narrowed. Women shown working outside the home were still more likely than men to be shown in white-collar occupations (60 percent male, 74 percent female). With regards to the setting of the commercial, the trend was to show fewer males in outdoor settings; although the proportion for females in these categories had not changed. The differences between the female and male portrayal had narrowed, but the direction involved showing more men in the home, not more women in out-of-home settings.

Schneider and Schneider concluded that there was still considerable difference in the portrayal of men and women in television commercials, but that the trend from 1971 to 1976 had been toward at least a more realistic portrayal in terms of census data. They considered that this was a measure of social and advertiser acceptance of changing sex roles in the United States.

In a related study Kenneth Schneider had fourteen male and female subjects rate a sample of forty-eight commercials shown on-air during 1976.[38] The subjects rated the commercials using semantic pairs designed to measure the personality characteristics of the men and women portrayed. As rated by Schneider's subjects, the female characters in the commercials

were more concerned about the appearance of their home and more dependent on the opposite sex than were male characters: this confirms previous
findings from content-analysis studies. However, Schneider's study is interesting because of the insight it gives about the portrayal of men and the differences between prime-time and daytime commercials. According to subjects' ratings, men were portrayed more positively than women in prime-
time commercials. Female characters were generally rated as less able
spouses, less mature, more foolish, and less successful than male characters.
In daytime commercials the situation reversed, and women were found to
be portrayed more positively than males on similar dimensions. Schneider
concludes that, with respect to portrayed personality traits, male characters
are portrayed as negatively as female characters. The real difference comes
with the time of day in which the commercial is shown.

   A very recent follow-up study by Sharits and Lammers extends these
findings about the male role in commercials.[39] Using a similar methodology
to Schneider's, these researchers asked male and female business-school
subjects to rate their perceptions of the roles portrayed in over one hundred
television commercials. Their results showed that women in the commercials were rated more favorably than were men: the female models were
perceived to be better spouses and parents, more mature, more attractive,
more interesting, and more modern. Little difference was found in the
perceptions of the models between male and female subjects. Of particular
interest is that Sharits and Lammers conclude that men are increasingly filling a sex-object role in commercials.

The Situation in the 1980s. One of the most recent content studies to be
reported added new data derived from a content analysis of 1,631 commercials aired on network television in July 1980.[40] The purpose of this
research, conducted by Pesch and others, was to assess changes in sex-role
portrayals since the mid-1970s and to focus on an issue not previously
stressed, the difference between daytime and prime-time television.

   In the findings for daytime television commercials, male voice-overs
had increased to 92 percent compared to earlier results, which are in the
mid-to-high 80s. On afternoon television 72 percent of the product representatives were female. Female product representatives were shown in fam-
ily/home occupations (83 percent), while the male product representatives
were portrayed in business or management occupations (67 percent).

   In the prime-time commercials 90 percent of voice-overs were male,
again dominating all product types. Males and females were equally likely
to be seen as product representatives in prime time. As in previous studies, a
relationship was found between sex of product representative and product

category; for example, all car advertisements studied employed male product representatives.

The researchers concluded that afternoon television still showed the traditional woman. While women predominated in the advertisements as characters and product representatives, they were still shown within the home and as subject to the male voice of authority. In prime time the majority of women were still shown in the home and the majority of men in business settings, but the margins of difference were less than those found in the studies of 1970s commercials.

The studies examined in this section confirm the existence of sex stereotyping in television commercials, paralleling similar stereotyping in print advertising. In both media, despite some minor improvements over time, women's place continues to be the home, where women serve their husbands and children and defer to male authority. On television, that male authority, exemplified by the voice-over, has, in fact, increased during the ten-year period under study.

It is important to note that stereotyping of women goes hand in hand with stereotyping of men. Unfortunately, little research to date has examined the details of the male portrayal in television commercials, nor the way in which that portrayal may be changing with changing times. However, this question does deserve more systematic research attention, particularly because public protest about male stereotyping is beginning to be heard. For example, a recent newspaper article entitled ''Wimps?'' concluded that men in television advertisements are becoming feminized: they do not walk, but slink; they are afraid of their children and submissive to their wives; ''They are seriously interested in the thought of Alan Alda.''[41] Whether such allegations can be substantiated is an empirical question that should be examined more carefully. Schneider's work suggests that day-part differences may be an important dimension.

The conclusions reached about the portrayal of men and women in television advertising should be viewed in the larger context of their portrayal in television programming. Here too, research indicates widespread stereotyping. As Gerbner and Signorielli concluded in their study of television drama from 1969 to 1978, ''Marriage, romance, and family are women's concerns in the world of television.''[42] Much research shows that, in television programming, as in its advertising, women perform traditional female activities such as cooking, cleaning, and childcare, while men engage in traditional male activities, such as drinking, smoking, and working in the backyard. Women, in addition, fill a smaller number of roles in programming than do men, are less likely to be shown as employed, are less likely to be shown in professional roles, are less likely to be shown as aggressive, and are more likely to be dominated and victimized.[43] In short, programming shows similar stereotypes to those revealed in the analyses of commercials.

The Portrayal of Children in Television Commercials

Several researchers have paid special attention to the portrayal of children in the television commercials which are directed to them. In children's commercials, as in adult-oriented advertising, there is evidence of significant sex bias. One of the earliest to research this area was Barcus in a report prepared for Action for Children's Television in 1971.[44] Barcus concluded that the characters in toy advertisements on Saturday morning television programming were usually identified by sex roles. He typically found commercials where girls played with dolls and boys with cars, planes, and mechanical devices. Products advertised to girls contained themes of popularity and beauty, while boy-oriented commercials centered around power, poise, and speed. A follow-up study by the same author in 1975 found that spokesmen for the products advertised on children's television were adult and male in 90 percent and 72 percent of cases respectively.[45] Moreover, male characters in the commercials outnumbered females two to one.

In 1974 Chulay and Francis reported a further study of the portrayal of girls on Saturday morning television commercials.[46] From analysis of almost three hundred commercials showing female children, they concluded that television advertising was orienting the girl to a traditional feminine role, as the wife and mother concerned about her appearance and accepting the role of sex object. Chulay and Francis noted that the independent woman and the woman who is successful in business is not shown in children's television commercials.

Research by Doolittle and Pepper in 1975 also examined the content of children's television advertising.[47] Comparing their recent study of commercials to two previous ones, they found no evidence of increasing efforts to portray a society in which the sexes are equal. They concluded, on the contrary, that sexual stereotyping in children's commercials was increasing. Similar results were reported by Verna in 1975.[48] She found that male-dominated advertisements made up more than half of those sampled, while female-dominant advertisements accounted for less than one-seventh (the remainder were sexually neutral). The female was placed in predominantly passive activities, and her behavior was almost always dependent on a role or activity involving another person or doll. Even the commercial style was stereotyped. Commercials for boys were marked by numerous cuts, loud sound tracks, and aggressive activity. Commercials for girls featured fades and dissolves and background music. A 1979 study by Cattin and Jain confirms and updates these findings.[49] Cattin and Jain reported an analysis of one hundred children's commercials in which they found that boys were portrayed more actively than girls and that boys are especially dominant in nonfood advertising.

These studies indicate that, like the adult female, the girl in commercials plays a stereotyped role. Girls are portrayed as more passive than boys. They are shown assisting their mothers in serving men and boys. They are shown learning household tasks and ways to become beautiful. They are not shown learning how to become independent and autonomous.

Conclusions: The Image of the Sexes in Television Commercials

This review of over ten years of content research into television commercials confirms that sex stereotyping exists and that it applies to both adult and child portrayals. The issues—in-home versus occupational portrayals; authority roles; product-category stereotyping; and so forth—are virtually identical to the issues found in the examination of print advertising. And the most recent content-analysis studies show that little progress and improvement have been made.

It is important to note again the limitations of the kinds of content studies examining television. While these studies have well documented the matter of the stereotyped portrayal, they fail to measure many aspects of the manner of portrayal that are relevant to understanding the true nature of the images of the sexes in commercials. Many critics of advertising have focused on manner. They note that women are often seen to be almost ecstatic in their reactions to products—their voices rise in joy over a new cleaner, they literally run to tell their neighbors about it, they wilt and almost cringe in embarrassment over faults in their housekeeping, they exult in having cleaner washes than their neighbors. While such criticisms may sound exaggerated, they have been confirmed by a Canadian advertising-industry task force on advertising and women.[50] The task force report noted that when commercials had been examined in storyboard form, they seemed acceptable. But in complete form, the same script seemed much less acceptable. The execution of the commercial, the task force found, had given a sexist tone arising from stereotypical acting styles, the quality of women's voices, and the general style of the commercial.

The reader undoubtedly has his or her own favorite example: the woman who happily 'Shouts' it out, the woman who is ashamed by ring around the collar, the woman whose life revolves around her dirty oven, the woman who finds sexual fulfillment by choosing a whitening toothpaste (or a deodorant, or bra, or perfume), the women who makes family life worth living and saves a marriage by serving a moist cake, the woman who happily tricks her family into using the foods that are 'best' for them. The examples are legion. While content research into television advertising has made major contributions in defining aspects of this portrayal, it has not effectively delineated these questions of manner of portrayal which constitute the most pervasive form of stereotyping. A recent example shows how the manner of portrayal can simultaneously show an unflattering portrait of both sexes.

In a recent commercial for Tide detergent, a male announcer convinces a housewife that she can write a commercial for Tide. The wife says that she tested Tide against another brand her husband bought on sale (wife indicates sheepish husband), and found that Tide worked better than the sale brand. Her conclusion: if you've got a husband who shops for you, better tell him to get Tide (husband hangs his head in shame). On paper, the commercial may seem innocuous, even slightly humorous, but in the actual advertisement, the tone of voice used by the woman makes the message very clear: daddy is a dummy; mommy is an expert—at washing clothes.

The Image of the Sexes in Print and Television Advertising

The overwhelming conclusion of content research is that advertising presents the typical woman in the home, while her labor-force role is underrepresented. She is shown as a housewife and mother dependent upon male authority for her decisions. She is shown as desperately in need of product benefits to satisfy and serve her husband and family, and it is from this service that she draws her self-esteem. In addition, she has a pressing need for personal adornment to help her attract and hold a man. Rosemary Scott, summarizing her review of this research, noted that the advertising portrayal as a whole showed two roles for women: attracting and attaining a man, and then serving him in the role of housewife and mother.[51] Three tables summarize the findings from this large body of research, organized according to the following areas: table 1-1, how the sexes are portrayed; table 1-2, presence of the sexes in advertising; and table 1-3, special issues and problems. Despite the fact that the issues summarized in these tables were first documented from empirical research by the authors in the early 1970s,[52] recent monitoring studies show that there has been only minimal improvement in advertising's portrayal of the sexes. Women and men in society today clearly are far different from their portrayed images in advertising. As sex roles continue to change and expand at a faster rate than the advertisers' response, the image of the sexes in advertising is not keeping pace with change. In fact, the image reflects the status quo of a time gone by.

Table 1–1
How the Sexes Are Portrayed

Areas of Stereotyping	Research Findings
Portrayals of housewives	Females are predominantly shown as housewives and mothers, while males are shown in many occupations.
	Females are almost three times more likely than males to be shown inside the home.
	Subservient role portrayals: women are most often seen performing domestic tasks, men demonstrate products but do not use them.
	Women serve men and boys; men and boys do not serve women.
	Dependent role portrayals: men tell women what to do; explain what products to buy; tell how to use them.
	Women are shown as isolated from other women.
Portrayals of girls	Girls are shown as more passive than boys.
	Girls are shown assisting mothers serving men and boys; girls are shown learning household tasks, beauty roles.
Portrayals of sexuality	Women are more likely than men to be shown in decorative or nonfunctional roles.
	Women are more likely to be portrayed through exaggerated acting, stereotyped voice tone and stereotyped body language.

Source: Alice E. Courtney and Thomas W. Whipple, *Canadian Perspectives on Sex Stereotyping in Advertising* (Ottawa: Advisory Council on the Status of Women, 1978), p. 83.

Table 1–2
Presence of the Sexes in Advertising

Areas of Stereotyping	Research Findings
Authorities	There is a very low level of use of females as announcers, voice-overs, and other authority figures.
Product representatives	Males dominate as product representatives during prime-time hours.

Table 1–2 continued

Areas of Stereotyping	Research Findings
Product representatives continued	Females dominate as product representatives only in female cosmetic advertisements.
	Male product representatives demonstrate products; women are shown in housewife roles using products.
	Women are more prominent in personal-product advertising (cosmetics and so on).
	There is a low presence of women in advertising for big-ticket products and services.

Source: Alice E. Courtney and Thomas W. Whipple, *Canadian Perspectives on Sex Stereotyping in Advertising* (Ottawa: Advisory Council on the Status of Women, 1978), p. 84.

Table 1–3
Special Issues and Problems

Areas of Stereotyping	Research Findings
Health issues	Active women and women engaged in sports are not shown.
	Drug advertising addressed to doctors shows women as passive, dependent, and with exaggerated or imagined symptoms.
Aging	Older men are shown, but not older women. The typical woman portrayed is younger than the typical man portrayed.
Minority groups	Female members of minority groups are not shown in advertising.
Liberation stereotyping	Liberation is belittled, used as a vehicle to show dominant women and stupid men, or as a vehicle to sell beauty products.
Personal product advertising	Women's undergarments and personal-hygiene products are advertised on television. Equivalent male products are not advertised on television.

Source: Alice E. Courtney and Thomas W. Whipple, *Canadian Perspectives on Sex Stereotyping in Advertising* (Ottawa: Advisory Council on the Status of Women, 1978), p. 85.

Notes

1. Betty Friedan, *The Feminine Mystique* (New York: W.W. Norton and Company, 1963).

2. Leslie J. Friedman, *Sex Role Stereotyping in the Mass Media* (New York: Garland Publishing, 1977).

3. Alice E. Courtney and Thomas W. Whipple, *Sex Stereotyping in Advertising: An Annotated Bibliography* (Cambridge, Mass: Marketing Science Institute, 1980).

4. Harold H. Kassarjian, "Content Analysis in Consumer Research," *Journal of Consumer Research* 4 (June 1977):8–18.

5. Alice E. Courtney and Sara Wernick Lockeretz, "A Woman's Place: An Analysis of the Roles Portrayed by Women in Magazine Advertisements," *Journal of Marketing Research* 8 (February 1971):92–95.

6. Louis C. Wagner and Janis B. Banos, "A Woman's Place: A Follow-up Analysis of the Roles Portrayed by Women in Magazine Advertisements," *Journal of Marketing Research* 10 (May 1973):213–214.

7. Ahmed and Janice Belkaoui, "A Comparative Analysis of the Roles Portrayed by Women in Print Advertisements: 1958, 1970, 1972," *Journal of Marketing Research* 13 (May 1976):168–172.

8. Maralinda Wolheter and H. Bruce Lammers, "An Analysis of Male Roles in Print Advertisements Over a 20-year Span: 1958–1978," in *Advances in Consumer Research,* ed. J.C. Olson (Ann Arbor: Association for Consumer Research, 1979), pp. 760–761.

9. Mark G. Weinberger et al., "Twenty Years of Women in Magazine Advertising: An Update," in *Proceedings: The 1979 Educator's Conference,* eds. N. Beckwith et al. (Chicago: American Marketing Association, 1979), pp. 373–377.

10. Donald E. Sexton and Phyllis Haberman, "Women in Magazine Advertisements," *Journal of Advertising Research* 14 (August 1974):41–46.

11. M. Venkatesan and Jean Losco, "Women in Magazine Ads: 1959–1971," *Journal of Advertising Research* 15 (October 1975):49–54.

12. Gunner Andrew et al., *Rhetoric and Ideology in Advertising* (Stockholm: Liber-Forlag, 1978).

13. Denise Warren, "Commercial Liberation," *Journal of Communication* 28 (Winter 1978):169–173.

14. Suzanne Pingree et al., "A Scale for Sexism," *Journal of Communication* 26 (Autumn 1976):193–200.

15. Yvonne L. Slatton, "The Role of Women in Sport as Depicted in Advertising in Selected Magazines, 1900–1968" (Ph.D. diss., University of Iowa, 1971).

16. Alison Poe, "Active Women in Ads," *Journal of Communication* 26 (Autumn 1976):185–192.

17. Diane McKnight, "Sexism in Advertising: What's a Nice Girl Like You . . . ," *Technology Review* 76 (May 1974):20–21.

18. Jean Kilbourne, *Killing Us Softly: Advertising Images of Women,* Film. Available from Jean Kilbourne, P.O. Box 385, Cambridge, Mass.

19. Trevor Millum, *Images of Women: Advertising in Women's Magazines* (Totowa, N.J.: Rowman and Littlefield, 1975).

20. Joseph E. Dispenza, *Advertising the American Woman* (Cincinnati: Standard Publishing, 1975).

21. Erving Goffman, *Gender Advertisements* (Cambridge, Mass.: Harvard University Press, 1979).

22. Judith Posner, "Sexual Sell: Or We Do It All For You," manuscript (Atkinson College, York University, Toronto, 1981).

23. Robert Seidenberg, "Advertising and Abuse of Drugs," *The New England Journal of Medicine* 284, no. 14 (1972):789–790; idem, "Drug Advertising and Perception of Mental Illness," *Mental Hygiene* 55 (January 1971):21–31; and idem, "Images of Health, Illness and Women in Drug Advertising," *Journal of Drug Issues* 4 (Summer 1974):226–267.

24. Gerry V. Stimson, "The Message of Psychotropic Ads," *Journal of Communication* 25 (Summer 1975):153–160; and idem, "Women in a Doctored World," *New Society* (May 1975):265–267.

25. Andrea Mant and Dorothy Broom Darroch, "Media Images and Medical Images," *Social Science and Medicine* 9 (November–December 1975):613–618.

26. Elissa Henderson Mosher, "Portrayal of Women in Drug Advertising: A Medical Betrayal," *Journal of Drug Issues* 6 (Winter 1976):72–78.

27. Jane Prather and Linda S. Fidell, "Sex Differences in the Content and Style of Medical Advertisements," *Social Science and Medicine* 9 (January 1975):23–26.

28. Courtney and Whipple, *Sex Stereotyping in Advertising: An Annotated Bibliography.*

29. Judith M. Bardwick and Suzanne L. Schumann, "Portrait of American Men and Women in T.V. Commercials," *Psychology* 4 (1967): 18–23.

30. Judith Adler Hennessee and Joan Nicholson, "NOW Says: Commercials Insult Women," *The New York Times Magazine,* 28 May 1972, pp. 12, 48–51.

31. Joseph R. Dominick and Gail E. Rauch, "The Image of Women in Network T.V. Commercials, *Journal of Broadcasting* 16 (Summer 1972): 259–265.

32. Leslie Zebrowitz McArthur and Beth Gabrielle Resko, "The Portrayal of Men and Women in American T.V. Commercials," *Journal of Social Psychology* 97 (December 1975):209–220.

33. Arthur Jay and Rebecca Silverstein, "The Portrayal of Women in

Television Advertising," *Federal Communications Bar Journal* 27 (1974): 71–98.

34. Alice E. Courtney and Thomas W. Whipple, "Women in T.V. Commercials," *Journal of Communication* 24 (Spring 1974):110–118.

35. Jeanne Marecek et al., "Women as T.V. Experts: The Voice of Authority?" *Journal of Communication* 28 (Winter 1978):159–168.

36. William and Karen J. O'Donnell, "Update: Sex-Role Messages in T.V. Commercials," *Journal of Communication* 28 (Winter 1978):156–158.

37. Kenneth and Sharon Barich Schneider, "Trends in Sex Roles in Television Commercials," *Journal of Marketing* 43 (Summer 1979):79–84.

38. Kenneth C. Schneider, "Sex Roles in Television Commercials: New Dimensions for Comparison," *Akron Business and Economic Review* (Fall 1979):20–24.

39. Dean Sharits and H. Bruce Lammers, "Men Fill More TV Sex Roles," *Marketing News,* 3 September 1982, pp. 1, 6.

40. Marina Pesch et al., "Sex Role Stereotypes on the Air Waves of the Eighties," (Paper delivered at the Annual Convention of the Eastern Communication Association, Pittsburgh, April 23–25, 1981).

41. Dick Dabney, "Wimps?", *The Toronto Star,* 18 January 1982, p. A 10.

42. George Gerbner and Nancy Signorielli, *Women and Minorities in Television Drama, 1969–1978* (Research report, Annenberg School of Communications, University of Pennsylvania, 1979), p. 17.

43. For a review of this literature, see Leslie J. Friedman, *Sex Role Stereotyping in the Mass Media;* and Bradley S. Greenberg et al., *Life on Television—Content Analysis of U.S. TV Drama* (Norwood, N.J.: Ablex, 1980).

44. F. Earle Barcus, "Saturday Children's Television: A Report of T.V. Programming and Advertising on Boston Commercial Television," (Report prepared for Action for Children's Television, Newton, Mass., July, 1971).

45. F. Earle Barcus, "Television in the Afternoon Hours," (Report prepared for Action for Children's Television, Newton, Mass., 1975).

46. Connell Chulay and Sara Francis, "The Image of the Female Child on Saturday Morning Television Commercials," (Paper delivered at the Annual Meeting of the International Communication Association, New Orleans, La., April 17–20, 1974).

47. John Doolittle and Robert Pepper, "Children's TV Ad Content: 1974," *Journal of Broadcasting* 19 (Spring 1975):131–142.

48. Mary Ellen Verna, "The Female Image in Children's TV Commercials," *Journal of Broadcasting* 19 (Summer 1975):301–309.

49. Phillipe Cattin and Subhash C. Jain, "Content Analysis of Children's Television Commercials," in *Proceedings: The 1979 Educator's*

Conference, ed. N. Beckwith et al. (Chicago: American Marketing Association, 1979).

50. Task Force on Women and Advertising, *Women and Advertising: Today's Messages Yesterday's Images?* (Toronto: Advertising Advisory Board, 1977).

51. Rosemary Scott, *The Female Consumer* (New York: John Wiley, 1976).

52. Alice E. Courtney and Thomas W. Whipple, *Canadian Perspectives on Sex Stereotyping in Advertising* (Ottawa: Advisory Council on the Status of Women, 1978).

2 Attitudes toward Sex Stereotyping in Advertising

In addition to being a subject of research investigation, the issue of sex stereotyping in advertising has received a great deal of public attention during the last decade. The presence of many articles in newspapers and magazines, complaining about advertising's portrayal of the sexes, testifies to the high level of general interest and public concern. The public reaction and press coverage have almost invariably been critical.

Polls of media audiences consistently find that the majority of consumers agree with the critics that advertising is insulting to both men and women. Government agencies and the advertising industry also have contributed to the public debate regarding the portrayal of the sexes in advertising. They have spoken out on the issue, conducted seminars, and sponsored research studies.

Attitudes and opinions toward sex stereotyping in advertising are reviewed from various perspectives in this chapter. The views of audiences of advertising, critics and other public spokespeople, industry self-regulatory and government agencies, and advertising practitioners are included.

Audience Attitudes

Although a segment of society has been openly critical of advertising's portrayal of the sexes for over a decade, are their complaints supported by the attitudes and opinions of real people? In other words, is this issue important to the general public or are only radical feminists concerned about the portrayal of women in advertising?

General Criticisms

Beyond the numerous content-analysis studies of advertisements, the empirical research which has examined the question of how the consumer in general, and women consumers in particular, view sex-role portrayals in advertising is rather limited. However, the results of public-opinion polls completed to date have shown consistently that significant numbers of consum-

31

ers agree that advertising is insulting to women. One of the first opinion polls, which focused on attitudes toward advertising, was conducted in 1971. A survey of *Good Housekeeping* magazine readers found that 40 percent of those responding felt that television commercials were insulting to women.[1] Kovacs concluded that many women simply do not recognize themselves in the advertising of the 1970s.

Significantly more *Redbook* than *Good Housekeeping* readers appeared to have negative attitudes ten years ago regarding the portrayal of women in advertising. Seventy-five percent of the people who responded to a 1972 *Redbook* survey agreed that the communications media downgrade women by portraying them as mindless sex objects.[2] However, seven years later, U.S. women who responded to another *Good Housekeeping* survey had changed their behavior and attitudes during the 1970s.[3] They claimed that they were watching less television than even a year ago. The biggest turnoffs, according to the sixty-thousand respondents, were too much advertising and too many offensive advertisements. The most common complaint cited was that commercials are stupid in the way they portray people.

Critics Specific Complaints

The critics of advertising report many of the specific problems already documented by empirical research and discussed in chapter 1. In addition, they have cited new areas of complaint not covered by formal research studies. In a 1978 report for the Canadian government's Advisory Council on the Status of Women,[4] Courtney and Whipple classified critics' complaints into three areas of criticism of sex stereotyping: portrayals of housewives, sexual portrayals, and liberation stereotyping.

Portrayals of Housewives. Public spokespeople have been particularly critical of unfavorable personality styles of housewives as depicted in advertisements. Women are shown as obsessive about cleanliness and as having exaggerated love for and need for household products. Other personality problems shown are women's isolation from, fear of, and jealousy of other women. Nagging wife portrayals receive their share of complaints too.

Critics are concerned also about advertising's condescending portrayal of women's intelligence and capabilities. Women are shown as low in intelligence and unable to make decisions about household or personal matters without the advice of a male. These condescending portrayals are enhanced with the use of language which is belittling to women. Phrases such as "little woman;" "my wife, I think I'll keep her;" and "I try to spend my husband's money well" are criticized as examples of language which keeps a woman in her place.

Sexual Portrayals. Concern about the way women are portrayed in advertising also has been expressed regarding sexual portrayals. In addition to the prevalent 1970s portrayal of women as homemakers in advertising, chapter 1 documented the existence of the female sex-object portrayal. The portrayal of women as sexual objects in advertising to specifically attract the attention of men is criticized as demeaning. This image of women has been attacked by a number of groups representing various audiences of advertising. For example, in 1971, the first European church-sponsored conference on the image of women in the mass media focused their criticism on sexual portrayals.[5] They specifically attacked the use of scantily clothed women to sell everything from liquor to automobiles. Beauty-product advertising to women also has been denounced for preying on female insecurities. Advertisements which exaggerate the need for personal adornment and the desire to get and hold a man are major targets for criticism. A variety of groups has concluded that a negative image of women contributes to the discrimination against women in filling important jobs.

Do other groups, composed of people of both sexes and varying in age, share this concern over sexual appeals in advertising, or are these attitudes limited to specific audiences? To explore the possibility that differences in consumer attitudes toward the use of sexual appeals in advertising may reflect the perceived gap separating the younger generation and their parents, Wise, King, and Merenski conducted a study to compare the attitudes of six hundred middle-aged consumers with those of their college-aged offspring.[6] The survey results indicated that the older group of consumers of both sexes and the younger females voiced the strongest agreement with the statement "advertisers make too much use of sex appeals in their advertisements." The more sexist attitudes expressed by the younger group of males were interpreted by the researchers to be a negative sign for those advocating changes in attitudes toward sex stereotyping in advertising. The study concluded that attitude changes, especially among males, are required to eventually achieve significant changes in advertising's portrayal of the sexes.

Liberation Stereotyping. Female liberation has been used, on occasion, as a rationale for greater use of women in advertising. However, the critics have complained that under the liberation banner women now can be exploited sexually in advertising by increasing the use of women as sex objects. In addition, the liberated female is either portrayed as the supermom who washes with three temperature detergent, the natural woman who uses hair color, or the innovator who uses new personal products such as feminine-hygiene spray. Besides complaints about the content of personal-product advertising, many women have criticized the media scheduling or timing of television commercials for such products.

Product Category Problems

In an attempt to identify the sources as well as the subjects of offensive
advertisements which turn off women, the Ontario Status of Women Council sponsored a study in 1974–1975.[7] They requested organizations and individuals on the council's mailing list to monitor advertising and to report
specific instances of advertising that respondents found offensive to
women. The report contained views from over five-hundred respondents on
approximately one-thousand advertisements, categorized by the offensive
aspect of the advertisement.

Objectionable advertisements were found in all major media, but television received the brunt of the criticism. Women objected to stereotyping or
demeaning roles in advertising, to intellectually patronizing portrayals, to
the use of women as sex objects, and to the public exposure of intimate
products. To provide further insight into the things that women found
objectional, the advertisements also were classified by product type. Complaints were received about advertising in a wide variety of product categories, with laundry and dishwashing advertisements leading the list. Feminine-hygiene advertisement examples were a close second in number of
complaints, followed by advertising for personal apparel, hair, and beauty
products; household cleaners; cigarettes; retail stores; and automobiles.

Studies conducted during the late 1970s and early 1980s supported the
concerns over the advertising of feminine-hygiene products, especially on
television. The 1979 *Good Housekeeping* study,[8] referred to earlier in the
chapter, found that high on the list of complaints were embarrassing advertisements for feminine-sanitary products, including the most recently mar-
keted deodorant-vaginal sprays. A 1980 survey by the Marschalk Company
found that feminine-hygiene advertising was the most disliked product
advertising on television.[9] However, the report notes that probably this
finding is due more to the product itself than to the advertising. Based on a
1981 study of product-category advertising, the researchers at Warwick,
Welsh, & Miller concluded that products such as feminine hygiene, laxa-
tives, bras, and girdles are inherently objectionable irrespective of the
advertising treatment.[10] Other less sensitive products, such as jeans and
pantyhose, were found not to be objectionable as such, but the manner in
which these commercials often are executed were considered in poor taste
by both men and women.

Another measure of public criticism comes from complaints received by
the Advertising Standards Council (ASC) of the Advertising Advisory
Board (AAB). The ASC administers the Canadian Code of Advertising
Standards, a code developed by the advertising industry for the purpose of
self-regulation, particularly in the area of untruthful and misleading advertising. Crandell stated that during the 1970s most complaints reaching the

council concerning women and advertising dealt with offensive sexual innuendo and advertising of specific products.[11] In 1977 the ASC received a
large number of complaints specifically about television advertising for
women's personal products. However, because it was beyond the council's
purview in 1977 to tell advertisers whether or not promotion of their products was permissible or to deny them access to any media of their choice, the
ASC took no further action at that time.[12]

It is important to note that the Canadian Code of Advertising Standards did not include any reference to sex stereotyping nor to insulting or
denigrating portrayals of the sexes in 1977. Such problems were considered
by the council to be matters of taste and opinion and thus were specifically
excluded by the code. It is reasonable to expect that the percentage of complaints concerning the portrayal of the sexes in advertising may have been
significantly higher if such concerns had been covered by the code in 1977.
Chapter 9 includes a more thorough discussion of the code and the changes
made since 1977, which now incorporates sex-stereotyping issues.

Changing Portrayals and Attitudes

In an attempt to determine if the controversy over the portrayal of women
in television commercials has had any real impact, Ogilvy and Mather, a
New York advertising agency, conducted interviews among consumers in
1978.[13] The results show that one-third of consumers feel that television
commercials' portrayal of women is better, while one-quarter think the
treatment of women has actually worsened during the 1970s. Forty percent
of the respondents mentioned older people as the group most often unfairly
treated on television, with women the next most mentioned group. In commercials for neutral products, such as headache remedies, and in advertisements for credit cards, cosmetics, and frozen dinners, a working-woman
presenter was found to be more believable. On the other hand, commercials
for home-oriented products were judged more believable if the presenter
was a housewife.

Although some advertisers are playing up women's new roles in their
advertisements, supposedly to their product's advantage, all attempts do
not meet with consumers' approval. In a 1980 survey of women's attitudes
toward advertising, conducted by J. Walter Thompson Company, criticism
of "new" women advertisements was expressed. Rena Bartos, a senior vice
president for the agency in charge of the study, said she found a "certain
resentment of tokenism and toward advertisements exploiting the women's
movement."[14]

A 1981 survey of three-hundred full-time homemakers suggests that
marketers should be wary of characterizing the working mother as today's

liberated superwoman.[15] Although the superwoman syndrome may account for the fact that nearly 70 percent of the respondents feel society is pressuring women to go to work to be a complete, independent woman, the results do not support the myth that stay-at-home moms are miserable, traditional women. According to Batten, Barton, Durstine & Osborn, Inc., the survey sponsors, millions of stay-at-home moms are turned off by the glorified working woman. They advise that advertisers must avoid moving from one stereotype to another and instead address the many facets of today's woman.

A report of a nationwide survey of public attitudes about television, prepared by Jones et al. for the U.S. Commission on Civil Rights, calls for a halt to such discrimination.[16] A random, cross section of U.S. viewers expressed a strong desire for changes regarding women and minorities. The survey developed by the Screen Actor's Guild, was sent to newspapers throughout the country. Of the viewers responding, two-thirds said they would like to see women appearing on television in positions of authority; for example, as spokeswomen for national products.

Profile of the Critical Consumer

In 1975 the National Advertising Review Board (NARB), the U.S. advertising industry self-regulatory body, released a study expressing very strong feelings on the advertised image of women. Evidence referenced by a NARB panel, which prepared the report, suggests that women vary markedly in their attitudes toward their role portrayals. The strongest critics, according to the report, are likely to be younger, more highly educated, and more prone to be opinion leaders. The document also noted that a United Nations committee reportedly blames advertising for "perpetrating the derogatory image of women as sex symbols and as an inferior class of human being."[17]

In 1981 the consultive NARB panel followed up their 1975 study when they commissioned a survey by the Gallup Organization on consumer complaints about advertising.[18] The findings indicated that half of the respondents had wanted to complain about an advertisement during the past year, but that only 16 percent of those who wanted to actually did so. Consequently, the real critical consumer segment, who finds faults with advertising and wants to complain about misleading or deceptive advertisements, women's personal product advertisements, and advertisements that insult the intelligence of the consumer, is significantly larger and broader than many profiles may indicate.

Carruthers' study of women who complained to the Canadian counterpart of the NARB, the Advertising Advisory Board (AAB), found that Canadian and U.S. advertising critics have similar profiles.[19] The ninety-three women who complained to the AAB in 1976 concerning the portrayal of women in advertising were, in general, young, well educated, and employed, many in professional occupations. Those who registered specific complaints about the advertising of personal-feminine products, on the other hand, were primarily married, aged forty-one or older, and only about one-half were employed, mainly in secretarial or clerical positions.

A published U.S. public-opinion survey provides further empirical evidence of the profile of critical consumers and their attitudes toward sex-role portrayals in advertising. Lundstrom and Sciglimpaglia investigated whether women and men are critical of the way they are shown in advertisements and whether the portrayal affects their attitudes toward products.[20] Their 1977 study results indicate that women generally have more critical attitudes than do men. Women, more than men, found advertising to suggest that they do not do important things, that they are portrayed offensively, and that their place is in the home. In addition, women felt that they are more sensitive than men to their role portrayals. However, women were less likely than men to agree that advertising treats women as sex objects. The authors conclude that the role portrayal of women is a problem in that a sizeable portion of women are critical. Those who were most critical appear to be more articulate and influential, younger, better educated, upper-status women who have rejected the values and stereotypes of the traditional role of women's place in society. Considerable proportions of the women surveyed indicated that they would alter their purchasing behavior due to advertising they considered offensive, but these women did not necessarily fit the profile of the strongest critics. The findings suggest that even though a product's advertising may be perceived as offensive to men and women, many would continue to purchase the particular product.

An experimental comparison of women's self and advertisement image, conducted by Witkowski,[21] produced results which concur with Lundstrom and Sciglimpaglia's survey findings regarding women's perceptions. Witkowski found that there is a significant difference between women's self-perceptions and their perceptions of women portrayed in magazine advertising. By showing women in a greater variety of useful roles and less often as decorations or housewives, he concluded that such advertising would be a more accurate reflection of how women view themselves and not how men picture them. His findings, however, differed somewhat from Lundstrom and Sciglimpaglia's results concerning the impact of advertisement image on the critical consumer. According to Witkowski, consumer opinion about the portrayal of women in advertising may not be limited to negative attitudes toward the medium or to a poor self-image. He concluded that significant perceptual differences indicate that certain advertisements alienate some female market segments, resulting in fewer sales and an increased public criticism of the advertising profession.

How the Public Concern Has Been Interpreted

During the 1970s government agencies at both the provincial and federal levels in Canada investigated the public concern about advertising expressed in reader surveys conducted by U.S. and Canadian magazines. Seventy-two discussion groups conducted in the province of Ontario during 1973 generated information concerning the effect of communications on personal and family life.[22] One significant finding was that several groups felt that commercials slight a number of social groups in our society, notably women, the aged, and immigrants.

In 1978 the Canadian government narrowed the research focus to attitudes toward television advertising in a nationwide survey of over three thousand Canadians.[23] The study found that 59 percent of the respondents believed television advertising to be insulting to women. This clear majority opinion is significant when compared to the results concerning the portrayal of men. Forty percent of respondents agreed that advertisements are insulting to men, 30 percent disagreed, and 30 percent neither agreed or disagreed. Although opinions are split over attitudes toward male portrayals, 80 percent agreed that commercials do not show people the way they really are in our society.

Although much of the criticism and research which sparked interest for the Canadian government investigations originated in the United States, similar U.S. government attitude and opinions surveys have not surfaced to date. U.S. government agencies, such as the Federal Communications Commission and the Federal Trade Commission, traditionally have avoided free-speech issues involving matters of individual interpretation. Sex stereotyping in advertising, as far as they are concerned, may fall under first amendment jurisdiction and consequently merit no governmental action.

Practitioner Attitudes

Appeals to marketing managers and advertising executives, that they must recognize the emergence of the liberated working woman as a distinct market segment and develop alternative promotional strategies to reflect changes in women's attitudes and roles, began in the early 1970s. DuBrin and Fram recognized that many women are offended by the sexist and/or chauvinistic nature of media advertising.[24] They also noticed that buyer behavior of the middle-class woman was changing, as evidenced by her avoidance of those products which reinforced the stereotype that women should be content to be homemakers. To successfully cope with women's liberation, they claimed advertisers must change media's portrayal of women. However, a panel discussion at a women and advertising symposium,[25] sponsored by *Glamour* magazine, concluded that the label *working woman* is, in fact, just another marketing stereotype. The panel contended that advertisers are missing the point with working-woman advertising. They emphasized that the typical career woman functions as a working woman, but also as a mother, homemaker, sports enthusiast, and as an individual.

By 1978 practitioners had stated that advertising's approach to women had changed and was still changing. But some of the old stereotypes, which many new women find annoying, were expected to appear in advertisements because they sell. It was predicted that advertising will reflect changes in roles, mainly where they are relevant to product use and the product user. If advertising portrays women in stereotypical roles, it is not necessarily a case of a male-chauvinist conspiracy, so claimed Jennifer Stewart, a spokeswoman for the industry.[26] In large part the reason for showing stereotyped portrayals, she argued, can be attributed to the advantage of being able to communicate instantly and nonverbally with stereotypes.

One explanation for differences in advertising strategies to male and female consumers is related to the sex orientation of the product being advertised. Some products are oriented toward consumers of one sex, while others can be used by both sexes. Although it is common and may be a sound strategy to introduce a product as polarized to one sex, after that market is penetrated the mass market of the other sex offers new opportunities for a marketer. However, Stuteville argues that the sequence of communication when moving a product from femininity to masculinity differs from the reverse.[27] He illustrates, for example, that to introduce hair spray to men necessitates the use of supermasculine symbols, while women accept many male-oriented products with fewer, less feminine symbols. This unequal communications process, according to Stuteville, may be indicative of the unequal status of masculinity and femininity in our culture and contribute to the underlying reasons the portrayal of the sexes in advertising has been criticized so extensively during the last decade.

Female advertisers, who have experienced discriminatory portrayals first hand from both sides of the television camera, could be expected to be more sensitive to sex-stereotyping issues in advertising than their male counterparts. However, interviews with seven high-placed women in the advertising world found that most of them take a middle-of-the-road position with respect to the controversy surrounding the portrayal of women in television commercials.[28] On the one hand the women executives all said they backed the basic goals of the women's movement, such as equal pay for equal work. But at the same time none of the women saw anything offensive about advertising campaigns which had been severely criticized by feminists. One of the female executives did state, though, that almost all advertising art directors are men; this, in her opinion, is one of the reasons advertising is often insulting to women.

The six winners of the American Advertising Federation's 1974 Advertising Woman of the Year award basically agreed with the women advertising executives and did not agree with the criticism voiced by feminists about the portrayal of women in advertising. They claimed that only a small percentage of women object to being shown as housewives and mothers. Further, Levere reported that their opinion is that modern advertising has responded a significant amount already to the women's movement.[29]

To empirically investigate whether in fact there are gender differences in socially responsible advertising decisions, Surlin asked eighty-five male and twenty-seven female advertising executives in Atlanta, Georgia to respond to a questionnaire.[30] The survey instrument measured attitudes toward socially responsible advertising-content decisions and respondents' self-reported professional behavior. The content decision areas which produced the most significantly different attitudes between the two groups dealt with married life portrayed as problems which can be solved by purchasing products and dealt with the use of sex-appeal advertisements. In general, advertising executives of both sexes stated that they would not act irresponsibly, although Surlin found the female executives to be more adamant. Differences in socially responsible behavior which were reported by the respondents indicate that women advertisers may perform in a more socially responsible manner, especially in areas of advertising content dealing with sex-related topics. Surlin concluded that, in fact, there may be differences in socially responsible professional behavior exhibited by male and female advertising executives, but all such behavioral differences are not admitted to and reported by the male respondents.

Concluding Comments

This review of attitudes and opinions toward sex stereotyping in advertising reveals that polls conducted by such diverse groups as consumer magazines and government agencies, plus other investigations of public criticism, consistently find that the majority of consumers agree that advertising is insulting to women. The aged and immigrants also are mentioned frequently as other minority groups who are discriminated against in advertising. The impact of offensive, stereotyped portrayals includes significant effects on purchasing behavior and employment for women. As more women enter the marketplace, the level of criticism will likely increase unless positive steps are taken. Public support has been expressed for more authoritative roles for women in advertising, such as off-camera announcers and on-camera spokeswomen for national products, to improve their image on television and in other advertising media.

It appears from the results of these studies that the variety of portrayals in advertising has increased, as has consumers' acceptance of various role portrayals. However, attitudes expressed toward the continued treatment of women in advertisements should indicate to advertisers and agencies that there is still plenty of reason and opportunity to improve the portrayal of the sexes in advertising. Interestingly, attitude studies among advertisers have found that the majority disagree that their advertising campaigns are offensive. Therefore, it must be concluded that the criticism leveled by feminists and other consumer groups during the 1970s has had only limited success.

Although recent public comment has recognized minor improvements in advertising over the years, many critics state that further improvements are needed. The general impression is that major broadcast and print media have made some attempts during the last decade to decrease sexism in their advertisements. Consequently, the complaints regarding television and consumer-magazine advertising do not cite as many extremely sexist portrayals as in the early 1970s. However, public criticism of other media advertising, including billboards, direct mail, and industrial magazines continues with great fervor. Examples of these advertisements regularly appear in the "No Comment" department of *Ms.* magazine. For those who believe that further changes are needed in advertising's portrayal of the sexes, significant efforts still are required to change attitudes and influence the behaviors of those responsible for content and media decisions in advertising.

Notes

1. Midge Kovacs, "Women Simply Don't Recognize Themselves in Many Ads Today," *Advertising Age,* 12 June 1972, p. 50.

2. Carol Tavris and Toby Jayaratue, "How Do You Feel About Being a Woman: The Results of a *Redbook* Questionnaire," reprint (New York: McCall Publishing Co., 1972).

3. "'GH' Readers Say Ads Turning Them Away from TV," *Advertising Age,* 29 January 1979, p. 65.

4. Alice E. Courtney and Thomas W. Whipple, *Canadian Perspectives on Sex Stereotyping in Advertising* (Ottawa: Advisory Council on the Status of Women, 1978), p. 87.

5. "European Women Hit Mass Media Image of Being Robots, Sex Objects," *Advertising Age,* 9 August 1971, p. 26.

6. Gordon L. Wise, Allan L. King, and J. Paul Merenski, "Reactions to Sexy Ads Vary With Age," *Journal of Advertising Research* 4 (August 1974):11–16.

7. Dorothy Aaron, *About Face: Toward a Positive Image of Women in Advertising,* (Toronto: Ontario Status of Women Council, 1975).

8. "'GH' Readers Say," p. 65.

9. *A Study to Evaluate Consumer Attitudes Toward Television Commercials* (New York: Marschalk Co., Inc., 1980).

10. *Study of Consumer Attitudes Toward TV Programming and Advertising* (New York: Warwick, Welsh & Miller, Inc., 1981).

11. Interview with Evelyn Crandell, Advertising Standards Council, 13 January 1978.

12. Robert E. Oliver to Nicole Strickland, 6 May 1977.

13. "Portrayals of Women in TV Commercials: Has the Controversy Had any Real Impact?" *Listening Post* (New York: Ogilvy and Mather Research, 1978).

14. Laurel Leff, "TV Ads Reflect Power of Working Women," *Wall Street Journal,* 30 October 1980, p. 25.

15. "Ads Glorifying Career 'Superwomen' Can Alienate Full-Time Homemakers," *Marketing News,* 1 May 1981, pp. 1–2.

16. Norma Jones et al., "The Media in Montana: Its Effects on Minorities and Women," (Report prepared by the Montana Advisory Committee to the U.S. Commission on Civil Rights, 1976).

17. *Advertising and Women: A Report on Advertising Portraying or Directed to Women* (New York: National Advertising Review Board, 1975).

18. "NARB Polls Public on Ad Gripes," *Advertising Age,* 23 March 1981, p. 42.

19. Margaret Carruthers, "Women Who Complain About the Portrayal of Women in Advertising," (Paper delivered at the University of Guelph, Guelph, Ontario, 1977), pp. 1–2.

20. William J. Lundstrom and Donald Sciglimpaglia, "Sex Role Portrayals in Advertising," *Journal of Marketing* 3 (July 1977):72–79.

21. Terrence H. Witkowski, "An Experimental Comparison of Women's Self and Advertising Image," in *New Marketing for Social and Economic Progress* ed. R.C. Curhan (Chicago: American Marketing Association, 1975), pp. 431–434.

22. *Communications in Ontario* (Ottawa: Ontario Mininstry of Transportation and Communication, 1973).

23. Canadian Radio-Television and Telecommunications Commission, *Attitudes of Canadians Toward Advertising on Television* (Hull, Quebec: Supply and Services, 1978).

24. Andrew J. DuBrin and Eugene H. Tram, "Coping with Women's Lib," *Sales Management,* 15 June 1971, pp. 20–21.

25. Lorraine Baltera, "Working Women Ads Often Off Target: Panel," *Advertising Age,* 31 January 1977, p. 33.

26. Jennifer Stewart, "Function of Women in Ads is to Sell the Product," *Marketing News,* 21 April 1978, p. 13.

27. John R. Stuteville, "Sexually Polarized Products and Advertising Strategy," *Journal of Retailing* 47 (Summer 1971):3–13.

28. J. Klemsrud, "On Madison Avenue, Women Take Stand in Middle of the Road," *New York Times,* 3 July 1973, p. 28.

29. Jane Levere, "Portrayal of Women in Ads Defended by Top Ad Women," *Editor and Publisher,* 8 June 1974, p. 11.

30. Stuart H. Surlin, "Sex Differences in Socially Responsible Advertising Decisions," *Journal of Advertising* 3 (Summer 1978):36–39.

3 The Social Effects of Sex Stereotyping

There is overwhelming evidence that advertisements present traditional, limited, and often demeaning stereotypes of women and men. It is recognized, of course, that stereotypes in advertising can serve a useful function by conveying an image quickly and clearly, and that there is nothing inherently wrong with using characterizations of roles that are easily identifiable. However, when limiting and demeaning stereotypes are as pervasive as those involved in advertising's portrayal of the sexes, it becomes important to question whether those stereotypes might result in negative and undesirable social consequences.

This chapter examines available evidence concerning the societal impacts of sex stereotyping in advertising. It will be shown that there is increasing evidence that advertising stereotypes, particularly those in television commercials, do influence children, women, and men. They reinforce, and perhaps also shape, our view of our own capabilities and achievements, of appropriate sex roles, and of career aspirations. However, this chapter will also point out evidence that advertising's influence is only one among a myriad of factors in our society that shape our images of men and women.

Measuring the Social Effects of Sex Stereotyping

Only recently has there been significant research attention paid to the social consequences of sex stereotyping. Interest in advertising sex stereotyping is even more recent. Most of the relevant research deals with television advertising and is part of a large and growing body of research about the effects of television in society. It is, of course, extremely difficult to examine the influence of television on attitudes and behaviors because television so pervades the culture and yet is only one of a myriad of influences. Nevertheless, over the past decades, a large body of research evidence has been accumulated which examines the way television does influence society. It is beyond this chapter's scope to discuss that literature in any detail, but it may be useful to set the stage for the review with some general comments.

A growing body of research shows that television does profoundly influence children and adults. It can influence intellectual development, change attitudes, contribute to aggressive behavior in children, teach children how to become consumers, encourage prosocial attitudes and behavior, be an agent of political socialization, and teach racial stereotypes, among many others.[1] The weight of evidence shows that television is profoundly important in reflecting and shaping society. It can be shown that one way its influence operates is to help to reinforce and/or to shape views about men and women.

There is agreement among psychologists that changes in attitudes and behavior can be brought about as a result of exposure to the symbolic models portrayed in books, films, television, and television advertising. Liebert and Poulos, reviewing many studies on the influence of television on children, concluded that the socialization effect is a natural result of children observing others' behavior. "Modeling . . . is a cornerstone in social development."[2] Comstock et al., in their comprehensive review, *Television and Human Behavior,* go even further and conclude that "there may be conditions under which observation via television constitutes a *stronger* stimulus to imitative learning than does real-life observation."[3]

That children and adults learn from television and from the sex-role models it portrays is a conclusion that will not be questioned here. However, the evidence for such effects should be reviewed carefully. The methodological problems involved in studying the effects of television are formidable, and the body of research linking television sex stereotyping with attitudes and behaviors is still recent and small.

Some of the evidence comes from correlational studies. Such studies examine the relationship between the amount of time spent with television and the degree to which subjects hold certain sex-typed attitudes or engage in sex-typed behaviors. Correlational studies offer useful insights, but they fail to establish causation. Gerbner and Signorielli, for example, have examined patterns of television viewing among adults and correlated them with responses to a series of questions measuring sexist attitudes.[4] Their conclusion is that there is a positive relationship between heavy television viewing and responding that women should stay at home and that a woman should not work if her husband can support her. The data must be interpreted with caution. Does television viewing cause the sexist attitudes, or are such findings revealed because people with sexist attitudes watch more television than less sexist people?

Experimental studies overcome the causation problem. In such studies the quantity and quality of television viewing can be held constant, other relevant variables can be controlled, and cause and effect can be established. But, despite the greater precision of experimental studies, methodological issues still arise. Sample sizes are usually small and often are not representative, exposure conditions are unrealistic, and usually only short-term effects of exposure can be measured, and the effect measures used are often unrealistic.

Research by Freuh and McGhee serves as a good example of the problems involved in examining the influence of television sex stereotyping.[5] They investigated the relationship between the amount of television watched by children and the strength of their traditional sex-role development. Their subjects were eighty children whose television watching was either self-reported or monitored by parents. Sex-role development was measured using a standardized paper and pencil test which measured the children's choices of sex-typed toys. The researchers found that children who were heavy television viewers had a greater propensity to give test answers which were sex-typed and which the researchers believed indicated traditional sex-role development. Freuh and McGhee also found that boys and older children made the greatest number of traditionally sex-typed choices on the test.

The conclusion of the study seems obvious: children learn about traditional sex roles from television. But a number of critical questions remain unanswered. Why are boys and older children more traditional? Was it their traditional attitudes that made some children heavy television watchers in the first place? What role did parents play, not only in teaching children about sex roles, but also in helping them to interpret what was seen on television? Was the standardized test a valid measure of the children's sex-role development? Were the forty boys and forty girls studied representative of their age groups?

Television and Observational Learning

Despite the methodological difficulties, researchers have concluded that television is a source of learning through observation. One of the ways children learn about the characteristics of their own sex is through modeling. Some theorists suggest that children learn from same-sex models because they are more often rewarded for behaviors imitating same-sex models. Others suggest that children learn to organize their self-concept and their world view along lines that reinforce their identification with their own gender. Both groups agree, however, that children are encouraged to emulate same-sex models, whether seen directly or experienced through the media. Thus, children generally recall more about same-sex models than about opposite-sex models. This tendency appears to be stronger in boys than in girls. Indications are that same-sex modeling has greater effects when the model behaves in ways that the children consider to be sex-appropriate; children tend not to recall the sex-inappropriate behavior of own-sex models.

A study by Sprafkin and Liebert demonstrated the influence of television models on same-sex learning.[6] Sprafkin and Liebert conducted observations of children while the children chose and watched selected television programs. They found that the children selected programs that featured characters of their own sex; girls watched female characters and boys watched males. However, attention was greater when the same-sex characters behaved in stereotypical ways. For example, girls attended 78 percent of the time to female characters who behaved stereotypically, and only half the time to female characters who engaged in other behaviors. Overall, the findings of the Sprafkin and Liebert study indicate that children selectively use television to find confirmation of previously developed stereotypes about their own sex.

Reeves and Greenberg used multidimensional scaling techniques to explore the cognitive dimensions used by children in judging television characters.[7] They found that children at three different age groups used virtually the same dimensions to describe the characters. Boys were more influenced by physical strength and activity; girls were more influenced by physical-attractiveness cues. Reeves and Greenberg concluded that the dimensions identified are strong predictors of the children's desire to model the social behavior of television characters behaving stereotypically.

The importance of such findings is underlined by content research by Sternglanz and Serbin who studied the sex-role models presented on children's television programs.[8] Their data indicated that males are much more visible on children's programs and that both male and female roles are sex-typed. A female child, they concluded, was shown that it was inappropriate for her to make plans or be aggressive and that she would be punished if she did not behave sedately. They concluded that television taught female children that the only way to be a successful human being was through magic, which enabled the female to manipulate effectively and subtly.

Occupational Stereotyping and Sex Roles

A group of studies has explored the way in which television programming may influence children's occupational aspirations. However, some early studies of children's responses to stereotyping of occupational roles are not themselves free of a degree of stereotyping. DeFleur and DeFleur, in 1967, demonstrated that children's knowledge of occupations increased linearly with age and that television is an important source of information for children, particularly about the social ranking of occupations.[9] They concluded that television is a more important source of children's occupational knowledge than personal contact. DeFleur and DeFleur began, however, with the assumption that in this society males will have to choose an occupation and will therefore be more aware of possible occupations than will females. Consequently, their study used flash cards showing cartoon characters in which the figures shown to have occupations were all male. From today's perspective it seems surprising that in this early study the researchers seemed unaware of the bias built into their experiment.

Children's consciousness of the occupational limitations for women was demonstrated by Beuf in 1974.[10] A sample of sixty-three children, aged three to six, was selected from a suburban middle-class neighborhood. Even though the children had been born since the advent of the woman's movement, they were found to have stereotyped career ideas: 70 percent of the boys and 73 percent of the girls chose traditionally stereotyped careers when asked what they would like to be. In addition, television viewing appeared to influence choices: 76 percent of the heavy television viewers chose stereotyped careers, while only 50 percent of the moderate viewers did so. An interesting feature of the study is that Beuf asked the children what they would like to be if they were of the opposite sex. The responses indicated a high degree of consciousness about sex roles (and limitations) even among preschoolers. The girls had thought about the opposite-sex question and had an answer. Sex was perceived by several of the girls as a barrier to what they would really like to be and as a limitation on their capabilities. The boys, on the other hand, regarded the question with mystification or suspicion; they had never thought about being a girl. One little boy said, "Oh, if I were a girl I'd have to grow up to be nothing."[11] As a result of this study, Beuf urged in her conclusion that positive efforts be made to present a wider choice of career possibilities in media role models, particularly for girls.

Miller and Reeves also examined the role of television programming on the degree of occupational stereotyping learned by young viewers.[12] They sampled two hundred third- to sixth-grade children to test three hypotheses: that boys would name more television role models than would girls, that boys would name more same-sex models, and that children who had seen women in nontraditional occupations on television would be more likely to see those occupations as appropriate for women. Their results indicate that children do choose television characters to emulate; all boys and 71 percent of the girls named same-sex characters. Girls were more likely to cite opposite-sex models, possibly because of the greater value placed on male roles in society. Both girls and boys had obviously learned that boys have wider options and are generally better off. The nontypical female roles which the researchers were able to find in television programming bear out the more limited roles for women: two female police officers, one female school principal, one female park ranger, and one female television producer (Mary Tyler Moore). There is hardly a wide variety here, particularly in the status of the occupations. Nevertheless, children who had seen the nontypical roles for women thought it more appropriate for women to be in those occupations.

Perhaps the Miller and Reeves findings can be further interpreted in the light of content analysis of television programming by Manes and Melnyk.[13]

They found in their analysis of prime-time television content, over two months, that working women portrayed at all job levels were represented as either unmarried or unsuccessfully married; only three of sixty-two female characters with jobs were shown as successfully married. Manes and Melnyk concluded that female characters with high job status were in evidence on television only as models not to be imitated if women wished to have successful marital and parental relationships.

These studies suggest that television may affect children's sex-role learning in two ways. First, television provides confirmation of previously learned stereotypes. However, indications are that nonstereotypical television can provide opportunities for new learning by providing new and innovative role models. In the next section studies are reviewed which indicate that not only programming, but also commercials serve as models for attitudes toward the sexes.

Television Commercials and Sex-Role Stereotyping

Difficult as it is to examine the effects of television programming, it is even more difficult to isolate the influence of the advertising portion of that programming. Most research in this area has therefore been conducted in experimental, laboratory settings. Most of it has focused on children.

Effects on Children

In the seventies a series of studies was conducted to examine the effect of nontraditional commercials on children's sex-role stereotyping. O'Bryant and Corder-Bolz tested sixty-seven girls and boys, aged five to ten years.[14] They used commercials of their own design, some of which showed women in roles reversed from the traditional female occupations. Over a four-week period these commercials and some additional ones were shown, interspersed with videotaped cartoons. In the commercials the women talked about the products they were selling and also about their jobs. The traditional occupations shown in the commercials were telephone operator, fashion model, file clerk, and manicurist. The nontraditional occupations were pharmacist, welder, butcher, and laborer. The children were tested for occupational knowledge, propensity to stereotype the occupations, and for their own occupational preferences. Changes from pre- to postexposure showed that the children had learned from the advertisements not only about the nature of the various occupations, but also about the sexual appropriateness of the jobs. The nontraditional roles were still seen as less common choices for women, and the commercials did not cause boys to prefer traditionally female jobs. However, girls exposed to the innovative commercials gave higher preference ratings to nontraditional occupations than girls who saw commercials with traditional roles. These results caused the authors to conclude that television commercials could have a significant impact on children's perceptions of occupational possibilities and therefore on their career aspirations.

A similar study by Atkin used commercials which showed women in the roles of court judge, computer programmer, and television technician.[15] The children who were exposed to these nontraditional commercials were more likely to select those occupations as appropriate for women. The results were particularly dramatic in the case of the woman seen as a judge. Just over half the children who had seen that commercial subsequently checked judge as suitable for a woman; only 27 percent of the control group did so.

In a related experiment Pingree showed third- and eighth-grade boys and girls commercials with either traditional or nontraditional occupations for women and measured their attitudes toward traditional roles for women against those of a control group.[16] The experimental groups were three: one group was instructed that the people in the commercials were real people; another group that the commercials contained actors; and a third group was given no instructions about the reality dimension.

Among the experimental groups children who believed the characters to be acting were less traditional in their attitudes toward the role of women. The two sets of commercials had a significant impact on the children's attitudes toward women only for those groups which had been instructed that the people in the commercials were real. For these groups, most children had less stereotyped attitudes about women after viewing the nontraditional commercials. However, for eighth-grade boys the pattern was reversed; after viewing nontraditional commercials they had more stereotyped attitudes toward women's roles.

Pingree's findings are puzzling. The complexity of her experiment, difficulties in finding appropriate nontraditional commercials to test, and problems with sample size and group comparability make the results difficult to interpret. For example, the control group was found to be less traditional in its views than any of the experimental groups. Pingree hypothesizes that this may be because this group was also found to watch less television than the experimental groups. Pingree's finding that eighth-grade boys became more stereotyped in their views suggests that nontraditional commercials may backfire with certain groups.

None of these studies demonstrate that traditional commercials create the occupational stereotypes held by children, but they all strongly suggest that such commercials play a role in reinforcing stereotypes. Despite the commonly held belief that socialization effects occur only after repeated exposures to stereotypes over long time periods, these studies show that the attitudes of children exposed to even one counter-stereotypical commercial can be affected, at least in the short term. Thus, these studies indicate the potential power of television commercials to educate children, particularly girls, about occupational opportunities and to influence occupational preferences.

An additional study examining the effect of commercials on children's attitudes is that of Cheles-Miller who examined children's acceptance of the stereotypes of husbands and wives shown in traditional advertising.[17] Cheles-Miller worked with fourth- and fifth-grade children. First, she measured her subjects' agreement with a series of stereotyped statements describing the good husband and the good wife, as well as their knowledge of commercials and general attitudes toward them. The children were then shown commercials running on prime-time television which typified the stereotyped wife and husband. After viewing the commercials, the children were asked to rate the accuracy of the portrayal they had just seen and to indicate how well they liked the characters portrayed. Cheles-Miller found that demographic and attitudinal variables were related to the children's acceptance of the stereotyped role models. A child was most likely to accept the stereotype if he/she liked the characters and if he/she had a relatively low self-concept. However, a child whose mother had a high-ranking job (Cheles-Miller rated housekeeper as a low-ranking job), scored low on the stereotype-acceptance test. Cheles-Miller's findings indicate that television's influence on children is filtered through the child's own first-hand experience and personality. Cheles-Miller concludes from her results that the more consistent the role portrayal on television, and the less the personal experience of the child, the greater is the power of the commercial to affect him or her.

Elementary-school-guidance teachers apparently share Cheles-Miller's concern. A study by Barry of the attitudes of 175 guidance teachers examined their perceptions of the effect of television on children.[18] Sixty percent of the counselors surveyed believed that children accept the stereotyped roles shown in commercials, 68 percent believed that the overall purpose of television advertising to children was to confuse them, and 54 percent thought that parents should monitor children's television viewing habits more closely. The counselors surveyed by Barry saw television commercials as a powerful and potentially harmful influence on children.

However, evidence exists that parental guidance and the role models found at home and at school can outweigh the influence of television commercials. In a study by O'Neil, Schoonover, and Adelstein, students at a Montessori school were tested and it was found that they were not significantly affected by the occupational stereotypes found on television.[19] These children, however, were atypical in several ways: their television-viewing time worked out to less than half the national average; their parents were also not heavy television watchers; the parents monitored their children's viewing; and the mothers of the children provided examples of counter-stereotypic social roles. The school itself fostered nontraditional sex-role perceptions. Left to itself, television can be a strong force maintaining the status quo, but when parents and school take positive action, they can apparently undo what television is teaching their children. There is an interaction between what is viewed on television and what is observed in reality.

Effects on Women

The research reported thus far has examined the effect of television and commercials on children who, most experimenters believe, are those in society most likely to be influenced by the role models they see there. However, recent work indicates that adult women also are affected. Jennings, Geis, and Brown have examined how television commercials influence college-age women.[20] The authors report that in their early work they showed college students traditional and nontraditional commercials and found that female subjects who saw traditional commercials expressed fewer career aspirations than those who saw nontraditional commercials. Building on these findings, they investigated whether commercials could have effects, not only on the attitudes of female college students, but also on their behavior. Eight commercials were devised by the experimenters: four showed women in traditional, dependent, and subservient roles vis-a-vis men; the other four exactly reversed the roles within the same script and showed women as dominant and men as subservient. After viewing one or the other set, subjects were questioned about the female and male roles depicted. Then, half the subjects were given and Asch-type conformity test: they were asked to rate cartoons and were shown a set of falsified average ratings; the degree to which subjects' final opinions differed from the falsified ratings was interpreted as a measure of independence of judgment. The other subjects were asked to give a short, impromptu speech, and their degree of confidence in doing so was rated.

The subjects who had seen the role-reversed commercial set tested as more independent in the cartoon test and more self-confident in the speech test. The experimenters also tested for the effect of the type of subject the women were studying in college and the number of hours the students said they normally watched television. These factors did not prove to be significant; only the version of commercials seen predicted the ratings of independence and self-confidence. Moreover, the women were asked if they identified with the people in the commercials. All reported a low level of identification regardless of the version of the commercial seen. Nevertheless, the experimental results showed a measurable behavioral impact of the commercials. The experimenters point to the power of the implicit message in commercials, learned unconsciously, to affect both the attitudes and behaviors of adult women.

The studies discussed in this section do not prove that commercials contribute to the development of our stereotypes of men and women; indeed, it would be almost impossible to so determine. They do show, however, that television commercials contribute to the perpetuation of sex stereotypes. Children are exposed to models of behavior in the media, and they learn from them. To the extent that those models are stereotyped, exposure will contribute to strengthen already sex-typed attitudes and behaviors. The reflection of reality shown on television is, therefore, a powerful and pervasive substantiation of the status quo, with all the force of a self-fulfilling prophecy. If commercial television were the only source of information, girls could grow up with no other aspirations than to be housewives and mothers simply because no other option is offered, no other possibility suggested, and no exploration in any other direction rewarded. However, television is only one of the many influences on a child's attitudes and behavior toward the sexes; television's impact is filtered through that of home, school, and other real-life models. Moreover, evidence suggests that television can begin to exert a more positive and broadening influence. Nonstereotyped commercials have the possibility of enlarging children's horizons and of achieving this with relatively few exposures. They also may have the possibility of influencing the attitudes and behaviors of women and of doing so without their conscious awareness of the influence.

The Social Effects of Prescription-Drug Advertising

As noted in chapter 1, several researchers have examined prescription-drug advertising addressed to physicians and have noted that such advertisements are more likely to show women than men, particularly in advertising for psychotropic-drug products. They have concluded that there is a sex bias in such advertisements which may lead doctors to prescribe mood-altering drugs for women, rather than helping the women to deal with real problems. McKee, Corder, and Haizlip tested those conclusions in a survey of twenty-three psychiatrists.[21] The psychiatrists were each sent copies of all advertising pages of an issue of *The American Journal of Psychiatry* that showed drugs used in treating depression and anxiety and which portrayed a patient. The psychiatrists were asked to review the advertisements and answer a series of questions.

The respondents indicated that they were more likely to be attracted to advertisements featuring an attractive female patient. Approximately one-half believed that physicians might be affected by such advertisements and to believe that women were more likely to be weak, sick, and crazy. However, three-quarters believed that they, as psychiatrists, were experienced enough to overlook the impact of the advertising and to direct themselves to the underlying causes of patients' behavior. The study is inconclusive. It cannot be said with certainty that the sexually biased content of some prescription-drug advertising adversely affects psychiatrists or other physicians. However, the survey does indicate that doctors themselves recognize the possibility that sex-biased advertisements may be dangerous. It suggests the need for caution on the part of the drug advertisers and physicians to counter the possible negative effects of the overrepresentation of women patients in such advertisements.

The Critics' View of the Economic and Social Consequences

Critics of advertising, particularly those with a feminist orientation, have posited many potentially damaging effects upon the social and economic fabric which may result from sex stereotyping in advertising. Many of these were reviewed in a 1978 paper by Whipple and Courtney and table 3–1 summarizes these criticisms.[22] As the table show, critics have contended that the occupational stereotyping seen in advertising is one of the factors that may limit the aspirations of men, women, and children by encouraging them to have stereotyped views of their personal opportunities and those of others.

Table 3–1
Social Welfare and Economic Consequences of Sex Stereotyping in Advertising as Viewed by Critics

Area of Stereotyping	Immediate Effects of Advertising Sex Stereotyping	Longer Range Effects to Which Advertising Contributes
How the sexes are portrayed in advertising	Advertising influences adult perceptions of male/female roles.	Women limit own access to, and are denied access to, a wide range of occupations; effects on salaries of women; working housewives forced to perform two jobs.
Portrayals of housewives	Advertising influences adults to believe housewives are unintelligent, dependent on men, subservient, have personality problems.	Affects individual self-esteem and others' perceptions of housewife; affects structure of family and divorce law; affects ability of women to organize; affects job access and salaries.

Table 3–1 continued

Area of Stereotyping	Immediate Effects of Advertising Sex Stereotyping	Longer Range Effects to Which Advertising Contributes
Portrayals of girls	Like adults, children similarly influenced in their perceptions of sex roles, capabilities, personalities.	Limits aspirations and levels of achievement of girls. Profound influence for both sexes in lifestyle, education, occupation, and other choices.
Portrayal of sexuality	Advertising may influence women to devote too much attention to personal appearance; may influence men to view women as sex objects.	May be linked to depersonalization of women as sexual objects.
Presence of the sexes in advertising	Advertising influences perception that women cannot exercise authority; make decisions independently. Also it has direct impact on employment of women as announcers.	Influences aspirations of, and abilities of, women to manage and take on other authoritative roles. Influences both sexes' perceptions of women's abilities to perform these roles competently.
Health	Advertising may influence doctors to misdiagnose and overprescribe for women patients. Passive stereotype discourages women from active participation in physical exercise.	May have profound effects both on individual health and also on the way medical profession views and treats all women.
Aging and minority groups	Absence of older and minority group women from advertising makes them an invisible part of society.	May have profound effects both on individual mental and physical well-being and also on the way society treats these groups.
Liberation	Advertising may influence society to believe that the women's liberation movement is a joke, unimportant, insignificant.	May act to slow progress of change for women and men.
Personal products	Contributes to irritation felt by many men and women.	

Source: Thomas W. Whipple and Alice E. Courtney, "Social Consequences of Sex Stereotyping in Advertising," in *Future Directions for Marketing,* ed. G. Fisk et al. (Cambridge, Mass.: Marketing Science Institute, 1978), pp. 339–340.

For this contention, as this discussion points out, some evidence exists. Thus, as the critics suggest, stereotyped advertising may be one of the factors that contributes to cause women to limit their access to various occupations, and it may thus contribute to various social and economic consequences, including the ghettoization of female work.

The critics have been particularly concerned about advertising's depiction of the housewife and mother. They contend that advertising sex stereotyping contributes to the view that all household work is, by definition, women's work. This, they believe, has effects on working wives who often find themselves fully responsible for two jobs. It may also affect those men who might otherwise aspire to participate more fully in caring for home and family. Critics believe that the depiction of housewives in commercials is a contributor to the belief that housewives are low in intelligence, unable to make decisions, dependent on men, superservants for their families, competitive with other women, neurotic about cleanliness, and acquisitive for material things. Such contentions have not yet been researched, but it does seem more than likely that advertisements play a role in perpetuating such stereotypes.

In addition, the critics have been very much concerned that advertising encourages us to view women as sexual objects, with resultant negative effects ranging from depersonalization to sexual violence. No research has as yet been specifically directed at measuring such effects. However, social scientists have examined the relationships among mass-media exposure, erotic content, and violent content and the resultant attitudinal and behavioral effects. Their data indicate that there may be cause for the critics' concern. As Feshbach has pointed out in his article, "Mixing Sex with Violence—A Dangerous Alchemy," erotic media content can both arouse sexual feelings and reduce inhibitions against aggressive behavior.[23] Feshbach's conclusion is based on analysis of the likely effects of television programming and cannot be generalized to the effects of advertising. Nevertheless, data do indicate that critics' concerns are not totally unrealistic.

These, and the other criticisms outlined in table 3-1, are indeed serious. While there is to date little or no data with which to examine them more fully, they are not totally unrealistic. Of course, the critics themselves would agree that stereotyped advertising is not the sole cause of such serious societal problems. However, they do view advertising as playing a contributing role, and possibly a major contributing role, in perpetuating and exacerbating such problems. The questions the critics raise deserve much more research attention in the future.

Conclusion

Concern over the effects of advertising stereotyping stems from the fact that advertising is an important force that reinforces perceptions of traditional, limited, and often demanding stereotypes of women and men. While there has been much criticism addressed to the likely effects of such stereotyping, there is as yet only limited evidence.

The effect of television and television commercials on children is the best researched topic. Researchers agree that television can be a relevant source of information for sex-role socialization, that incidental learning about the labor force takes place among children viewers, and that children model themselves after the characters portrayed in programming and advertising. There is evidence that children accept the stereotyped roles shown in television advertising, select them as appropriate for males and females in general, and select stereotyped careers for themselves. Boys have higher propensities to stereotype than do girls, as have heavy television watchers. Studies also demonstrate that girls are likely to prefer and select for themselves a wider choice of careers and more unusual occupations if they have seen women portrayed in those roles on television or in advertising. Studies have also demonstrated, however, that television and its advertising work among a wide range of other influences which can alter and outweigh the stereotypes portrayed on air.

Evidence of the effects of sex-role stereotyping on adult men and women is more limited. However, nontraditional advertisements may help women to greater independence of judgment and greater self-confidence. Evidence also indicates that stereotyped advertising may affect doctors and lead them to overprescribe for women patients, treating symptoms with tranquilizers while ignoring the real causes of their difficulties.

These tentative findings only touch on the list of potential far-reaching effects of sex stereotyping which have been raised by advertising critics. About these possible effects there is, as yet, no evidence. Nevertheless, it is indisputable that advertising is at least one contributing influence affecting the way children and adults view their roles in society. Indeed, the importance of advertising in this regard has been recognized explicitly in the report of an advertising industry task force on sex stereotyping by the National Advertising Review Board.[24]

It would be, of course, a gross exaggeration to claim or imply that advertising sex stereotyping is the sole, or even a major, cause of societal problems. However, there is mounting evidence that sex stereotyping in advertising does play a role in reflecting societal ills and helping to sustain them. There is also mounting evidence, however, that more responsible advertising could play a positive and beneficial role in helping to change them.

Notes

1. The most important studies in these areas are cited and discussed in George Comstock et al., *Television and Human Behavior* (New York: Columbia University Press, 1978); Robert M. Liebert and Roberta Wicks Poulos, "Television and Personality Development: The Socializing Effects

of an Entertainment Medium," in *Child Personality and Psychopathology: Current Topics,* vol. 2 (New York: John Wiley, 1975); Richard P. Adler et al., *The Effects of Television Advertising on Children* (Lexington, Mass.: Lexington Books, 1980); and Richard M. Perloff et al., "Mass Media and Sex-Typing: Research Prospectives and Policy Implications," (Paper delivered at the Annual Convention of the American Psychological Association, Toronto, Canada, 1978).

2. Robert M. Liebert and Roberta Wicks Poulos, "TV for Kiddies: Truth, Goodness, Beauty and a Little Bit of Brainwash," *Psychology Today* 6 (November 1972):123–127.

3. Comstock et al., *Television and Human Behavior,* p. 430.

4. George Gerbner and Nancy Signorielli, *Women and Minorities in Television Drama, 1969–1978* (Research report, Annenberg School of Communications, University of Pennsylvania, 1979).

5. Terry Freuh and Paul E. McGhee, "Traditional Sex Role Development and the Amount of Time Spent Watching Television," *Developmental Psychology* 11 (1975):109.

6. Joyce M. Sprafkin and Robert M. Liebert, "Sex-Typing and Children's Television Preferences," in *Home and Hearth: Images of Women in the Mass Media,* ed. G. Tuchman et al. (New York: Oxford University Press, 1978), pp. 228–239.

7. Byron Reeves and Bradley S. Greenberg, "Children's Perceptions of Television Characters," *Human Communication Research* 3 (Winter 1977):113–127.

8. Sarah H. Sternglanz and Lisa A. Serbin, "Sex Role Stereotyping in Children's Television Programs," *Developmental Psychology* 10 (1974): 710–715.

9. Melvin L. DeFleur and Lois B. DeFleur, "The Relative Contribution of Television as a Learning Source for Children's Occupational Knowledge," *American Sociological Review* 32 (October 1967):777–789.

10. Ann Beuf, "Doctor, Lawyer and Household Drudge," *Journal of Communication* 24 (Spring 1974):142–145.

11. Beuf, p. 144.

12. Mark M. Miller and Byron Reeves, "Dramatic TV Content and Children's Sex-Role Stereotypes," *Journal of Broadcasting* 20 (Winter 1976):35–49.

13. Audrey L. Manes and Paula Melnyk, "Televised Models of Female Achievement," *Journal of Applied Social Psychology* 4 (October-December 1974):365–374.

14. Shirley L. O'Bryant and Charles R. Corder-Bolz, "The Effects of Television on Children's Stereotyping of Women's Work Roles," *Journal of Vocational Behavior* 12 (April 1978):233–243.

15. Charles K. Atkin, *Effects of Television Advertising on Children:*

Second Year Experimental Evidence, Report No. 2 (East Lansing, Mich.: Michigan State University, 1975).

16. Suzanne Pingree, "The Effects of Nonsexist Television Commercials and Perceptions of Reality on Children's Attitudes about Women," *Psychology of Women Quarterly* 2 (Spring 1978):262–277.

17. Pamela Cheles-Miller, "Reactions to Marital Roles in Commercials," *Journal of Advertising Research* 15 (August 1975):45–49.

18. Thomas E. Barry, "Children's Television Advertising: The Attitudes and Opinions of Elementary School Guidance Counselors," *Journal of Advertising* 7 (Fall 1978):9–16.

19. Nora O'Neil, Sandra Schoonover, and Lisa Adelstein, "The Effect of TV Advertising on Children's Perceptions of Roles," summarized in *Children and Television: A Report to Montessori Parents,* ed. T.W. Whipple, mimeographed (Cleveland, Ohio: Cleveland State University, 1980).

20. Joyce Jennings, Florence L. Geis, and Virginia Brown, "Influence of Television Commercials on Women's Self-Confidence and Independent Judgment," *Journal of Personality and Social Psychology* (1980), pp. 203–210.

21. Christine McKee, Billie F. Corder, and Thomas Haizlip, "Psychiatrists' Responses to Sexual Bias in Pharmaceutical Advertising," *American Journal of Psychiatry* 131 (November 1974):1273–1275.

22. Thomas W. Whipple and Alice E. Courtney, "Social Consequences of Sex Stereotyping in Advertising," in *Future Directions for Marketing,* ed. G. Fisk et al. (Cambridge, Mass., Marketing Science Institute, 1978), pp. 332–350.

23. Seymour Feshbach, "Mixing Sex with Violence—A Dangerous Alchemy," *New York Times,* 3 August 1980, p. D. 29.

24. *Advertising and Women: A Report on Advertising Portraying or Directed to Women* (New York: National Advertising Review Board, 1975).

Part II
Advertising Effectiveness

The New Market

There is a simple demographic fact at the heart of a quiet revolution that has affected almost every man, woman, and child in the United States. The ripple effect of that one demographic fact could eventually touch almost every institution in our society and every aspect of our daily lives.

This paragraph is the opening to Rena Bartos's 1982 book, *The Moving Target: What Every Marketer Should Know About Women.* [1] The details of Bartos's work will be discussed later in this chapter, but it is appropriate to begin with her announcement of the quiet revolution among consumers. The demographic fact she refers to is the entry of large numbers of women into the work force; the ripple effect she refers to has had, and will continue to have, profound implications for almost every aspect of marketing and advertising. In this chapter the changing consumer will be discussed through Bartos's work and through the work of other advertisers, marketers, and academics who are studying the behavior of female consumers.

Demographic, Attitudinal, and Behavioral Changes

Since the 1970s there has been a growing literature documenting changes in the female consumer. These studies have focused on three kinds of change: changing demographics, attitudinal changes, and changes in buyer behavior. A thorough survey of this literature would be sufficient material for a different book and is inappropriate to the main task here. This chapter will, however, include a summary of the highlights and general conclusions that have emerged from recent studies.

Demographic Changes

The observer of the academic and industry literature would have noted in the early 1970s the appearance of a number of articles dealing with changes in women, all reflecting the rapid growth in the numbers of women in the labor force. A typical article of this period was that of Miles, who discussed the new woman. [2] Miles contended that the new woman was becoming a personal rather than a family consumer and was beginning to find new status symbols. A similar article by Baltera concluded that women were changing and that advertisers did not understand how the new female consumer lives or learns.[3] A major problem with both reports is that they were primarily impressionistic, rather than empirical.

By 1977 a major change in the literature had occurred. At this time there appeared many articles documenting demographic changes among women.[4] Typically, such articles showed the trends in the female population and concluded that such trends had an important and growing significance for the marketer. Statistics reported how the female population had changed in total and by age groups, what the projected changes would be to the year 2000, what changes were occurring in the position of women in the labor force, and what the future would hold for the female consumer. The most recent and comprehensive summary of such demographic statistics can be found in Bartos's work.[5] The census data Bartos reports show that 42 percent of the U.S. labor force (in 1980) is made up of women, that 52 percent of all women work outside the home, and that 50 percent of all married women work outside the home. Bartos also found that all women who are not in the work force are not necessarily housewives; some are too young or too old or infirm to work. Conversely, being a working woman does not in the majority of cases keep a woman from doing housework. Four-fifths of all women who work are also responsible for cleaning house.

Bartos's study not only looks at the statistics which document the changes in the past, but also projects future trends. One of her most striking conclusions emerges from a look at changes in women's attitudes and aspirations. These data reveal that 90 percent of women younger than thirty-five do not anticipate being homemakers for their entire lives. Among older women only 30 percent regard the best life-style choice as that of mainly homemaker. Bartos concludes:

> This means that the majority of women of all ages believe that women should participate in the workforce in some combination with marriage and motherhood.[6]

Thus, demographic analysis documents a profound change in women, and analysis of their aspirations suggests that such trends are likely to continue into the future.

Attitude and Buyer-Behavior Changes

Not only have demographics changed, but with them attitudes have changed. Another series of studies about changing women has documented these developments. Studies by Mason et al., for example, contrast women's sex-role attitudes as measured by five surveys conducted between 1964 and 1974.[7] The results show considerable movement toward more egalitarian role definitions in that decade, with this change occurring equally among higher- and lower-status women. Other studies have looked at such factors as the new woman's attitudes toward men,[8] the sexual division of labor within the household,[9] and the influence of sex-role attitudes on younger consumers' views of leisure activities.[10]

From a marketing perspective the most significant group of studies about the new woman has investigated the way the change in female consumers has affected buying attitudes and behaviors. Consumption behavior, retail shopping, and household decision making are among the topics researched. In one of the earliest studies of female buying behavior Scott did a detailed analysis of the buying habits and attitudes of women in Great Britain.[11] Scott observed that, before 1976 when her work appeared, there was virtually no discussion at all about the female consumer in the major international marketing and advertising textbooks. It is hoped that the new and growing research interest in women consumers will soon remedy that glaring defect.

The typical marketing study of female consumers looks at the effects of role and life-style variables. Venkatesh used a feminism scale to divide 333 women respondents into three attitudinal groupings—traditionalists, moderates, and feminists—to investigate the significance of the women's movement for marketing.[12] He concluded that there were important differences among the three groups with respect to attitudes toward advertising appeals, innovative behavior, and magazine readership.

Green and Cunningham, Reynolds et al., and Scanzoni have also examined the marketing effects of women's attitudes toward their roles.[13] These studies show differences between traditional women and those with more modern attitudes. In Green and Cunningham's study of family decision making it was discovered that in households with more liberated views husbands made fewer purchase decisions and played a lesser role in deciding the amount of money to spend on purchases. Scanzoni, in reviewing the literature on changing sex roles and family decision making, concluded that whereas modern women negotiate with their families in terms of individualistic interests, traditional women try to persuade their husbands to compromise on the basis of collective, family interests. Douglas and Urban also examined the influence of sex-role attitudes on women consumers.[14] In comparing samples of women from the United States, the United Kingdom, and France, they concluded that the main factor differentiating the consumer attitudes and behavior of women was the degree to which they adhere to the traditional cultural norms concerning the homemaking role.

The Effect of Employment Status

While these studies focused on attitudinal and life-style variables, many investigations into changes in women's consumer behavior have concentrated on the differences between working and nonworking women. Strober has been engaged in studies examining the effect of female employment on the division of family income between consumption and savings, and on family spending on durables.[15] In her study with Weinberg it is reported that the wife's employment is less important than total income and family assets in understanding the amount families spend for labor-saving durables.[16] Strober and Weinberg find that, if income is held constant, working and nonworking wives are similar also with respect to shopping behavior and meal preparation.

In contrast, studies by advertising agencies have generally concluded that the working/nonworking dimension is an important one in predicting purchase behavior.[17] The general thrust of such studies is that working and professional women make up a new market which has enormous potential. Women in the professions, it has been found, are buying as much liquor and insurance, purchasing as many cars, taking as many trips, and making as many investments as their male counterparts. Employment status has also been found to influence retail-shopping behavior. Studies by Anderson and McCall have both shown significant differences in shopping patterns between working and nonworking women.[18] For example, working women tend to make fewer trips to the grocery store per week, and husbands often share the shopping tasks. Joyce and Guiltinan have found that the shopping behavior of professional women differs from that of women with nonprofessional jobs.[19] The professional group is less concerned with factors such as store atmosphere and more concerned about convenience.

The influence of employment status and life-style variables has also been examined in studies of purchasing behavior toward specific product categories. Douglas has studied purchase behavior for grocery products and women's clothing.[20] In both the United States and France, working wives were found to have more liberated attitudes than nonworking wives, and working wives were found to be less house-proud. A surprising finding was that in France, working wives are less interested in cooking than nonworking wives, but the reverse is true for the United States. These findings are paralleled by those of Roberts and Wortzel whose studies of U.S. women have concluded that employment status is a poor predictor of food-shopping behavior.[21] Their conclusion is that attitudes toward food preparation are more useful predictors.

The changed media patterns that have resulted from the influx of women into the labor force have also been studied. Both Douglas, and Sosanie and Szybillo compared the media habits of working versus nonworking wives.[22] Douglas found no major differences in the frequency and types of magazines read by working and nonworking wives in either the United States or France. Sosani and Szybillo, however, did find differences. Working wives were found to have somewhat less exposure to prime-time television and much less daytime television exposure; they were heavier magazine readers. Many industry studies in the late 1970s have confirmed the finding that working women watch significantly less television than their nonworking counterparts.[23]

Women Consumer Segments

Taken as a whole, this literature indicates that employment status, marital status, and lifestyle and attitudinal variables all affect women's consumer behavior. The most recent and most thorough synthesis of all these variables can be found in *The Moving Target,* Rena Bartos's 1982 book about the new woman consumer and the implications she has for marketers.[24] Bartos's studies show that marketers' traditional view of women needs a good deal of refining. Advertisers have traditionally aimed their messages at any housewife, eighteen to forty-nine, assuming that the motivations of this woman are to prove herself a competent housewife, to get the job of housework done faster than her neighbor, and to persuade those around her that she is not taking shortcuts in performing household chores when she really is. The other picture of the buying female is any girl, eighteen to twenty-five, and her primary motivation is presumed to be to find a man and get married.

Bartos shows that the female consumer comes in many more than these two varieties and that her consumer attitudes and behaviors will vary depending on which segment she falls into. The female consumer can be segmented into the working and nonworking woman, but within these large segments, there are significant subgroups. Bartos has found a different mind set in terms of buying behavior, for example, between women who are not working but plan to enter the work force in the future, and those who never plan to work. Among working women she also finds significant differences between women who have careers and those who are doing jobs. Plan-to-work housewives, according to Bartos, have much more in common with working women (both those with jobs and those with careers) in terms of their social values, than they have with housewives who never plan to leave home. This finding points to the fairly dramatic conclusion that the majority of women today share a set of consumer values and motivations which are at odds with the motivations advertisers have assumed any housewife, eighteen to forty-nine, will have.

Bartos shows how the segments of women she has identified vary with respect to buying behavior for many products, both in their attitudes toward their homes and housework and their media behavior. For example, housewives who plan to work view housework as a never-ending task, but plan-to-work housewives consider it a challenge to be completed quickly so they can get on to other activities. Career women put less emphasis on the perfect household and more on convenience: they are significantly more likely than any other segment to purchase cooking appliances such as a microwave oven.

Bartos analyzes the motivations and behaviors of these groups with respect to many product classes. Fashion, cosmetics (an area in which she believes the traditional marketing assumptions are particularly outdated), cars, and money management get particular attention. In each case Bartos shows the importance of understanding the changing motivations and behaviors of each of the new demographic segments. Another major point Bartos makes is indicated by the title of her book. Not only has today's woman undergone many changes, but also she is continuing to change, and Bartos believes it is advisable for marketers and advertisers to monitor future changes, as well as to catch up with the current situation. It is not this chapter's purpose to repeat the detailed analysis and conclusions that are described at length and with excellent documentation in *The Moving Target*. Bartos's work could well be regarded as essential reading for any marketer interested in the female consumer today. It is highly recommended to readers who are seriously concerned with more effective marketing and advertising to U.S. women.

The Male Perspective

Much research attention has been lavished on the changing roles and status of women, but it is only recently that marketers have begun to consider the impact on the men in their lives. One field of current research interest is the dual-earner household, families where both husband and wife work. A recent Stanford Research Institute (SRI) survey of six thousand U.S. households concluded that two-earner families buy more goods and services than families with only one earner.[25] Dual-earner couples are also more willing to spend money on quality leisure and entertainment activities and are good targets for marketers of products such as boats, ski equipment, and recreational vehicles.

Two recent research studies looked at what the changes mean for husbands. A Benton and Bowles study of 452 married men revealed that men are taking on a wide variety of nontraditional roles within the household: 32 percent are doing food shopping, 47 percent are cooking for the family, 29 percent are doing the laundry, and 80 percent are caring for children younger than twelve.[26] The study indicates that advertisers of products usually aimed at women would best consider aiming at a mixed-sex audience. They recommend, for example, airing detergent advertisements on football games and putting recipe advertisements in magazines such as *Playboy* and *Esquire*. Cunningham and Walsh also conducted a recent survey of husbands' behavior.[27] Demographic and attitudinal variables were used to divide their sample of one thousand husbands into five groups. The largest segment, new breed husbands, representing 32 percent of all married men, is willing to share such chores as grocery shopping, cooking, and cleaning. The next largest segment, classics, share household responsibilities, but insist on having the final decision-making power. Cunningham and Walsh's report says that although advertising often depicts men under great strain in the kitchen, research shows men do not think it is emasculating to cook.

Although behavior is changing, many men still hold traditional attitudes. In a 1979 survey of two hundred men, a leading advertising agency discovered that while men describe the ideal woman as intelligent and self-confident, they also prefer her to be family oriented and to continue to perform traditional household chores.[28] The majority of married men feel that cleaning the bathroom is women's work, as is doing the laundry, washing the dishes, cooking dinner, and doing grocery shopping.

Conclusion

This chapter has given a brief overview of the literature describing the changes in both female- and male-consumer behavior. It has been brief because it is the purpose in this book to focus on sex stereotyping in advertising, rather than on the dimensions of the new and changing market. However, the research reviewed here shows that it is critical to effective marketing to study and comprehend the demographic, attitudinal, and behavioral changes that are taking place. They impact on product-development strategy, retailing, media planning, and have profound implications for the content of advertising messages. Because research shows those changes to be rapid, complex, and often counter-intuitive, advertisers would be well advised to examine this growing body of data in detail.

Although attitudes and behaviors are changing dramatically and on a wide scale, most advertisers have not yet tailored their depictions of men and women to fit the new picture. Yet there is a growing body of research data which examines the advertising implications of these changes and which reveals a great deal of information that can be extremely useful to the advertisers who wishes to communicate more effectively with the changed consumer. The remaining chapters in this section discuss those advertising effectiveness issues.

Notes

1. Rena Bartos, *The Moving Target: What Every Marketer Should Know About Women* (New York: Free Press, MacMillan Publishing, 1982), p. 3.

2. V. Miles "The New Woman: Her Importance to Marketing," *International Advertiser* 12 (Fall 1971):13–16.

3. Lorraine Baltera, "The Working Woman's Come a Long Way, But Can Advertisers Find Her?" *Advertising Age,* 22 July 1974, p. 2.

4. George Fisk and Alladi Venkatesh, "Marketing Implications of the Women's Movement," (Paper presented at the Macromarketing Services Seminar, University of Colorado, Boulder, Colorado, August 1977); William Lazer and John E. Smallwood, "The Changing Demographics of Women," *Journal of Marketing* 41 (July 1977):14–22; Marianne A. Ferber and Helen M. Lowry, "Woman's Place: National Differences in the Occupational Mosaic," *Journal of Marketing* 41 (July 1977):23–30; and Rena Bartos, "What Every Marketer Should Know About Women," *Harvard Business Review* 56 (May–June 1978):73–85.

5. Rena Bartos, *The Moving Target.*

6. Rena Bartos, *The Moving Target,* p. 37.

7. Ken O. Mason, John L. Cxajka and Sara Aber, "Change in U.S. Women's Sex-Role Attitudes 1964–1974," *American Sociological Review* 41 (August 1976):573–596.

8. Bernice Kanner, "BBDO Finds What Women Think of Men—Wow!" *Advertising Age,* 4 June 1979, pp. 3, 108.

9. John P. Robinson, "The 'New Home Economics': Sexist, Unrealistic, or Simply Irrelevant?" *Journal of Consumer Research* 4 (December 1977):178–181; Harry L. Davis, "Dimensions of Marital Roles in Consumer Making," *Journal of Marketing Research* 7 (May 1970):168–177; Robert Ferber and Lucy Chao Lee, "Husband-Wife Influence in Family Purchasing Behavior," *Journal of Consumer Research* 1 (June 1974): 43–56.

10. James W. Gentry and Mildred Doering, "Masculinity-Femininity Related to Consumer Choice," in *Contemporary Marketing Thought,* ed. B.A. Greenberg and D.N. Bellenger (Chicago: American Marketing Association, 1978), pp. 423–427.

11. Rosemary Scott, *The Female Consumer* (New York: John Wiley, 1976).

12. Alladi Venkatesh, "Changing Roles of Women—Some Empirical Findings With Marketing Implications," in *Contemporary Marketing Thought,* ed. B.A. Greenberg and D.N. Bellenger (Chicago: American Marketing Association, 1977), pp. 417–422; and "Changing Roles of Women—A Life Style Analysis," *Journal of Consumer Research* 7 (September 1980):189–197.

13. Robert Green and Isabelle Cunningham, "Feminine Role Perception and Family Purchasing Decisions," *Journal of Marketing Research* 12 (August 1975):325–332; Fred D. Reynolds, Melvin R. Crasky, and William D. Wells, "The Modern Feminine Life-Style," *Journal of Marketing* 41 (July 1977):38–45; and John Scanzoni, "Changing Sex Roles and Emerging Directions in Family Decision Making," *Journal of Consumer Research* 4 (December 1977):185–188.

14. Susan Douglas and Christine D. Urban, "Life-Style Analysis to Profile Women in International Markets," *Journal of Marketing* 41 (July 1977):46–54.

15. Myra H. Strober, "Wives' Labor Force Behavior and Family Consumption Patterns," *American Economic Review, Papers and Proceedings of the 89th Annual Meeting of the American Economic Association* 67 (February 1977):410–417.

16. Myra H. Strober and Charles B. Weinberg, "Working Wives and Major Family Expenditures," *Journal of Consumer Research* 4 (December 1977):141–147.

17. Jennifer Alter, "Working Women 'Neglected'—Study," *Advertising Age,* 4 May 1981, p. 50; "Working Women Now More Attractive—Y&R," *Advertising Age,* 11 January 1982, p. 76; and *The Female Culture* (Toronto: Vickers & Benson Ltd., 1976).

18. Beverlee B. Anderson, "Working Women Versus Non-Working Women: A Comparison of Shopping Behaviors," in *1972 Combined Proceedings,* ed. B.W. Becker and H. Becker (Chicago: American Marketing Association, 1973), pp. 355–359; and Suzanne H. McCall, "Meet the Workwife," *Journal of Marketing* 41 (July 1977):55–65.

19. Mary Joyce and Joseph Guiltinan, "The Professional Woman: A Potential Market Segment for Retailers," *Journal of Retailing* 54 (Summer 1978):59–70.

20. Susan P. Douglas, "Cross National Comparisons and Consumer Stereotypes: A Case Study of Working and Non-Working Wives in the U.S. and France," *Journal of Consumer Research* 3 (June 1976):12–20.

21. Mary Lou Roberts and Lawrence H. Wortzel, "New Life-Style Determinants of Women's Food Shopping Behavior," *Journal of Marketing* 43 (Summer 1979):28–39; and "Wives' Employment and Shopping Goals as Determinants of Information Gathering Strategies for Food Purchasing and Preparation," in *1979 Educators' Conference Proceedings,* ed. N. Beckwith et al. (Chicago: American Marketing Association, 1979), pp. 220–225.

22. Susan P. Douglas, "Do Working Wives Read Different Magazines from Non-Working Wives?" *Journal of Advertising* 6 (Winter 1977):40–43, 48; and Arlene Sosani and George J. Szybillo, "Working Wives: Their General Television Viewing and Magazine Readership Behavior," *Journal of Advertising* 7 (Spring 1978):5–13.

23. Colby Coates, "Growth of Working Women a Boon to NBC Radio," *Advertising Age,* 7 August 1978, p. 32; Sheri Cragi, "TV Day: Just One Thing Missing," *Marketing,* 10 November 1980, pp. 3, 57; and Bill Katz, "The Influence of Lifestyle on Women's Media Habits," *Marketing,* 21 April 1980, pp. 20–28, 30.

24. Reno Bartos, *The Moving Target.*

25. Michael E. Pralle, "Survey Dispels Myths About Growing Dual-Earner Market," *Marketing News,* 16 May 1980, p. 17.

26. 'B&B Study Says Males Domestic," *Advertising Age,* 6 October 1980, p. 53; and *Men's Changing Role in the Family of the '80's,* (Toronto: Benton & Bowles Canada, Ltd., 1980).

27. "'New Breed' Husbands Are Happy Cookers: New Research Identifies Subsegments of Married Men," *Marketing News,* 14 November 1980, p. 7; "C&W Discovers a 'New Breed' of Husband," *Advertising Age,* 10 November 1980, p. 64; and Bernice Kanner, "C&W Finds Males Doing More at Home," *Advertising Age,* 14 July 1980, p. 84.

28. "BBDO Discovers Women Have It Tougher," *Advertising Age,* 26 November 1979, p. 3.

5

Preferences for Sex-Role Portrayals in Advertising

It has been documented in chapter 1 that advertisers, for the most part, continue to show stereotyped portrayals of the sexes in their advertising campaigns. This advertising, in the process of selling products and services, tends to sell supplemental images as well. As noted in 1975 by the National Advertising Review Board, these images may contribute to the maintenance of some undesirable aspects of the status quo in society.[1] Advertising polls which measured the criticisms leveled against advertising (chapter 2) and research which demonstrated that sexist advertising results in negative social consequences, especially among children (chapter 3), have had only limited impact on advertisers. Despite the dramatic evidence of major attitudinal and behavioral changes among men and women (chapter 4), advertising has continued to show sex-stereotyped portrayals because advertisers believe they are more effective in selling their products.

One way to convince advertisers to use more liberated portrayals of men and women in their advertising is to demonstrate to them that modern, less stereotyped advertisements are equally or more effective than the copy approaches currently in use. Thus, to achieve change in advertising's portrayal of the sexes, it was necessary to show advertisers that progressive, more liberated advertising can be an effective communications and selling tool. Consequently, the advertising effectiveness of stereotyped advertising emerged as an important research issue during the late 1970s. Researchers began asking the question, "Can more progressive portrayals of men and women communicate effectively?"

The area of greatest research interest concerns the advertising effectiveness of different kinds of role portrayals of women in advertising. This research has examined whether, and under what conditions, more progressive, less stereotyped portrayals may be preferred to traditional ones. This chapter reviews the research evidence regarding preferences for sex-role portrayals in advertising. Many of the studies incorporated laboratory or field experimental designs to test the effectiveness of variations in sex-role portrayals. Preferences for advertisements in both print and broadcast media are considered, as well as how preferences relate to: the gender of the model in the advertisement; the product advertised; and audience characteristics, including gender, employment status, liberatedness, and advertising expertise.

Gender of Human Models in Product Advertisements

In 1963, David Ogilvy, president of Ogilvy and Mather Advertising, asserted that "when you use a photograph of a woman, men ignore your advertisements, and when you use photographs of a man, you exclude women from your audience."[2] One explanation for the use of human models in advertisements is that they provide a meaningful context for the advertised product. As a result, consumers may pay attention to the advertisement and thus have the opportunity to form positive attitudes toward the product. Of interest to advertising researchers wishing to test Ogilvy's claim is what differences in consumer attention and attitudes are expected when male and female models in product advertisements are compared? And do the results of the model comparison apply to all kinds of products, or do certain products fair better with a specific model type? To answer these questions through systematic experimental exploration, Kanungo and his colleagues at McGill University designed and conducted two studies to measure the effects of variation in the use of human models in advertisements on the perceptions of and attitudes toward both durable and nondurable products.

Kanungo and Pang selected four frequently advertised consumer durables (car, sofa, stereo, and television) for their 1973 study.[3] To obtain meaningful measures of the effect of human models on the attitudes of potential customers towards the products, twenty adults were asked what product qualities or characteristics they would look for when buying each of the products. Kanungo and Pang selected the eleven most frequently cited qualities of the automobile and eight most frequently stated qualities for each of the other three products as the relevant quality dimensions. A rating sheet was then designed for each product to measure on a seven-point scale the attitude toward the product on each quality dimension.

Advertisements were prepared, using clippings from magazines and catalogs, such that each product advertisement included either a male model, a female model, a male-female pair, or no model (control treatment). Each of the sixty-four randomly selected student respondents was randomly assigned to rate an advertisement for each product with a different model treatment. The experimental design provided that the four model treatments be evaluated independently by male and female groups of subjects, which allowed the quality ratings of each product to be analyzed separately by treatment condition for male and female subjects.

The findings of Kanungo and Pang's study revealed that the effects of the gender of human models on consumer attention and attitudes are not as simplistic as Ogilvy's assertion. The results suggest an interaction between the model's gender and the product because the three variations of model gender have differential effects for different products. An overall favorable attitude toward the product was created among all subjects when a male model was used for the car and a female model was used for the sofa, while using opposite-sexed models resulted in unfavorable attitudes toward the car and sofa. All respondents also were in agreement that gender of the model did not effect attitudes toward the stereo because the three treatment conditions including models produced similar favorable responses. Gender of the subject did, however, effect the ratings of the advertisements for the television. When compared to the control-treatment condition, any model caused an unfavorable attitude toward the television among the male subjects. Female subjects, on the other hand, responded favorably only when a male-female pair was used.

Kanungo and Pang explained the product-model interaction as a function of the fittingness of the gender of the model to the stereotyped masculine/feminine image of the product. A separate sample of thirty-five students, who had previously judged the car as more masculine, the soft as more feminine, the stereo as equally masculine and feminine, and the television as neither masculine nor feminine, provided the researchers with the image measures required to make the comparisons. They found that the congruity of a product-model match results in an increased favorable attitude for the product, while the incongruity of a product-model mismatch produces unfavorable responses. From an advertising effectiveness point of view, the researchers advised that it is important to determine the perceived qualities of a specific product and the corresponding image they convey to potential consumer segments before deciding the gender of the model to use in advertising. Of course, the best match between the product and the model is the goal of such considerations.

In 1975 Kanungo and Johar designed a follow-up study to extend the generalizability of the fittingness-of-model hypothesis which was suggested by the results of the experiment with the four high-priced consumer durables.[4] They tested whether a match or mismatch between the product image (masculine or feminine) and the sex of the human model in an advertisement creates in the mind of the consumer a favorable or unfavorable product image. Kanungo and Johar used three low-priced consumer nondurables: coffee, bath soap, and toothpaste. Each of the products was judged in a preliminary test by twenty male students to have neither an exclusively masculine nor feminine image. Since the products are used frequently by both sexes, these results do not imply that the product images are neutral or sexless, but that they evoke equally masculine and feminine images.

The effects of human model characteristics on consumer attitudes were investigated by utilizing three common attitude measures: the consumer's perceived credibility or believability of the message, his perceived interest in the product, and his buying intentions. Advertisements for each of the three nondurable products were prepared with a male model, a female model, a male-female pair, and no model (control), following a process similar to that used to prepare the advertisements for the durable products. Employing a counterbalanced procedure involving a factorial design, subsets of the advertisements were randomly allocated to ninety-six adult-male-office workers who rated the advertisements on seven-point scales. Analysis of variance was then performed on the ratings of the subjects to determine the effect on attitudes by variations in model gender.

The results of the analysis of variance revealed that in advertisements for all three consumer nondurables studied, the use of the male-female pair model significantly increased the credibility of the advertised message, the likeableness of the product, and the intention-to-buy score. The positive effects of the male-female pair corroborate the earlier findings for durable products—that the model effect on attitudes toward the product is a function of the fittingness of the model for the product. For all three consumer nondurables and their associated advertisements both the product and the male-female pair model were perceived as equally masculine and feminine. Kanungo and Johar suggest that this explanation, based on matching gender images, is more tenable than others considered as to why a male-female pair is the most appropriate gender model for each of the products.

Kanungo and Johar's experimental findings do appear to extend the generalizability of the fittingness-of-model hypothesis to nondurable products, at least to those with equally masculine and feminine images. However, masculine, feminine, and sexless-imaged nondurable products were not tested. Also, the experiment was limited to male subjects who based their ratings on a single exposure of each advertisement. Consequently, to generalize the results to female consumers or to multiple exposure situations would require further empirical investigations with products of variously perceived gender-related images.

Although the results of these experiments fall short of providing specific guidelines for determining the appropriate gender of model to use in advertisements for durable and nondurable products, they do suggest that advertisements could be created to be more effective if the model matched the image of the product advertised. For example, instead of traditional, stereotyped model-product pairings, male-female pairs may be more effective as models for nondurable goods and for some durable items as well. However, as documented in chapter I, the state of the art is such that women are still portrayed predominantly in print advertisements for nondurable products (for example, food items, cleaning aids, and personal-care and cosmetic products), while men are overrepresented in advertisements for durable, big-ticket items (for example, cars, televisions, and stereos). The research findings from Kanungo and his colleagues' experiments provide practitioners with tentative empirical evidence that model changes in print copy can result in advertising which is a more effective communications vehicle.

Recognition of Gender Stereotypes

Although stereotyped advertising issues involve portrayals of both genders, the majority of media-content analyses (chapter 1), most of the negative attitudes toward sexist portrayals (chapter 2), and the major concerns expressed regarding social-conditioning effects (chapter 3) have focused on the roles of women rather than men. Lull, Hanson, and Marx extended this female orientation by researching the question, "Do viewers recognize the discriminatory sex-role portrayals inherent in so many television commercials; and if so, what types of portrayals do they find most objectionable?"[5] They explored the degree to which college men and women are sensitive to sex-role stereotyping of females and the types of which they are most aware.

Six color commercials were chosen from a videotape of three-hundred because they represented common negative stereotypes of women cited in the literature.[6] The selected television advertisements typified woman as fulfilling usual domestic tasks (for example, household expert, dependent on men, demeaned housewife), in appearance-role portrayals (for example, dumb broad, growing old), and in an unhappy marriage (for example, powerless to change).

A sample of sixty-seven women and fifty-seven men, drawn randomly from a university population, viewed the six commercials and then described their immediate reactions to each one by responding on an open-ended questionnaire. Each written response was coded by three raters for viewer recognition or nonrecognition of the stereotype. The 124 subjects also completed a seven-item feminism scale designed to measure the degree of personal affiliation with principles of the women's liberation movement.

Lull, Hanson, and Marx found that women were generally more aware than men of the stereotypical female portrayal and recognized the stereotypes significantly more often than the men in four of the six commercials. Women were far more sensitive to two of the domestic-task portrayals (for example, household expert, dependent on men) and to both of the appearance-role portrayals. Although fewer than half of the subjects recognized these portrayals as sexist, over three-fourths of the college women recognized the dumb-broad stereotype, while approximately four men in ten classified the powerless-to-change and growing-old advertisements as sexist.

The study also provided evidence that recognition of sex stereotypes depends to some degree upon reported agreement with the ideals of women's liberation. The correlations between sexism recognition and the feminism score were significant for both male and female subjects, but the relationship was stronger for women. Therefore, while Lull and his colleagues did not find widespread recognition of sex-role stereotyping among all their college students, those who had cognitively committed to feminism were more aware of outmoded cliches in female role presentations.

In addition, it was discovered in the analysis of the written responses that women were more critical of the female stereotypes than were men. While men often commented on the stereotypical roles of male characters in the commercials, even when they were only peripherally displayed, women expressed strongest disapproval of the dumb-broad portrayal. This degree of recognition and criticism of traditional advertising portrayals of women, among both male and female young adults, should signal to advertisers that today's woman and today's man are different. This growing segment of consumers has modern attitudes and is sensitive to outdated advertising appeals. The results of this study suggest that many of today's young adults would be less critical of advertising if it rid itself of those irritating sex-role stereotypes of women and portray females in modern, nonsexist roles.

Preferences for Sex-Role Portrayals in Magazine Advertisements

By the late 1970s advertisements depicting new roles for women had appeared in some magazines. The promotional effectiveness of these changes, however, had not been tested. What remained to be answered was whether the liberated forms of nonstereotyped models used in the new advertisements were attaining the desired objectives of the advertisers.

To evaluate the newer life-style themes in advertising, Bettinger and Dawson conducted a pilot study in 1977 to assess the differing degrees of liberated life-styles in ten full-page advertisements for cigarettes and hair-coloring products.[7] Liberated life-styles were regarded as those portraying women as individuals expressing independence in nontraditional occupations and emphasized emerging roles of women in society. A panel of twenty-one women ranked the advertisements. One-half of the advertisements were discarded in the pretest due to a lack of agreement among the panel members, while the remaining five advertisements exhibited consistent and different levels of liberated life-styles.

Next, 226 female subjects from five widely dispersed geographical areas ranked the five advertisements on the basis of overall preference and rated them on other descriptive qualities. The empirical data collected from these respondents were used to test the hypothesis that women favor the utilization of liberated life-styles in magazine advertising. Bettinger and Dawson expected that advertisements which catered to this preference would produce a more favorable product orientation. However, preference for the advertisements was found to be inversely related to the degree of liberated life-style expressed by the advertisements. Women respondents did not find a sex-object role to be offensive, annoying, or undesirable, while a female model portrayed in a traditionally masculine occupation was regarded as distasteful. The researchers concluded that magazine advertisers may have gone too far with the role-reversal concept.

Because of the importance of the issues investigated and the unexpected findings, Bettinger and Dawson recommended that a more extensive study be conducted. The limited availability of advertisements with differing degrees of liberated life-styles necessitated that they restrict their research to only two products to reduce costs. They admitted that since the purpose of hair dye is to enhance beauty, the hair-color advertisements by their very nature are subject to criticism. They may suggest to some that a female is a sex object, regardless of the portrayal. Based on their own admission, plus the importance of product differences in Kanungo's studies on model preference, it is recommended that different products be used in any follow-up research. Also, randomly selected respondents, rather than volunteer subjects, should be utilized.

Bettinger and Dawson's pilot study did demonstrate that advertising which depicts a liberated life-style may be as displeasing to certain females in the U.S. market as some traditional role portrayals. Advertisements varying in life-style portrayal for a number of products need to be evaluated to determine if there are product category/advertising style interactions which influence the preferences of these women. However tentative these findings, though, the researchers' cautions are worth heeding: feminists' demands may exceed the requirements of women customers, and subconscious desires of female product users can be exceeded by advertisers who liberalize life-style themes too much for the majority of their consumers.

Role Preference in Relation to Product Advertised

Criticism that Bettinger and Dawson restricted their research to only two products was overcome in two studies which specifically examined the preferences for female role portrayals in magazine advertisements as they relate to a wider range of advertised products. Using two different research methodologies, both studies addressed the question: What role portrayals are most likely to make the product being advertised most desirable?

In 1974 Wortzel and Frisbie asked a convenience sample of one-hundred demographically dispersed, young women to design print advertisements, by matching pictures of products with pictures of women, so the advertisements would be most likely to make each subject want to buy the products. The women selected product pictures from a portfolio containing pictures of three products in each of seven product categories for a total of twenty-one pictures. Small and large appliances, food, and household items represented products used by families; women's products were categorized separately as grooming aids and personal products; while pictures of male products, which women may purchase, were grouped into one category—men's grooming and personal products. A second portfolio of twenty-five pictures selected by a jury of women consisted of five pictures depicting women in each of five roles: neutral, career, family, fashion, and sex object.

Analysis of the subjects' 2,100 constructed advertisements revealed across product categories no consistent preference for specific female roles that always increased product desirability. Instead, preferred role portrayals appeared to have been chosen on the basis of specific product classes. For the four types of products used by both male and female household members, the family role was preferred. For women's products the product's desirability was increased when the woman in the advertisement was portrayed in a neutral or career setting, although the fashion role was also acceptable. The sex-object role was not considered to be the most effective role portrayal for any of the seven products. Even for men's grooming and personal products, the sex-object role was ranked third behind fashion and career-role portrayals. Wortzel and Frisbie concluded that women react primarily to the product-use situation and do not wish to be stereotyped to any particular role which can be generalized across product lines.

Although subjects were warned in the Wortzel and Frisbie study to avoid selecting product-women role pairs that they would expect from exposure to current advertising, Buchanan and Reid questioned whether the construct-an-advertisement methodology completely negated such socializing effects.[9] Therefore, to substantiate Wortzel and Frisbie's findings, Buchanan and Reid developed an alternative experimental approach for implementation.

Sixteen male and sixteen female college students were each asked to evaluate one of four portfolios, each containing four specially designed advertisements in which a product is matched with a female role portrayal. The four product categories were: an instant-breakfast drink, a bath cleaner, a set of golf clubs, and a blood-center-donation appeal. The female model in the four advertisements portrayed either a housewife, a grade-school teacher, a cab driver, or a Ph.D. in physics. The Latin Square, factorially designed experiment, with repeated measures across both product categories and role portrayals, specified that each subject rate each of the four advertisements in the portfolio on the basis of twenty evaluative semantic differential scale items. Following a factor analysis of the item scores, a scale score was computed for each subject by summing those items which loaded on the good/bad factor. The summated scale score served as the dependent variable in the analysis of variance of the four products by four roles Latin Square design.

The results indicated that there was a significant difference among the role portrayals in each product category, as well as among the product categories for each of the four roles. The significant main and interaction effects led Buchanan and Reid to conclude that perceptions of the advertisements were not based solely on the role portrayals of the female models. Instead, perception of each advertisement varied according to the product, the role and their interaction, because no role was consistently the best across all four product categories. According to the authors of this follow-up study, the value of their experimental findings is that they substantiate Wortzel and Frisbie's earlier conclusion that no one role portrayal for women, be it traditional or nontraditional, is the most influential over all product categories.

Buchanan and Reid suggest that copy research be directed to specifying which cues are picked up from various female models so that more effective advertising can be developed for specific products. They proposed that successfully tested nontraditional portrayals could make advertising messages more representative of modern women in certain target groups. Implementing such portrayals, they claim, may offset some social criticism in addition to contributing to the development of more effective advertising messages.

*The Relationship between Feminist Orientation and
Role Preference*

Chapters 1 and 2 contain documentation that much of the pressure to show women in advertisements in nontraditional roles was generated by proponents of the feminist movement. It is, therefore, worthwhile to investigate whether women who believe most strongly in the tenets of women's liberation also tend to perceive a product as more desirable if the woman in the advertisement is portrayed in a nonstereotyped role. In other words, does the positive relationship between personal affiliation with principles of the women's liberation movement and consequent recognition of sex stereotypes extend to preferences for sex roles in print advertisements?

Using advertisements disguised for brand name, Mazis and Beuttenmuller investigated attitudes toward women's liberation and the perception of advertisements among a group of college women.[10] They found that female students react to favorable and unfavorable role portrayals, as defined by feminists, in accordance with their positive or negative attitudes toward liberation issues. However, their results should be interpreted with caution as the respondents were limited to college women.

In Wortzel and Frisbie's design-a-print-advertisement study, the researchers also tested the hypothesis that "those women who most strongly agree with the tenets of the women's liberation movement will most strongly consider a product's desirability enhanced when a woman appearing in the advertisement is portrayed in a career or neutral (less traditional) role, rather than in a sex-object, family, or fashion-object (more traditional) role."[11] While their sample of one hundred young women was not drawn randomly, it was not limited to college women. Instead, every effort was made to insure that a sample with a representative distribution of demographic characteristics of females between the ages of twenty-one and thirty-five would be achieved. Wortzel and Frisbie felt that the younger women would be more sympathetic than older women to nontraditional roles in advertisements, but not as sensitive as college women.

Their results, however, showed that the role-preference pattern was similar for women with positive attitudes toward women's liberation and for those respondents with negative attitudes. Women with feminist attitudes did not show a consistent preference for neutral or career roles for the different product lines. In fact, these respondents selected the family role for small and large appliances, household items, and food more frequently than did the more traditional women. Another interesting pattern that Wortzel and Frisbie observed was that feminist-oriented women were more opinionated than their counterparts about sex-role preferences; they were more likely to select a specific role than to indicate no preference.

Wortzel and Frisbie's interpretation is that the product seems to be more important than attitudes toward the liberation movement in determining which role portrayal most enhances a product's desirability. They concluded that women appear to be both reasonable and rational in their preferences, selecting role preferences on the basis of product function, not on the basis of ideology. Their message to advertisers is that if a product is one which is normally used in a household environment, then nonliberationists as well as liberationists prefer to see it in that type of setting in advertising. On the other hand, if the product is one which women use personally to improve their self-concepts, then nontraditional roles are preferred by both liberationists and nonliberationists.

As an extension of the Wortzel-Frisbie study, Ducker and Tucker undertook research to investigate further the relationship between profeminist predispositions and the perception of advertisers' portrayal of women in different roles.[12] They went a step further than their predecessors by developing a more rigorous model of profeminism, incorporating into the research a previously tested personality characteristic that was based on Barron's independence-of-judgment test and served as a moderating variable.[13] Through the use of this personality measure, Ducker and Tucker statistically controlled socially desirable transitory attitude statements, resulting in a more stable measure which relates to a central personality characteristic.

Rather than rely on the use of the Wortzel and Frisbie design-and-advertisement technique, Ducker and Tucker used actual advertisements from national magazines as stimuli. They selected seven print advertisements and pretested them to insure that they projected the image of women as: mother, sex object, glamour girl, housewife, working mother, modern woman, and professional. A convenience sample of 104 female college students evaluated each of the seven advertisements by reacting to the woman and/or her role in the advertisement. Responses were coded as either liking or disliking the advertised image of women. In addition, the young women completed the independence-of-judgment test and the Wortzel-Frisbie feminism scale.

Analysis of covariance procedures adjusted the variance on the women's liberation scale for subjects' individual differences on the independence-of-judgment test, which enabled Ducker and Tucker to classify the respondents on the basis of adjusted feminism scores as either traditionalist, neutral, or profeminist. Further statistical analysis of the advertising-evaluation scores indicated that reactions to the women in the advertisements were not different among the members in each of the three respondent categories.

Ducker and Tucker concluded that their results show that holding profeminist opinions, even by younger, educated, independent women, does not affect their regard for the roles assigned to women in print advertisements. If these findings could be extrapolated to other segments than college women, then certain advertising policy problems and dilemmas would be minimized. Advertisers would need to worry less about channeling different advertisements into different media to accommodate the profeminist consumers. Instead, they could focus their efforts on determining the appropriate image of women for a specific product so as to increase the clarity of the product's positioning for both profeminist and traditional consumers.

The fact that Ducker and Tucker using different research procedures and advertising stimuli reached conclusions similar to Wortzel and Frisbie's counter-intuitive findings does not resolve all the concerns regarding the validity of their results. For example, their women's liberation scale has not been validated as a sensitive measure of profeminist orientation. Instead, its application has been limited to two convenience samples of young women who, the authors admitted, were most likely biased toward including a high proportion of women sympathetic to portrayals of nontraditional roles in advertising. Until a better measure of profeminist orientation is developed and tested on a probability sample of women, the caution relating to Mazis and Beuttenmuller's significant results should be heeded for the Wortzel-Frisbie and Ducker-Tucker nonsignificant findings as well. At this point in time, the question of the relationship between feminist orientation and role preference of advertising's portrayal of women remains open.

The Relationship between Demographic Descriptors and Role Preference

The present uncertainty regarding what influences role preference in advertising hinders practitioners who may wish to channel nontraditional advertisements into magazines. To obtain estimates of different segments' responsiveness to alternative advertising copy, appropriate segment descriptors are needed. Advertisers typically rely on geographic variables and demographic descriptors, such as gender, age, education, employment, and income as segmenting variables for media-selection decisions. If these market descriptors were also related to role preferences in print advertisements, guidelines for developing copy for specific media could incorporate common audience descriptors into the market-segment definitions.

In Bettinger and Dawson's study, the authors investigated geographic and age influences on preferences for role portrayals.[14] They anticipated some differences due to location and size of metropolitan areas because of the stereotyped, liberal big-city image. However, differences in attitude toward liberation-oriented advertising themes were not found to exist among the five diverse and geographically different test markets. Furthermore, an analysis by size of metro area did not reveal a large-city tendency to prefer nontraditional feminine life-style themes. Their data also failed to support the existence of age differences significantly affecting preferences for the various life-styles portrayed in the print advertisements for cigarettes and hair-coloring products. When differences did appear, younger women expressed more traditional views than did the older group, especially toward the advertisement depicting women in the dual role of wage earner and homemaker.

When Wortzel and Frisbie conducted further analysis of their data, they also controlled the two descriptive variables among their sample of young women.[15] They reached similar conclusions about education and employment. Their analysis revealed no significant demographic-segment deviations from the overall preference patterns for specific female roles.

However, in the follow-up study to Wortzel and Frisbie's design-an-advertisement study, Buchanan and Reid did find demographic differences in role preferences.[16] They measured both male and female responses to the sixteen test advertisements and found that female subjects were more critical of the advertisements in general. An interesting observation they made concerning the housewife portrayal was the significant trend for women to be more critical of this particular role portrayal than of the others. Results of a pair-wise analysis of the similarity of the advertisements showed the females perceived all of the advertisements differently to a significant degree, while on the other hand male subjects perceived all of the advertisements differently, with the exception of four pairs.

It appears that of the various demographic variables which have been studied with respect to their relationship to recognition of and preference for role portrayals in advertisements, only gender of the respondent has consistently produced significant differences. As reported earlier, Kanungo and Pang found sex differences in preferences for the gender of the model in television advertisements.[17] Lull, Hanson, and Marx, when studying recognition of stereotypes in television commercials, found that female subjects were more aware and critical of stereotypical portrayals than were men.[18] And Buchanan and Reid corroborated these results for print advertisements.[19]

Preferences for Sex-Role Portrayals in Television Commercials

Do sex differences in recognition of stereotypes in television commercials, according to Lull's conclusions, extend to preferences for role portrayals in television advertisements too? To determine if gender and/or other demographic characteristics are meaningful segment descriptors of broadcast audiences, the research which has used television advertisements as stimuli must be studied. Overall television advertising role preferences, plus differences based on segment characteristics, will be examined in this section.

In chapter 1 it was pointed out that conducting monitoring research studies of role portrayals in television commercials was extremely difficult when compared to the content-analysis procedures for print advertisements. A similar increase in complexity applies to sex-role-preference research involving television commercials versus print advertisements. Not only must television commercials representing appropriate sex-role portrayals be found after a painstaking search or designed with extreme care, but respondents must base their preference ratings on both video and audio components of the advertisements. The added difficulty associated with broadcast commercial evaluations probably has been a significant contributing factor to the small number of such sex-role preference-studies.

Courtney and Whipple overcame many of the aforementioned difficulties with the assistance of the Advertising Advisory Board (AAB) and Spitzer, Mills, and Bates advertising agency and conducted a study in 1976 of the reaction to traditional versus liberated portrayals of women in television advertising.[20] The AAB, through its task force on advertising to women, made funds available for the research and provided substantial research advice. Spitzer, Mills, and Bates Advertising prepared the creative work used in the study and participated actively in the definition of creative goals for the project. Four national advertisers made these contributions even more valuable by permitting the use of their products in advertisements for the study. Their cooperation contributed significantly to the realism of the research. In addition, Contemporary Research Center assisted in the field-work design and conducted the interviews. The efforts and cooperation of these various organizations enabled the researchers to design and execute a study to gather the action-oriented information that advertisers require in order to make creative decisions concerning the portrayal of women in their advertising.

Six commercials—two on-air and four new ones—were prepared for evaluation. The on-air control commercials were advertisements previously prepared by the agency for two of its clients. They were chosen because they represented the extremes of traditional and liberated advertising styles being shown on television at the time. The traditional control advertisement depicted an overbearing mother-in-law complaining to her daughter-in-law about the unsightly spots left on her son's glassware by an inferior brand of dishwasher detergent. The mother-in-law suggests that the sponsor's brand should be used to prevent spotting. The liberated control advertisement, on the other hand, showed a female television director, surrounded by her male assistants in the booth, who is too busy to worry about underarm perspiration. She uses the advertised brand of personal deodorant so she will not have to be concerned while she works.

The agency also prepared the creative work and produced four test commercials especially for the study. Two test advertisements for each of two products—a food product and a household cleaner—were designed. These products were chosen because commercials in these product categories had received many complaints regarding the way they portrayed women. A breakfast-food advertisement and a floor-cleaner advertisement, each developed to reflect conventional advertising style with regard to role portrayal, were labeled traditional. Alternative versions for each product, considered to be liberated by the researchers and advertising agency, represented creative attempts to portray modern sex roles without being extreme. The two versions of each advertisement differed with respect to the major components of role portrayal, including the gender of the voice-over and the product representative, the occupation of the product spokesperson, and the tasks and activities performed by the product representative.

The traditional breakfast-food advertisement portrayed a full-time housewife preparing breakfast for and serving it to her husband and two children. A male voice-over was used. The liberated version for the identical brand showed the same family cooperating in breakfast preparation as the mother prepares to go to work. A female voice-over was used. The same copy points are made in both versions.

The traditional and liberated versions of the floor-cleaner advertisement differ in the gender of the product representative, the product demonstrator, and the voice-over. The traditional version showed two women competing in a male-conducted mopping contest. The liberated counterpart showed a husband and wife competing in the same contest, conducted by a female product representative, with a female voice-over.

All advertisements were prepared for showing on a portable audio-video player which is commonly used in advertising pretesting. The agency recorded the commercials on an audio-video tape that contained art-work main frames for each advertisement and that were coordinated with recorded audio.

Preference for the advertisements was based on respondent ratings on a five-point scale of how well fourteen evaluative items described each advertisement. Nine of the items were selected from a reaction profile of stable copy-testing factors used for describing advertisements.[21] The remaining five items included two persuasive communication attributes and three sex-role related phrases. The final list of items was determined on the basis of pretest results.

Female respondents, selected to rate the commercials on each of the fourteen items, represented a cross section of demographic groups from a small, conservative city located in a rural area. A systematic random selection procedure was used to draw a multistaged, geographically stratified proportionate area-probability sample of households from a sample frame of census-enumeration areas. Interviewers were instructed to call back as many times as was necessary to make contact at each designated household. In each household the woman who was between the ages of eighteen and forty-nine and who did the major grocery shopping was interviewed. A total of 144 eligible women, typical of area residents with respect to age, marital status, and occupation agreed to evaluate the commercials. Three fourths of the women indicated they were married, while 54 percent classified themselves as full-time housewives. Of the 46 percent who worked outside the home, over 60 percent had full-time jobs.

The subjects were randomly allocated to one of two groups to form two matched subsamples on such demographic characteristics as age, education, income, marital status, and occupation. Both groups rated the liberated and the traditional control advertisements. In addition, subsample one rated the traditional breakfast-food advertisement and the liberated floor-cleaner advertisement, while subsample two evaluated the remaining pair of test commercials—the liberated breakfast-food and the traditional floor-cleaner advertisements.

The fourteen-item ratings for each of the six advertisements were factor analyzed separately to determine the underlying advertisement-rating factor structure. Two independent evaluative dimensions were derived for each advertisement and labeled: effectiveness and irritation. Advertising-effectiveness scores were then computed for all respondents by summing the following eight-item ratings for each advertisement: realistic situation, original, intelligent, for women like me, worth remembering, meaningful to me, convincing, and makes me want to buy. An advertising-irritation score was also computed in a similar manner for each respondent by summing the ratings on three items: insulting to men, insulting to women, and irritating. The remaining items appeared to be three separate factors of minor importance and, therefore, were omitted.

All six commercials received high levels of playback of the advertising message because over 80 percent of the subjects were able to do so without being aided. The role depictions in the advertisements did not seem to affect playback of the major selling points.

Subsample comparisons of the traditional dishwasher-detergent and the liberated, personal-deodorant on-air commercials resulted in no significant sample differences in advertising-effectiveness scores for either of these two control advertisements. But when effectiveness scores for test advertisements were compared, subjects were found to have evaluated the breakfast-food advertisement showing liberated role portrayals as significantly more effective than its traditional counterpart. They agreed that the liberated version was significantly more original, worth remembering, and more likely to make the consumer want to buy the product. The two versions of the floor-cleaner advertisement were rated as equally effective, as the women only slightly preferred the liberated version, judging it to be significantly more convincing. The effectiveness scores indicate that both versions of the mopping-contest commercial were considered to be relatively ineffective by the respondents. However, overall, for the two product categories studied, the liberated advertising style was rated at least equal to, if not superior in effectiveness to, the traditional style.

When the analysis turned to the irritation-scale scores, subsample comparisons resulted in virtually no sample differences in the irritation ratings of the two on-air, control advertisements. Furthermore, all respondents agreed that the traditional dishwasher-detergent control advertisement was by far the most irritating of the six commercials tested. Irritation ratings for the traditional and liberated versions of both the breakfast-food and the floor-cleaner test advertisements also were very similar.

Courtney and Whipple concluded that liberated sex-role portrayals in television commercials are at least equally preferred to, and in some cases more preferred, than traditional advertising approaches. While many of the differences among the individual-item ratings of the six commercials were not of great magnitude, it is striking that all liberated advertisements scored higher than their traditional counterparts on several measures of advertising effectiveness. Commercials portraying female product representatives, showing working housewives, depicting men participating in household tasks, and using female voice-overs were rated as more effective than matched commercials employing more traditional portrayals. When compared on irritation level, the liberated commercials were just about as likely to be rated as irritating as the traditional versions. The subjects agreed that it is possible to create television commercials with modern portrayals and to do so effectively without causing consumer irritation; but that exaggerated or unreal presentations of the sexes, be they traditional or liberated in style, cause significant irritation. While liberated may be better, it is apparent from the findings that some kinds of liberated commercials are more effective than others. The real issue from the advertising effectiveness point-of-view is not whether to be liberated, but rather how to be liberated without being irritating. These findings suggest that advertisers should be exploring more modern approaches to the portrayal of both men and women as they demonstrate products and relay product benefits to television audiences.

The Relationship between Feminist Orientation and
Role Preference

In addition to examining differences among the commercials tested, Courtney and Whipple also investigated the way respondent differences effected ratings of the advertisements.[22] They investigated whether the women in their sample who believed most strongly with the principles of the feminist movement would also tend to favor a commercial if the women in the advertisement were portrayed in a liberated, more modern manner.

To obtain respondents' attitudes toward female liberation, they selected eight items from the Traditional Family Ideology Scale which measures exaggerated masculinity/femininity.[23] Seven of these items proved to be sufficiently correlated to develop a summary liberation score for each respondent. When the liberation scores were correlated with advertising-effectiveness scores, Courtney and Whipple found that respondents' attitudes toward women's liberation were not significantly related to the effectiveness evaluations of either test or control advertisements. Instead, more positive attitudes toward liberation seemed to be associated with more negative evaluations of the effectiveness of both liberated and traditional commercials. Also, women with a feminist orientation were more likely to find the advertisements irritating. In general, liberated women were more critical of all the commercials. This relationship was particularly evident in the reactions to the traditional breakfast-food test advertisement and the traditional dishwashing-detergent control commercial.

In an attempt to ascertain if another personality variable was related to advertising effectiveness and irritation, respondents were asked to rate eight items selected from the Berger Self-Acceptance Scale.[24] Three of the items measured self-confidence and were sufficiently correlated to form a sub-scale. However, there was little or no relationship between self-confidence and the evaluations of advertising effectiveness and irritation. On the whole, the only consistent finding was that the higher a woman was in self-confidence, the less likely she was to find the test and control advertisements irritating.

Overall, attitudes toward women's liberation and individual self-confidence were not highly correlated with ratings of advertising effectiveness or irritation. Consequently, Courtney and Whipple turned to demographic descriptors to determine if other respondent measures were related to the advertising effectiveness and irritation scores.

*The Relationship between Demographic Descriptors and
Role Preference*

Demographic measures, including age, education, income, marital status, and work status, were used to classify the respondents in the Courtney-Whipple study. First, the evaluations of the two on-air, control commercials were examined for the different demographic groups of subjects. The liberated, personal-deodorant advertisement scored higher in effectiveness than the traditional, dishwashing-detergent advertisement with all groups of women. In addition, the traditional on-air advertisement was rated as highly irritating by all groups of respondents and was significantly more irritating than the liberated control advertisement.

Next, both versions of each test commercial were compared with respect to each demographic group of respondents. Although most respondents considered both liberated commercials to be more effective than their traditional counterparts, the liberated advertisements appealed especially to certain segments of women. For example, the liberated breakfast-food advertisement was judged significantly more effective by women under thirty-five years old, those who did not have a college education, married women, and women who work full-time as a housewife or in the labor force. It is important to note that full-time housewives found the liberated version the more effective of the two, despite the fact that the commercial made a clear appeal to the busy working mother. Only among women who worked part-time was the traditional version judged more effective by a nonsignificant margin. The liberated floor-cleaner advertisement, on the other hand, was rated significantly more effective by only one group of women, part-time labor force participants. Moreover, no group of women found either traditional test advertisement more effective than its liberated counterpart.

Irritation scores across the demographic segments were very similar for the traditional and liberated versions of both test advertisements. Yet two groups of respondents, unmarried women and full-time workers, considered the traditional breakfast-food commercial to be significantly more irritating than the liberated version. When the irritation scores for the two cleaner commercials were compared, the traditional advertisement had significantly better ratings among two segments. Women with a family income of $15,000 or more and unmarried women judged the liberated floor-cleaner advertisement as more irritating than the traditional version. Otherwise, all other differences were nonsignificant.

Results of these demographic-segment comparisons indicate that one style of commercial, even if rated better overall, may not be best suited for all groups of women. Therefore, while advertisers determine how to be more liberated without being irritating, careful consideration and research must go into defining the target market for the advertised product. Only then can the most appropriate and effective advertising be created. If more than one segment is substantial enough to warrant separate commercials, then the portrayal of the sexes may differ depending on the segments involved. While more liberated approaches appear to be favored by most women sampled, the best particular variation of a portrayal will most likely differ from product to product and from segment to segment.

Of the demographic variables examined in the Courtney-Whipple study, working status of the respondents appeared to be the segment descriptor which most frequently produced significant differences in preference for liberated versus traditional role portrayals. Three other studies also have investigated whether housewives and employed women have similar or different preferences with respect to the way women are portrayed in television advertisements.

In a study of two-hundred women Leavitt found that both housewives and employed women rated commercials using working women as role models higher than they rated commercials using housewives.[25] Each woman who took part in the experiment viewed a commercial from each of two pairs, one with a housewife model and one with a working-woman model. As a result of his findings, Leavitt hypothesized that the housewives in his sample probably did not want to be typecast in traditional roles, whereas the employed women found the commercials depicting working women more convincing.

Another research study, undertaken by D'Arcy MacManus and Masius advertising agency, revealed preferences of women regarding their occupations as portrayed in commercials.[26] The advertising agency undertook group discussions among housewives (half labor-force workers, half not) to whom they showed two versions of the same basic commercial. In the first advertisement the woman plays her traditional role (giving her family breakfast, then waving them all off to work and school; suffering from a headache after a morning of cake baking; being admired for a shiny table). In the second advertisement the product representative is a modern woman (mother and father getting breakfast together and leaving home at the same time; coming home from work with a headache; polishing a table while her husband cooked). All the housewives agreed that small children were more likely to cause headaches than a day at work. Most of the respondents, in fact, saw work as a privilege rather than a burden.

The following conclusions emerged from the research: women do not wish any longer to be portrayed as enjoying domestic work, they bitterly resent domestic tasks being considered the main focus of their days, they do not with to occupy the supporting role in the lives of others, and more passionately than anything else, they object to being portrayed as gullible and uncritical.

In another attempt to find out how consumers feel about the imagery of women in advertising, Bartos conducted a study of four demographic segments: stay-at-home housewives, plan-to-work housewives, just-a-job working women and career-oriented working women.[27] To determine whether the female respondents reacted positively or negatively to the commercials they viewed, a like/dislike measure was used. Because like/dislike, according to Bartos, relates to the credibility of advertising, it was selected to measure women's emotional and attitudinal responses to the commercials.

Bartos concluded that the most striking result of the study was that all segments of women have much more in common than she assumed. The surprise was that all groups responded most positively to contemporary imagery in commercials and most negatively to traditional ones. Whether or not women are living modern life-styles, they endorse the new values and respond very positively to symbols of change.

All four segments responded positively to advertisements which: elicited emotional involvement and identification with contemporary roles; identified a woman playing many roles in the course of the day; showed father and mother sharing in child-caring duties; depicted women in work and achievement situations; reflected diversity in women with respect to age, life-style, and motivations; and implied respect for women's intelligence and judgment as consumers. Regarding the negative reactions, the commercials disliked most were those that: implied that family laundry or housework are a women's sole responsibility; put down her performance of chores as being less than perfect; treated men and women as incompetent, childish, or dim-witted; and showed women as sex objects. The most negative responses of all, however, were received for commercials which were considered to have a sexist tone. Some advertising was perceived as sexist because of semantics, for example, the use of girl instead of woman, or because the commercial epitomized a certain kind of protective approach toward women.

Some other issues relating to the role of women in commercials received mixed reviews from the four segments. Commercials with a sexy treatment elicited controversy. The most negative responses came from stay-at-home housewives, while the most tolerance of sexy treatments came from the career woman. Also, the notion of advertising personal products on television is a sensitive one to many women. This concern over privacy was particularly important to stay-at-home housewives. Career women, on the other hand, resented that advertisers focus on the intimate aspects of women's lives, but not those of men. They were the most outspoken group in expressing the view that: "If they can advertise sanitary napkins for women, why not condoms for men?"

Based on the results of her research, Bartos suggested that to make advertising directed to women more effective: separate strategies are probably not required, unless there are important differences in product needs, uses, or benefits among the four segments; new/working/career women should be advertised to with relevance, respect, and recognition of changing roles and attitudes; and women do not have to be shown in their occupational roles to reach them, just as housewives respond favorably to seeing working women in advertisements. Her study also suggests that career women, who have more disposable income than other segments and thus are extremely valuable customers of many products and services, are acutely sensitive to sexist portrayals. Bartos concluded that constructive action is necessary in the 1980s to meet the increasing challenge the career-women segment poses for advertisers.

A 1977 study, which examined demographic differences in preferences for sex-role portrayals in television advertisements, focused on the gender of the audience. Taking the position that a communication strategy should not offend an important portion of the market that advertising is attempting to reach, Kelly, Solomon, and Burke compared male and female responses to women's roles in advertising.[28] While some products are purchased almost exclusively by either males or females, they argued that a large number of household products are purchased by members of either sex, that the attitudes of both male and female segments should be of concern when the role portrayal of female models is under consideration for sex-neutral or dual-use products.

Kelly, Solomon, and Burke used a convenience sample of 328 students, 201 women and 127 men, for the experiment. Subjects were shown eight thirty-second commercials which were regularly being shown on television during the testing period, seven depicting women in various roles and one with no specific role portrayal. After viewing each commercial, respondents evaluated the advertisement, the product, and the sponsoring company, each on a set of four semantic differential scales. The three sets of semantic scores were then averaged to provide a single mean score for the advertisement, the product, and the company. The mean evaluations of the seven advertisements, the products advertised, and the sponsoring companies were then analyzed by sex of respondent through the use of difference in means tests.

The results suggested that there are male/female differences in preferences for the role portrayals of women in advertising. When women appear in traditional roles, male viewers rate advertisements, products, and sponsoring companies lower than do females. The lower male scores were most evident when the products advertised had appeals for purchasing by either sex. Advertisements with nontraditional role portrayals and those with both traditional and nontraditional women were rated very similarly by both males and females.

These experimental findings suggest that when women are portrayed in advertising which is targeted to a male audience, the most effective copy approach employs a combination of a traditional role with a nontraditional role or uses a nontraditional role alone. When appealing to male viewers, traditional roles used alone should be avoided. This conclusion is surprising, as studies of role preference in magazine advertising consistently have shown that females are more critical than males of traditional portrayals of women.

Kelly, Solomon, and Burke also found that the men in their study were more critical of traditional advertisements than were the female respondents. In addition, their finding is contrary to Lull, Hanson, and Marx's results regarding recognition and criticism of female role portrayals in television commercials.[29] Since the methodology employed and the advertising stimuli evaluated in these two limited television studies differed, the issue involving male versus female preferences for traditional roles in television advertisements will have to be left for future studies to resolve. At this point, however, it is safe to say that when developing television-advertising copy which portrays women in either traditional or more liberated roles, advertisers should not overlook the attitudes of males in the intended audience segment.

Portraying the New Woman and Man in
Television Commercials

Advertisers' efforts to portray the new woman in their advertising have resulted in fresh copy in some cases, while in other cases their advertisements have been criticized as unsuccessful attempts. One segment which has become upset by new-women portrayals is the U.S. male. In a national study conducted by Doyle, Dane, Bernbach, fewer than one-third of the men surveyed approved of the changes in the role of women in U.S. society.[30] Married men were especially concerned about how the changes may affect their personal comfort and well-being. According to these men, the biggest negative effect is that they have to spend more time on household chores which they do not like. Except for lawn care and home repairs, all other household tasks fall into the do-not-like category.

The agency report notes that since men are becoming more involved in household tasks, whether they like them or not, it is very appropriate to portray men in advertising for household products and to direct such advertising to the modern husbands of the United States. To avoid alienating males in the audience, the report suggests that the house-working husband be portrayed as a no-nonsense person, taking on a household job because it has to be done. His pleasure over the completion of the task should be expressed as an accomplishment in itself, not portrayed as an aesthetic fulfillment to him, as so many housewives have been depicted for years in highly criticized commercials. The report further warns against portraying the husband as helping his wife with household chores. This traditional role portrayal may please some husbands, but at the same time it may alienate the working wives who prefer a portrayal of sharing household duties.

Advertising Practitioners' Preferences for
Sex-Role Portrayals

Practitioners who determine the content of commercials in advertising campaigns and those experts who implement the decisions have been criticized for not responding to the complaints about the way the sexes are portrayed in television advertisements. Are the role preferences of agency personnel and their clients so different from those of consumers? To answer these questions and many others, Courtney and Whipple replicated their consumer-preference study among respondents with considerably greater advertising expertise.[31] To determine professionals' preferences for commercials with variations in sex-role portrayals, Whipple and Courtney chose a representative sample of advertising practitioners for their follow-up study.[32] A sample of sixty-eight advertisers from consumer-product companies and advertising agencies was selected to represent individuals in the marketing and advertising community with direct impact on the creative-development process in television advertising. The practitioners, including marketing and advertising directors, brand managers, account representatives and supervisors, and creative directors were all interviewed at their places of work. The sample of thirty-two company representatives and thirty-six agency representatives was randomly split to form two sub-samples, which were not significantly different with respect to age, sex, marital status, or employment tenure.

Without identifying the real purpose of the study, practitioners were asked for their professional opinions of the same six advertisements rated by the female respondents in the original study. In addition, for each advertisement evaluated, the advertising professionals were asked, "If in your present occupation you decided to run this advertisement, would you receive any opposition?" For those cases where practitioners expected opposition, the reason for the opposition was sought.

The practitioners were similar to the consumers in their ability to play back the advertising messages of the control commercials. However, while the sex role depicted did not seem to affect consumer playback of the major selling points in the test advertisements, it did affect the professionals' responses. They recalled the more liberated test advertisements better than the traditional versions. The practitioners also agreed that the so-called liberated version of each test advertisement was really not so liberated at all. Rather than being a radical departure from the traditional version, they suggested that the liberated advertisements would be more accurately represented by the term *progressive*.

Practitioner evaluations of the two control advertisements resulted in no significant differences in advertising effectiveness nor in irritation scores for the two professional subsamples. These findings paralleled those from the consumer-preference study, but evaluations of the test advertisements differed somewhat between the practitioner and the consumer samples. While consumers were consistent in rating both progressive test advertisements as more effective and slightly more irritating, the professionals did not always agree with the consumers nor were they in agreement among themselves. Only the consumer-product-company representatives concurred with the consumers by rating the progressive breakfast-food commercial as significantly more effective. They agreed that the progressive version was significantly more original and more likely to make the consumer want to buy the product. Agency representatives were of the opposite opinion, but not significantly so. The two versions of the floor-cleaner commercial, by comparison, received lower effectiveness scores from both consumers and practitioners. They were rated as equally ineffective, but contrary to consumer opinion, the practitioners (especially the company representatives) favored the traditional advertisement, though not significantly.

Practitioners' professional opinions differed from consumer preferences the most when the advertising irritation scores of the test commercials were compared. The professionals, especially those from consumer-product companies, rated the traditional version of both the breakfast-food and the floor-cleaner commercials significantly higher in advertising irritation than the progressive version. They agreed that the progressive portrayals were significantly less insulting to women and significantly less irritating than the traditional advertisements tested. Consumers had previously judged the two versions to be very similar in irritation scores, rating the progressive versions as slightly more irritating.

Professional evaluations of the six advertisements also were analyzed by various practitioner segments, based on demographic characteristics such as age, sex, marital status, employment tenure, and employer of the advertiser. The only comparison within the practitioner group which resulted in significantly different advertising evaluations was based on the employer classification: consumer-product company versus advertising agency. When these two groups of advertisers are examined separately, it is evident that the more favorable advertiser evaluations of the progressive test commercials are due primarily to better ratings by representatives of consumer-product companies. For both test advertisements the company advertisers agreed that the progressive versions are significantly more suitable for women in the target group, more original, less irritating, and less insulting to women.

Practitioners' views of the likelihood of objections to running the six commercials also varied considerably by the role portrayal employed. The progressive version of the breakfast-food commercial received the least number of likely objection votes, as less than 20 percent of the advertisers expected any opposition to the advertisement. The personal-deodorant on-air advertisement followed closely in least number of objections, being considered potentially objectionable by approximately one-third of the professional sample. Over one-half of the advertisers expected some objection to each of the remaining four commercials. Generally, both the company and the agency respondents expected greater opposition to the traditional advertisements. However, of the most common reasons cited for expecting opposition to the advertisements, execution problems were cited much more frequently than role-portrayal problems or improper target appeals.

Based on the findings of the Whipple-Courtney study, it appears that the more traditional sex-role preferences of advertising-agency practitioners may be one of the major reasons why sex-stereotyped television commercials are still being produced. The research evidence seems to indicate that the clients may be more progressive than their respective agencies regarding the issue of portraying men and women in advertising.

Conclusions from Sex-Role Preference Research

The major conclusion which can be discerned from the many research studies of preferences for sex-role portrayals in print and broadcast advertising is that no one role portrayal is preferred by consumers and advertisers. While this general finding does not support across-the-board use of liberated magazine and television advertisements, it does provide evidence that the continued use of traditional, sexist portrayals of men and women in advertising is also not preferred. Traditional roles are not displeasing to everyone, but they do tend to irritate many consumer segments and some professional advertising groups. More progressive advertisements which depict liberated life-styles have been rated at least equal to, and in some cases better than, more traditional portrayals. When more up-to-date roles for women and men have been portrayed in a realistic environment, without being irritating, these progressive attempts have been accepted by most male and female segments.

Another consistent finding which emerged from the research was that the sex of the product representative in the advertisement, the role portrayed, and the setting for the advertisement should match the product image, the usage environment, and the perceived product benefits to be most effective. The realism is important whether the roles are more traditional or liberated in style. The supermom, the woman's libber, and the helping-though-inept-husband roles certainly do not meet these criteria. On the other hand, advertisements portraying female product representatives, showing working housewives, depicting men participating in household tasks, and using female voice-overs have been evaluated by both consumers and advertisers as effective and nonirritating departures from traditional, stereotyped advertising.

The research studies, which sought to define those segments of consumers that are more or less in favor of progressive role portrayals, produced inconsistent findings when viewed together. Although personality variables, such as feminist orientation, independence of judgment, and self-concept, showed no consistent relationship to preferences for role portrayals, the measures themselves are as much in question as the findings. Some consumer demographic variables, including geographic region, age, education, income, and marital status, appear to have little or no relevance as segment descriptors. Other demographic variables, such as gender and employment status, were related to preferences for sex-role portrayals in some studies. Typically, females were more critical of traditional, sexist portrayals and preferred more liberated advertisements. However, one study came to the opposite conclusion because men criticized the traditional commercials. The findings regarding the moderating effects of employment status on role preferences also were inconsistent. Some research found that employed women preferred more progressive advertisements, while other studies produced results which showed that full-time housewives, as well as those employed, favored more liberated portrayals.

Overall, the men and women whose preferences were obtained are more contemporary, both in their attitudes toward themselves and toward the tested advertisements, than advertisers have generally reflected in their advertising. Since the research studies showed that it is possible to create advertisements without the stereotyped, traditional, sexist portrayals and to do so effectively without causing irritation, more advertisers should explore modern approaches to making unexaggerated, realistic presentations of the sexes.

Despite some inconsistent research findings and because no one role is preferred for all products and situations, it is most desirable for advertisers to conduct their own research directed toward the creation and evaluation of advertising with more progressive sex-role portrayals. Since today's men and women identify best with advertising that portrays the sexes as they are now in various segments of society, careful consideration must go into target-market definition and value assessment. As copy approaches for more liberated sex-role presentations are developed, advertisers also should test their relative effectiveness in test-market environments. Apparently, advertising practitioners, especially those from consumer-product companies, favor these newer approaches to the traditional way the sexes have been portrayed. Thus, the time may be right during the 1980s for such progressive efforts. With the assistance of research, advertisers should be able to create advertisements which are effective and more accurately reflect the changing values and life-styles in our society.

Notes

1. *Advertising and Women: A Report on Advertising Portraying or Directed to Women* (New York: National Advertising Review Board, 1975).

2. David Ogilvy, *Confessions of an Advertising Man* (New York: Dell, 1963), p. 148.

3. Rabindra N. Kanungo and Sam Pang, "Effects of Human Models on Perceived Product Quality," *Journal of Applied Psychology* 57, no. 2 (1973):172–178.

4. Rabindra N. Kanungo and Jotindar S. Johar, "Effects of Slogans

and Human Model Characteristics in Product Advertisements," *Canadian Journal of Behavioral Science* 7 (April 1975):127-138.

5. James T. Lull, Catherine A. Hanson, and Michael J. Marx, "Recognition of Female Stereotypes in TV Commercials," *Journalism Quarterly* (Spring 1977):153-157.

6. Alice E. Courtney and Thomas W. Whipple, "Women in TV Commercials," *Journal of Communication* 24 (Spring 1974):110-118.

7. C.O. Bettinger III and Lyndon Dawson, "Changing Perspectives in Advertising: The Use of 'Liberated' Feminine Life-Style Themes," in *Developments in Marketing Science,* ed. H.S. Gitlow and E.W. Wheatley (Coral Gables, Florida: Academy of Marketing Science, 1979), pp. 111-114.

8. Lawrence H. Wortzel and John M. Frisbie, "Women's Role Portrayal Preferences in Advertisements: An Empirical Study," *Journal of Marketing* 38 (October 1974):41-46.

9. Lauranne Buchanan and Leonard N. Reid, "Women Role Portrayals in Advertising Messages as Stimulus Cues: A Preliminary Investigation," in *Sharing for Understanding,* ed. G.E. Miracle (East Lansing, Mich.: American Academy of Advertising, 1977), pp. 99-104.

10. Michael B. Mazis and Marilyn Beuttenmuller, "Attitudes Toward Women's Liberation and Perception of Advertisements," *Advances in Consumer Research* (Chicago: Association of Consumer Research, 1973), pp. 428-434.

11. Wortzel and Frisbie, "Women's Role Portrayal Preferences in Advertisements," p. 42.

12. Jacob M. Ducker and Lewis R. Tucker, Jr., "'Women's Lib-ers' Versus Independent Women: A Study of Preferences for Women's Roles in Advertisements," *Journal of Marketing Research* 14 (November 1977): 469-475.

13. Frank Barron, *Creativity and Psychological Health* (New York: Van Nostrand, 1963).

14. Bettinger and Dawson, "Changing Perspectives in Advertising."

15. Wortzel and Frisbie, "Women's Role Portrayal Preferences in Advertisements."

16. Buchanan and Reid, "Women's Role Portrayals in Advertising Messages in Stimulus Cues."

17. Kanungo and Pang, "Effects of Human Models on Perceived Product Quality."

18. Lull, Hanson, and Marx, "Recognition of Female Stereotypes in TV Commercials."

19. Buchanan and Reid, "Women's Role Portrayals in Advertising Messages as Stimulus Cues."

20. Alice E. Courtney and Thomas W. Whipple, *Reaction to Traditional Versus Liberated Portrayals of Women in TV Advertising* (Toronto: Advertising Advisory Board, 1976).

21. William D. Wells, Clark Leavitt, and Maureen McConville, "A Reaction Profile for TV Commercials," *Journal of Advertising Research* 11 (December 1971):11–18.

22. Courtney and Whipple, "Reaction to Traditional Versus Liberated Portrayals."

23. D. Levinson and P. Huffman, "Traditional Family Ideology and Its Relation to Personality," *Journal of Personality* 23 (1955):251–273.

24. Emanuel M. Berger, "The Relation Between Expressed Acceptance of Self and Expressed Acceptance of Others," *Journal of Abnormal and Social Psychology* 47 (1952):778–782.

25. Clark Leavitt, "Even Housewives Prefer Working Women in TV Ads," *Marketing News,* 19 May 1978, p. 10.

26. "Women in Advertising," *Marketing Research Society Newsletter* (April 1980).

27. Rena Bartos, *The Moving Target: What Every Marketer Should Know About Women* (New York: The Free Press, 1982); idem, "Sales, Company and Brand Image Can Suffer if Ad Research Ignores Like/Dislike Dimension," *Marketing News,* 16 May 1980, p. 13; and idem, "What Women Like and Don't Like, in Ads," *Advertising Age,* 8 March 1982, pp. M-2—M-3.

28. J. Partick Kelly, Paul J. Solomon, and Marie Burke, "Male and Female Responses to Women's Roles in Advertising," in *Sharing for Understanding,* ed. G.E. Miracle (East Lansing, Mich.: American Academy of Advertising, 1977), pp. 94–98.

29. Lull, Hanson, and Marx, "Recognition of Female Stereotypes in TV Commercials."

30. "Males Don't Like New Women: DDB," *Advertising Age,* 20 October 1980, p. 60.

31. Courtney and Whipple, "Reaction to Traditional Versus Liberated Portrayals."

32. Thomas W. Whipple and Alice E. Courtney, "How to Portray Women in TV Commercials," *Journal of Advertising Research* 20 (April 1980):53–59.

Decorative and Sexual Portrayals

Sexuality in the form of nudity, sexual imagery, innuendo, and double entendre is employed as an advertising tool for a wide variety of products, ranging from personal-care products to heavy-industrial machinery. The use of sexual appeals in advertising stems from the widely held belief that sexual portrayals are effective in calling attention to the advertisement itself, in creating interest for the advertised product, and in motivating consumers to buy.

Sexual Appeals in Advertising

Content research has documented the extensive use of decorative models in advertising as evidenced in chapter 1. Women are depicted in the decorative role for products ranging from personal-care items to otherwise unglamorous products which are advertised in trade publications to mostly male audiences. One of the most blatant uses of females in the decorative role is in industrial advertising. In many industrial advertisements women are employed to call attention to parts and equipment. In those advertisements it is not uncommon to see bikini-clad women lounging near machine tools or electronic equipment.

The use of sexual portrayals is also extensive, but it has not been addressed in detail by content research. Portrayals of sexuality promise, either explicitly or implicitly, that the advertised product will heighten the sex appeal of the purchaser or offer some other sexually oriented reward. Such advertisements are targeted both to men and women.

Many advertisements targeted to men use partial or complete female nudity, sexual suggestiveness, and innuendo. For the most part these are used to imply that the sexy female shown in the advertisement is the man's reward for using the advertised product. Often, men are also portrayed in such advertisements. A sexual relationship is then implied between the male product user and his female companion, such that the advertisement promises, in effect, that the product will increase his appeal to her. Not only will it give him a closer shave, it will also provide a sexually available woman. This implication is seen in a variety of advertising, but it is most

103

common for products whose benefits are not easily described, such as the smell of a cologne and the taste of a beer or cigarette.

Implied or overtly suggestive sexuality is by no means confined to advertisements targeted to male audiences. Advertisements aimed at women also employ sexual appeals. Scantily clad, nude, and sexually provocative women appear here as well, particularly in cosmetic, fashion, and personal-care advertising. For example, advertisements for women's personal-care products and clothing employ female sexuality as an integral part of the advertising message. Often the advertisements imply that the product's main purpose is to improve the user's appeal to men, as in the panty-hose advertisement which claims, "gentlemen prefer Hanes." The underlying advertising message for a product advertised in this manner is that the ultimate benefit of product usage is to give men pleasure.

Another commonly used approach in advertisements targeted to women is to imply that the product increases female sexuality and that a woman's sexuality is a definite statement of her personality. The product makes her free, uninhibited, and sexually adventurous. This kind of sex appeal is seen frequently in perfume advertisements. Senchal cologne, for example, expresses that the world is the female's pearl; she may actively choose among the featured roles in the advertisement because of her increased sex appeal, thanks to Senchal. In other television commercials for perfume, sexual acts are suggested. In one advertisement the visual portion shows a speeding car and glimpses of parts of a woman's body as she shifts gears to throbbing music. After the music's climax, the woman is seen running her fingers through her hair in satisfaction while watching the sunrise, an image which suggests the afterglow of sexual intimacy. In another commercial for Chanel No. 5, a woman is shown sunbathing next to a pool. A man appears magically across the pool, swims toward her, and disappears between her legs as he emerges from the pool.

Less blatant suggestions of sexual acts are used for products designed to improve physical attractiveness, such as low calorie foods, diet drinks, and products positioned as healthful and slimming. Among the more well known are the advertisements for Diet Pepsi. The audio states, "Now you see it, now you don't," while the video cuts back and forth from the soft drink can to torsos of scantily clad women and men. These advertisements feature four or five female body shots to one male. Such advertisements, offering the promise of slender, sexually attractive bodies, are aimed almost exclusively at women.

It is significant that the nearly nude or provocative female model is used commonly in advertisements targeted to women, as well as in those targeted to men. Berger, in his classic study of the use of women in advertising, showed that advertising's portrayal of women presents a very passive view designed to attract a male spectator.[1] Yet advertisers apparently believe that women, as well as men, prefer to see female bodies. The use of female bodies in advertisements targeted to women implies that advertisers believe women define their sexuality in male terms and that they accept an objectified and passive view of themselves.

In the last decade there has been a trend in advertising toward advertisements depicting men in decorative roles. A very recent development is the increasing use of nude and suggestive male models. Males in sexual roles are seen now with some frequency in advertisements targeted to male as well as female audiences. It may be that the advertising of the 1980s is moving toward greater objectification of male sexuality.

Sex in advertising is, of course, also used to advertise products directly related to sexual activities. Such advertising is most common in print advertisements in specialty publications. It is also seen, however, in mass media; for example, in many newspaper movie advertisements. Nudity or partial nudity are frequently seen in advertisements for such products as sexually oriented books and magazines, pornographic films, and videotapes. The advertisements are deliberately intended to be sexually arousing to the viewer in order to indicate what the consumer might expect from product usage. The widespread use of sex as a technique to advertise products has elicited significant consumer protest, particularly from groups concerned about the societal effects of such advertisements.

Recent Organized Reactions and Advertiser Response

The U.S. lobby group, Women Against Pornography (WAP), is worried about the sexual images of women portrayed in advertisements and their effect on sexual violence against women. One of their major concerns is the use of young girls as symbols of sexuality in advertising and the contribution this portrayal may make toward the sexual exploitation of children.[2] WAP fears that people will begin to regard such images as normal, rather than recognizing them as the eroticized portrayal of little girls. This concern, fostered perhaps by the successful use of Brooke Shields in advertisements for Calvin Klein jeans, has caused WAP to initiate an annual awards program to call attention to what it regards as pornography in advertising. The first advertisers to be 'honored' by WAP were singled out as sexist. Those receiving the dubious distinction were Calvin Klein and Jordache jeans, Maidenform bras, The Texas Brand Boot Company, and the Jamaica Tourist Board. The tourist board advertisement, for example, was cited for showing the bikinied bottoms of native women and a baby's naked bottom.

In a more positive honor WAP presented shoe designer Joe Famolare with the Ms. Liberty Award for the campaign that "best exemplified how an advertiser can effectively market a product without sexist overtones.[3]

Famolare advertisements had once depicted a seminude woman in a racer's starting block, and a man who was shown pointing a starter's gun at her. These advertisements elicited many consumer complaints because of their implicit violence against women. Because of the complaints and WAP pressure, Famolare dropped the campaign. Instead, advertisements now feature Mr. Famolare's smiling face surrounded by his designer shoes. Famolare reports that the increased product exposure in the new, nonsexist campaign has improved sales.

Several recent tourism advertising campaigns have used sexual themes to lure travelers to vacation spots to the disgust of many observers. One of the advertisements in a print campaign to boost travel to Alaska depicts a bikini-clad model and her male companion declaring, "Summit conquered . . . here we are, half naked on an ice field, and loving it."[4] Two male representatives of the Alaska state legislature were quoted as saying, "They're using sex to sell Alaska. Silly and unforgiveable." A spokeswoman for the National Organization for Women added, "It's neither realistic nor relevant. I am offended they find it necessary to sell Alaska with a woman's body."

The Miami-Metro "Miami—See it like a native" poster, which depicts the back of an attractive woman wearing only a bikini bottom received similar reactions.[5] The Metropolitan Dade County Commission, acting on a request from the Commission on the Status of Women, passed a resolution limiting the advertising agency from reordering more posters after about 25,000 had already been distributed to travel agencies. Although the campaign generated publicity and requests for vacation materials, some of the female county commissioners reported being offended by the poster.

The advertisers who create these advertisements usually respond to the criticisms leveled at their sexual campaigns with amazement, disbelief, and a plea of innocence. The Alaska Division of Tourism's official reply claimed "the intent was not to make it appear that sex is a wholesale commodity in Alaska."[6] The account supervisor on the Miami-Metro account insisted, "It's sexy, but in a tasteful way, and it wasn't intended to be exploitive."[7] Advertisers repeatedly deny all claims that advertisements are created with any intent of exploiting women, but WAP spokespeople believe that the similarity of the portrayal of women in pornography and advertising is no accident.[8] For example, at a forum discussing advertising's sexual content, Edward McCabe (senior vice-president, copy chief, Scali, McCabe, Stoves) answered charges that women are portrayed in a demeaning manner in television commercials by arguing "that the use of sexy women in commercials was not manipulative or exploitive . . ."[9]

Sex has even been incorporated into the sales pitch for women's sports. The advertising campaign for the 1982 Chevrolet World Championship of Women's Golf elicited varied opinions. In a radio commercial for the event, a man's voice was heard to say he was going to attend to see talented athletes and also to watch the ladies, especially golfer Jan Stephenson, "a real eyeful." The professional golfers differed in their opinions about the advertisement.

> Jan Stephenson: She thought it was cute. After all, "today everything is sold with sex appeal."
>
> Beth Daniel: "Well, at least it says we're talented."
>
> Nancy Lopez: "They put this on the radio? I don't like it at all." She grimaced and said it demeaned the seriousness of the tournament.
>
> Amy Alcott: "Selling sex in women's athletics is an easy way out. I think it does cheapen the sport. But the people who are marketing the product (tournament) feel that is the mentality of America."[10]

Hans Kramer, tournament chairman and vice-president of the sponsoring organization, responded to questions about the commercial by saying, "I suspect that some people might find it sexist. But I don't think it will attract the lewd types. We're trying to appeal to those who attend professional sporting events. The cute parts of the advertisement are good attention-getters." Sharyn Hinman, copy chief for the public relations firm who wrote the script, said the commercial did not exploit the golfers. Its purpose was to make people aware of the tournament and the quality of the participants; the references to legwatching and Stephenson being an eyeful were just attempts to attract listeners' attention. She explained that, "(the male in the commercial) can't help himself, so he gives a nod to the fact that women are attractive." She did confess, however, that her firm would probably not have used the same approach if it were making an advertisement for a men's golf tournament. The advertisers of the tournament insist that they did not set out to deliberately demean or offend the golfers or members of the radio audience. Their purpose was to be sexy, cute, and attract attention. But, as with other examples, many golfers and listeners did not perceive the advertisement the same way the advertiser claims to have intended it.

According to the director of university events at the California university, heavily sexist advertising is a big turnoff for young, college-level adults. As a result, he reports that campus newspapers have rejected many advertisements because they are concerned about possible feminist reaction.[11] Other media are also rejecting advertisements they consider offensive to women. For example, a commercial for Calvin Klein jeans was pulled off stations in New York and elsewhere because it failed to meet minimum standards of acceptability. According to the American Broadcasting Company (ABC), which provided statistics for 1979, 3 percent of all advertisements were rejected outright at first screening, while 43 percent were sent back for revisions. The remaining 54 percent were accepted without changes on the basis of complex and subjective criteria.[12]

All major networks subscribe to the television code of the National Association of Broadcasters, but they apply the code in different ways as far as taste is concerned. Consequently, application of the standards varies among networks and from station to station. The networks argue that they are just trying to hold their ground against many of the new suggestive advertisements. According to one broadcast executive, "Our rule of thumb is that the advertising agencies will try to get anything they can by us."[13]

Consumer Reactions to the Use of Sex in Advertising

A general, negative attitude toward the use of sex in advertising on the part of advertising critics was documented in chapter 2. Advertising was blamed by the critics for perpetrating the derogatory image of women as sex symbols. The general attitude studies and public-opinion polls, also reported in chapter 2, support the critics' overall concern regarding sexual suggestiveness in advertising. According to those studies, women are generally more sensitive than men in their critical attitudes toward the use of sexual imagery. However, both men and women agree that advertising treats women as sex objects and as an inferior class of human beings. In recent years additional research has focused specifically on consumer reactions to the use of sexual appeals in advertisements.

Consumer reaction to the use of sex appeals in advertising was studied by Wise et al. in 1974.[14] College-aged students and their parents were asked to rate the extent of their agreement with the statement, "Advertisers make too much use of sex appeals in advertisements." The overall tendency of both groups was not to give solid support to the statement. However, older females did agree that there was too much use of sex appeals. Three years later Lundstrom and Sciglimpaglia's study produced more negative findings.[15] They found that 42 percent of the women responding to their questionnaire felt that women were treated as sex objects in advertising. This position was especially espoused by the younger, more educated women.

The overall concern about sex on television in the late 1970s and the mixed consumer reaction to it, encouraged Needham, Harper, and Steers advertising agency to investigate attitudes toward the use of sex in commercials. Johnson and Satow of Needham, Harper, and Steers first turned to agency data from a 1977 life-style study of four thousand married men and women from Market Facts' mail panel.[16] One question in the study directly concerned attitudes toward sex in commercials. Respondents were asked to indicate the extent to which they agreed with the statement, "TV commercials place too much emphasis on sex." The majority of the respondents

(77 percent of the women and 68 percent of the men) agreed with the statement. Furthermore, strong agreement tended to increase with age and decrease with education for both men and women.

Demographic Segments

Johnson and Satow then conducted six focus interviews with married homemakers, chosen because they agreed that television commercials place too much emphasis on sex. The interviews were designed to provide further insight into what were the specific objections to advertisements. The women criticized many advertisements for using overtly sexual appeals, including: Noxema shave cream, Bic lighter, Bic razor, Ultra Bright toothpaste, Muriel cigars, Pearl Drops tooth polish, Underalls panty hose, Aviance perfume, Shower Massage, Chicago Health Club, Tickle deodorant, and a variety of intimate feminine products. To determine what the women considered to be especially offensive in the commercials and why, the researchers showed the groups four of the criticized advertisements (Bic razor, Underalls, Muriel, and Aviance) and explored their reactions in more detail.

The younger women in the groups considered the Bic commercial a prime example of sexual innuendo, characterizing it as crude, locker-room humor. To them the advertisement was offensive and embarrassing. However, older women considered the Bic commercial "kind of cute." Further probing revealed that the innuendo in the commercial went over the women's head. When it was pointed out to them, the women concluded that only people with dirty minds would think the advertisement had sexual overtones.

In discussion of the Underalls advertisement women repeatedly mentioned that intimate products should not be advertised on televison at all. While panty hose to them seemed less intimate (and thus less offensive) than sanitary napkins, the Underalls advertisement still focused on what they saw as one of the inherently offensive parts of the body—the rear end. However, the women agreed that as long as featuring rear ends in the advertisement focused the viewer's attention on the product's primary benefit, then the advertisement was not offensive. It appears that in advertising for intimate products focusing on a product's primary benefit rather than on sex is important in mitigating offensiveness.

The Muriel-cigar commercial was classified by Johnson and Satow as a classic male-fantasy advertisement, characterized by the presence of a foxy lady in a very sexist scenario. Reaction to this advertisement differed significantly between the younger and older women in the focus groups. Older women liked the commercial, asserting that sex is all right for traditional men's products advertised to men. It never crossed most of their minds to be offended. One of the older women claimed, "At my age, anything that will get him excited just ain't half bad.'' Younger women, on the other hand, found the Muriel advertisement most offensive of the four. In addition to objecting to the depiction of a woman in a demeaning role, they found the advertisement personally threatening. Some admitted that the sexy woman in the advertisement made them wonder what their husbands did when they stayed late at the office.

The Aviance commercial was an example of a female-fantasy advertisement. The older women in the groups varied in their opinions of the striptease performed by the young housewife in the commercial. Some couldn't relate to the scene, others liked it, and the remainder were neutral. The opinions of the younger women, however, were decidedly split according to their husbands' occupations. Women whose husbands had white-collar jobs judged the commercial as one of their favorites. They liked the situation and fantasized about their husbands being so handsome. Younger women whose husbands had blue-collar jobs disagreed. They hated the commercial because the advertisement portrayed a situation they found unrealistic and unattainable. They found the advertisement threatening and offensive.

When the researchers raised the question of the morality of such advertisements, women of all ages shared the opinion that immorality in advertising offends them. The focus group participants felt that both the Bic-razor and the Muriel-cigar advertisements violated their moral standards and they were offended that the consenting adults in the advertisements were not married. The Aviance advertisement was more acceptable, apparently because the couple was married.

This in-depth examination of consumer reactions to sex in advertising enabled Johnson and Satow to formulate a set of guidelines for the use of sex in advertising. They concluded that sex is permissible: for products whose main purpose is to increase allurement, such as cosmetics, perfumes, and aftershare; for traditionally masculine products advertised to nonliberated women, including beer, cars, and liquor; in male fantasies for older women and in female fantasies for young white-collar women; in morally acceptable (married) situations; and when the sexuality in the advertisement is closely tied to the products' primary benefit.

Bartos' in-depth research on the four new demographic women's groups (discussed in chapters 4 and 5) showed that any commercial with an overt sexy treatment elicits controversy among women as to whether it was appealing or offensive.[17] Disagreements on this score were noted in the group most critical of sexy treatments (stay-at-home housewives) and among those who were most tolerant (the career women). According to Bartos, response differences were caused primarily by women's feelings about the potential embarrassment of the advertising treatment. Stay-at-home housewives were most likely to be personally embarrassed, while career women were least likely to find sexy advertisements embarrassing. All groups, however, were intensely negative to an advertisement that took the woman-as-sex-object approach to its ultimate implication.

Perceptual Segments

Morrison and Sherman also investigated how various subgroups of the population respond to the elements of a sexy advertisement.[18] Their sample included both men and women respondents who rated a total of one hundred product advertisements on six criteria. Interpretation of findings was made on the basis of clustering, followed by multiple discriminate analysis. The analysis derived five groups of women who were distinguished primarily by the degree to which they recognize nudity in advertisements. Two groups, comprising 45 percent of the women, rated the advertisements high in nudity, the majority of which reported being sexually aroused by the advertisements. However, 35 percent of the women sampled generally saw nothing. The results also indicated that suggestiveness of copy is an important variable, but recognition of this factor was rather uniform among the women.

Among the men, Morrison and Sherman found the situation to be more complex. For 45 percent of the men, nudity was not a major discriminating characteristic; they simply were not aware of the nudity in the advertisements. Furthermore, when these men were aroused by the advertisements, it was apparently connected with perceiving masculine romantic themes and suggestiveness of copy, but not with nudity. However, for another third of the sample, nudity and suggestive copy were recognized and were arousing. The remaining members of the sample were aroused by nudity alone, but not by suggestive copy. The authors concluded that the perception of sexual overtones in advertisements and the degree of sexual arousal they produce varies dramatically among different groups of the same sex, as well as between the sexes.

Communication Effectiveness of Sex in Advertising

Among the reasons cited by advertisers for employing sexual strategies are to gain product-category and brand attention, recognition, recall, favorable brand attitudes, and eventually sales. Data permitting direct measurement of the sales effects of sexually oriented advertisements are generally unavailable, so research studies have relied on communication measures to evaluate the effectiveness of using sex in advertising. Psychological concepts, such as arousal, perception, self-concept, distraction, and aggression, have provided a theoretical framework upon which some researchers have based their studies. Others have conducted empirical studies from a strictly pragmatic point of view. Both approaches have provided an interesting and complementary set of findings about the communication effectiveness of decorative and sexual portrayals.

The Impact of Decorative, Attractive, and Sexy Models

Several studies have been conducted during the 1970s which provide experimental evidence on the communication effects of decorative, attractive, and sexy models. In 1977 Chestnut, LaChance, and Lubitz examined the communication impact of a decorative model.[19] They tested the effect of the presence or absence of a decorative model using two recognition tests: one for the entire advertisement and the other for brand name only. Using these tests, they distinguished between model-related and brand-name-related memory of the advertisement. Four groups of approximately twenty-five male students each were administered both tests after being exposed to fifty different magazine advertisements. The results indicated that the presence of a decorative model influenced the memory for model-related information but had no influence on the recognition of brand-name information. The researchers posited that a decorative model exerts an influence on a product's image, thus facilitating recognition of the entire advertisement. However, a decorative model will not result in increased recall of all aspects of the advertisement. Consequently, the presence of models had no significant effect on brand-name recall.

Derrick and Wolken criticized this research for the way the dependent variables were measured and scored and for possible uncontrolled order effects in the design.[20] It is difficult to assess whether these internal validity concerns are more or less important than some external validity limitations, including a subject sample of male undergraduates and the artificiality of a laboratory setting. Nevertheless, Chestnut and his associates present fairly convincing evidence that decorative models do not impact on brand-name recognition.

Reid and Soley investigated whether the presence of women as decorative models affects recognition for visual-advertisement components, such as an illustration, but not for verbal components, such as body copy.[21] They hypothesized differential effects of visual and verbal stimuli on cognitive responses to advertising. To investigate they used Starch component scores for illustration and copy to represent visual and verbal-recognition responses. One hundred eleven cigarettes, liquor, and automobile advertisements were chosen which featured a decorative female whose primary function was as a sexual or attractive adornment for the product. Although prior research had suggested that the presence of female decorative models enhances recognition for the entire advertisement, Reid and Soley found that decorative models do not have equivalent effects on recognition of all advertisement components. Analysis of the Starch recognition scores revealed that the presence of decorative female models significantly affects recognition of the illustration, but not recognition of body copy in the advertisements. The authors explain that their results are consistent with psychological research which suggests that "visual stimuli facilitate superior memory performance for processed information."

These results confirm that using a sexy or an attractive woman as a product adornment is an effective attention-getting device. However, Reid and Soley also found that the improved advertisement recognition does not also mean that attention will extend to reading the body copy. The visual component, not the verbal component, accounted for improved advertisement recognition.

Baker and Churchill extended the previous research in several important ways.[22] They specifically focused on the effects attributable to the degree of a model's physical attractiveness, rather than mere presence or absence. Furthermore, they tested mock print advertisements which included male as well as female models. Three components of attitudes toward the advertisements (cognitive, affective, and conative) were measured using a set of thirteen semantic differential scale items. Both male and female subjects evaluated a coffee advertisement and a cologne advertisement. The effects of the physical attractiveness of the model, the sex of the subject, and the product type were determined by performing an analysis of variance for the cognitive, affective, and conative scores separately.

None of the experimental manipulations had any effect on cognitive evaluations of the advertisements. The affective scores, on the other hand, produced significant main effects for model attractiveness and subjects' sex, for both male and female model advertisements. The more attractive the male or female model, the more both sexes like the advertisement. The male-model advertisement received higher affective scores from female subjects, while the reverse was true for the female model advertisement. Greater intention to buy was expressed only for the advertisement featuring a male model evaluated by female subjects. His degree of attractiveness, however, did not influence the womens' evaluations in any significant fashion. It was his presence that mattered to the women. In only one case did the product type produce any significant effects and that was in interaction with the female model's attractiveness as judged by male subjects. For cologne, an attractive female model produced higher intention-to-buy scores among men; however, when coffee was the product advertised, an unattractive female model proved to be more persuasive.

Baker and Churchill's experiment suggests that physical attractiveness and gender of a model used in advertising can influence advertising evaluations. The right model can increase the chances that an advertisement is liked and in certain circumstances also affect intentions to buy. However, the findings do not support the use of attractive female models to the exclusion of male models or less attractive females.

The understanding of model effects was furthered by Patzer who combined the elements of previous experiments into a research study on the influence of the sexiness of a female model.[23] Patzer defined sexiness by liberal dress, a seductive pose, or suggestive stance. Both males and females were selected as subjects and asked to evaluate mock-up advertisements for a nonexistent new body soap. Half the subjects rated a sexy advertisement, half a nonsexy advertisement. Patzer took cognitive, affective, and conative measures on a semantic differential scale. In addition, measurements of aided recall, perceptions of the advertised product, and of the female model were obtained.

For male subjects the results showed that a sexy model increased advertising effectiveness. This finding held for both cognitive and conative scores, as well as for the affective measures. Aided recall of copy detail, however, was not related to model sexiness. Model sexiness also was positively correlated with perceptions of product expensiveness and evaluation of the model's physical attractiveness, credibility, truthfulness, intelligence, and expertise. For female respondents sexiness of a female model did not improve advertising effectiveness. Both the cognitive and conative evaluations for the sexy conditions were significantly lower than those for the nonsexy condition.

Patzer interpreted these results to mean that: males and females employ different standards to rate the sexiness of female models; for males sexiness is equated with physical attractiveness, but not for females; males attribute favorable characteristics to a sexy female including credibility, trustworthiness, intelligence, and expertise, while females do not; model sexiness, as perceived by males only, does have a positive impact on evaluation of product characteristics; and males apparently find sexy advertisements more effective overall, whereas females find them to be unbelievable, uninformative, confusing, and not influential. From a practical standpoint Patzer's results imply that to influence males an advertiser should use a sexy female model. However, that same model may produce negative effects on females.

The Effectiveness of Nude Models

Five studies have distinguished between the effect of models who are perceived as attractive or sexy and the effect of those who are sexually suggestive or erotic because of nudity. These studies have examined the effects of nudity and partial nudity on advertising-effectiveness measures, including brand recall and attitudes.

Smith and Engel systematically varied the presence or absence of a partially clad female model and asked subjects to rate a variety of product attributes associated with the advertised automobile.[24] In comparison to the control advertisement, both males and females rated the car better on psychological and functional variables after seeing the advertisement using a partially nude model. The car was perceived to be more appealing, livelier, more youthful, better designed, higher priced, faster, less safe, and higher in horsepower when the model was present. The researchers considered this an unconscious phenomenon because few subjects reported themselves aware of any bias toward the advertisements containing partial nudity.

Steadman hypothesized that a sexually suggestive advertisement will attract attention but that the increased attention will not be associated with recall of the brand name of the advertised product.[25] He constructed twelve advertisements by selecting six photographs of neutral subjects and six photographs of female models in various stages of undress depicting varying degrees of overt sexual suggestiveness. Twelve well-known brand names were randomly allocated to the pictures to complete the mock advertisements. An attitude measurement concerning the use of sex in advertising was taken, and a portfolio of the twelve advertisements was left with each of the sixty male participants for one day. Upon return of the book of advertisements, subjects were asked to recall the brand names associated with each picture and then to rank order the six sexual advertisements from most to least erotically suggestive. A second recall procedure was administered seven days later to measure delayed brand-name recall.

The research results indicated that nonsexual illustrations were more effective than sexually suggestive ones in achieving brand-name recall. Immediate brand recall was not affected by the type of picture used, but in measurements after one week, the sexual pictures inhibited correct brand-name identification. Steadman hypothesized that participants had been distracted by the models from paying attention to the accompanying brand names. He also reported that an attitude favorable to the use of sexual illustrations in advertising was positively related to the correct recall of brand names. Apparently many male viewers in the highly favorable attitude group attended primarily to the illustrations of the nude or partially nude models and ignored the brand names.

Alexander and Judd concluded a follow-up study in 1978.[26] However, they incorporated several methodological improvements in their design. They increased the sample size from sixty to 181 male volunteers, used an eight-item scale instead of a one-item measure to evaluate attitudes toward nudity in advertising, and prepared three advertisements for each of the five nudity levels. Each advertisement was viewed twice before respondents were asked to list the brand name remembered.

Significantly fewer brand names were recalled for those advertisements with a nude female than for those containing a nonsexual illustration of a pastoral scene. Surprisingly, brand recall did not significantly decrease as the degree of explicit nudity in the advertisements increased. Alexander and Judd suggest that the presence of a model, rather than the degree of nudity as such, may have been responsible for the number of brands recalled. To this point the results of the original and follow-up studies are similar. In the second study, however, the number of brand names recalled was not related to respondent attitudes toward nudity in advertising. Alexander and Judd pointed out that in a more realistic setting "learning may in fact be enhanced due to higher attention to the nude ads." Yet, in answer to the question, "Should a nude female be used in advertisements directed toward men?", Alexander and Judd responded no, especially when brand recall is the main objective.

Peterson and Kerin designed an experiment to explore some of the relationships between degree of model nudity, product type, and gender of respondent.[27] They examined the effect of these variables on perceptions of the advertisement, the advertised product, and the company producing the product. Mock-up advertisements were prepared using no model, a demure model, a seductive model, and a nude model. The advertisements promoted either a body-oil product or a ratchet-wrench set. Respondent attitudes were elicited during in-home personal interviews from 224 adult males and females who had examined a portfolio containing an experimental and two control advertisements.

In general males gave higher ratings to the advertisements, the products, and the producing companies than did females. The most important finding, however, was that significant differences in respondent evaluations of the advertisements were a function of the type of model; advertisements portraying a nude model were consistently perceived to have the least appeal. Products and companies also associated with a nude model were rated lowest in quality and reputation. Additionally, interaction between model type and product was significant. The seductive model/body-oil advertisement elicited the best evaluations on advertising appeal, product quality, and company reputation, while the worst evaluations were received for the nude model/body-oil combination. A significant model by respondent interaction revealed that women rated the nude model/ratchet-set advertisement as least appealing. The data for all model/product combinations support the concept that when the model and product are appropriately matched, the evaluations for advertisements, products, and companies are more favorable. Better evaluations were obtained from both males and females when the ratchet set was presented with no model or a demure model. Peterson and Kerin concluded that the use of nudity may produce negative effects, not only with respect to evaluation of specific advertisements, but to perceptions of product quality and corporate image as well.

Additional empirical evidence is provided by Sciglimpaglia, Belch, and Cain who studied the impact of variations in nudity, suggestiveness, and model gender on male and female perceptions of print advertisements.[28] Sciglimpaglia et al. used actual print advertisements, varying in degree of nudity and suggestiveness, rather than using the mock-up advertisements as in other studies. In making this methodological change, however, they paid a price for the realism of their experiment. For example, they could not control attractiveness and other characteristics of the different models presented. Each of the 142 subjects completed three self-administered instruments which measured the following factors: an individual's sexual values, both in a societal and personal context; attitudes toward role portrayals in advertising; and personal orientation with respect to social roles. They then rated nine test advertisements and eight control advertisements on four affective scales: good taste, appeal, interest, and offensiveness.

Evaluation of the advertisements generally improved as the levels of suggestiveness and nudity decreased. The sexually suggestive advertisements were perceived as being in poor taste by males and females alike but were particularly offensive to the women. Men and women varied to a greater extent in their evaluations of advertisements showing nudity. Women tended to evaluate female nudity negatively; men, on the other hand, evaluated female nudity significantly better. The opposite was true for male nudity.

For the males in the study the measures of sexual and social values were significantly related to advertising evaluations, and the relationships became more pronounced as sexual explicitness increased. For example, males with conservative social values rated the nude and suggestive advertisements negatively. In most instances female advertising perceptions were not significantly related to these measures. The authors concluded that the evaluation of the appropriateness of nude models in advertising is likely to be affected by the sex of the model and the predispositions and gender of the receiver.

Sexual Appeals and Advertising Effectiveness

In 1977 Britt warned advertisers to be cautious and avoid overt or direct use of sexual appeals because they might promote sex at the expense of the product itself.[29] Others agree with Strong who believes that up to the point where anxiety begins to impair the reception of the message, the sexier it is, the greater the effect.[30] Researchers who have reviewed the literature on sexual appeals and effectiveness agree that the issue is complex and that use of sexual appeals is risky. Wilson and Moore,[31] Alpert,[32] and Joseph[33] all call for extensive additional research to assess the communications effectiveness of sexual appeals. On the basis of the limited information available to date, however, some working conclusions about the use of sexual appeals in advertising can be posited.

Decorative, attractive, partially clad, and nude models do facilitate recognition of an advertisement, and female models have a particularly strong attention-getting impact among male consumers. However, decorative and attractive models are probably just as effective in getting attention as nude or partially clad models. The research evidence suggests that it is the presence of an attractive person in the advertisement which accounts for attention-getting value, not the nudity or sexual suggestiveness as such. Although decorative, sexy, and nude models do increase attention to the advertisement, they do not increase brand recall. In most cases the attention is focused on the model to the detriment of brand name and copy recall.

Attractive, sexy, and nude models tend to have positive effects on affective evaluations of advertisements. When the model is perceived favorably, the advertisement, the advertised brand, and the producing company benefit from more favorable attitude ratings. In some cases under rather complex conditions these favorable ratings may result in greater intentions to buy the advertised product. However, in other cases, a model rated as less attractive and less sexy produces higher intentions to buy. It would appear that consumers look for an appropriate congruence between the model used and the advertised product.

Studies focusing on the effects of seductive, partially clad, and nude models produce varying results. In some cases researchers have found that these models appear to enhance effectiveness. Other research, however, finds that the sexier the model, the less the effectiveness. In one study nude models resulted in unfavorable brand and company evaluations.

There are significant differences between the two sexes in rating attractive and sexy models; what is appealing to men may be ineffective with women and vice-versa. In addition, there are significant differences within sex in evaluation of such models. Age is an important variable to be considered, as are social values and attitudes toward sex in advertising.

In total, the research reviewed indicates that a model perceived as sexy and attractive may enhance communications effects if that model is perceived as appropriate to the product-use situation. However, overtly seductive, partially clad, and nude models are as likely to create unfavorable as favorable effects. Moreover, there will be strong segment differences in evaluation of such models. The sexier the advertising message, the more risky it becomes in terms of communications effectiveness. In the absence of further research, therefore, advertisers would be well advised to use presenters who are perceived as attractive and sexy, but to avoid overtly seductive, nude, or partially clad models.

Additional research with more and better measures is badly needed to investigate a variety of products across a wider selection of consumers.

Researchers also should extend their studies to investigate a number of more subtle questions and interactions among factors influencing communication effectiveness. A discussion of the research needed in this area is included in chapter 8. The research findings and their implications then must be communicated to and be implemented by advertising practitioners to make a significant impact on the future use of sex in advertising. That process is discussed in some detail in chapter 10.

Notes

1. John Berger, *Ways of Seeing* (Baltimore: Penguin Books, 1972).
2. "Children on the Block," *The Globe and Mail,* 9 March 1981, p. 6.
3. Pat Sloan, "Women WAP Wanton Ads," *Advertising Age,* 15 February 1982, pp. 3, 85.
4. "Sexy Alaskan Tour Ad Draws Heated Reaction," *Advertising Age,* 12 March 1979, p. 48.
5. "Miami Poster Fires Up Locals," *Advertising Age,* 3 December 1979, p. 44.
6. "Sexy Alaskan Tour Ad Draws Heated Reaction," p. 48.
7. "Miami Poster Fires Up Locals," p. 44.
8. Pat Sloan, p. 85.
9. John J. O'Connor, "Sex Roles in Advertising Draw Hisses and Boos," *Advertising Age,* 12 March 1979, p. 48.
10. Lorenzo Benet, "Sex: An Effective Sales Pitch or Sell-Out in Women's Golf?", *The Plain Dealer,* 19 August 1982, p. 2-E.
11. Marilyn Adler and Kathleen Bronder, "Real Market Muscle," *Advertising Age,* 28 April 1980, p. S-4.
12. Tracie Rozhon, "Racy Ads Do An End Run Around Network Censors," *The Plain Dealer,* 7 December 1980, p. 16-17.
13. Tracie Rozhon, p. 17.
14. Gordon L. Wise, Alan L. King, and J. Paul Merenski, "Reactions to Sexy Ads Vary With Age," *Journal of Advertising Research* 14 (August 1974):11-16.
15. William Lundstrom and Donald Sciglimpaglia, "Sex Role Portrayals in Advertising," *Journal of Marketing* 41 (July 1977):72-79.
16. Deborah K. Johnson and Kay Satow, "Consumers Reactions to Sex in TV Commercials," in *Advances in Consumer Research,* ed. H.K. Hunt (Chicago: Association for Consumer Research, 1978), pp. 411-414.
17. Rena Bartos, *The Moving Target: What Every Marketer Should Know About Women* (New York: The Free Press, 1982).
18. Bruce John Morrison and Richard C. Sherman, "Who Responds

to Sex in Advertising?'' *Journal of Advertising Research* 12 (April 1972): 15–19.

19. Robert W. Chestnut, Charles C. LaChance, and Amy Lubitz, ''The 'Decorative' Female Model: Sexual Stimuli and the Recognition of Advertisements,'' *Journal of Advertising* 6 (Fall 1977):11–14.

20. Frederick W. Derrick and John D. Wolken, ''Comment on The 'Decorative' Female Model: Sexual Stimuli and the Recognition of Advertisements,'' *Journal of Advertising* 7 (Spring 1978):60, 57.

21. Leonard N. Reid and Lawrence C. Soley, ''Another Look at the ''Decorative'' Female Model: The Recognition of Visual and Verbal Ad Components,'' in *Current Issues and Research in Advertising,* ed. J.H. Leigh and C.R. Martin, Jr. (Ann Arbor: The University of Michigan, 1981), pp. 123–133.

22. Michael J. Baker and Gilbert A. Churchill, Jr., ''The Impact of Physically Attractive Models on Advertising Evaluations,'' *Journal of Marketing Research* 14 (November 1977):538–555.

23. Gordon L. Patzer, ''A Comparison of Advertisement Effects: Sexy Female Communicator vs. Non-Sexy Female Communicator,'' in *Advances in Consumer Research,* ed. J.C. Olson (Ann Arbor: Association for Consumer Research, 1980), pp. 359–364.

24. George Horsley Smith and Rayme Engel, ''Influence of a Female Model on Perceived Characteristics of an Automobile,'' Proceedings of the 76th Annual Convention of the American Psychological Association, 1968, pp. 681–682.

25. Major Steadman, ''How Sexy Illustrations Affect Brand Recall,'' *Journal of Advertising Research* 9 (February 1969):15–19.

26. M. Wayne Alexander and Ben Judd, Jr., ''Do Nudes in Ads Enhance Brand Recall?'', *Journal of Advertising Research* 18 (February 1978):47–50.

27. Robert A. Peterson and Roger A. Kerin, ''The Female Role in Advertisements: Some Experimental Evidence,'' *Journal of Marketing* 41 (October 1977):59–63.

28. Donald Sciglimpaglia, Michael A. Belch, and Richard F. Cain, Jr., ''Demographic and Cognitive Factors Influencing Viewers' Evaluation of 'Sexy' Advertisements,'' in *Advances in Consumer Research,* ed. W. Wilkie (Ann Arbor: Association for Consumer Research, 1979), pp. 62–65.

29. Stewart Henderson Britt, ''The Use and Misuse of Sex in Advertising,'' in *Sharing for Understanding,* ed. G.E. Miracle (East Lansing: American Academy of Advertising, 1977), pp. 163–165.

30. Edward C. Strong, ''Prisoner of Sex in Advertising,'' in *Advances in Consumer Research,* ed. W. Wilkie (Ann Arbor: Association for Consumer Research, 1979), pp. 78–81.

31. R. Dale Wilson and Noreen K. Moore, ''The Role of Sexually-

Oriented Stimuli in Advertising: Theory and Literature Review," in *Advances in Consumer Research,* ed. W. Wilkie (Ann Arbor: Association for Consumer Research, 1979), pp. 55–61.

32. Mark I. Alpert, "Sex Roles, Sex and Stereotyping in Advertising: More Questions Than Answers," *Advances in Consumer Research,* ed. W. Wilkie (Ann Arbor: Association for Consumer Research, 1979), pp. 73–77.

33. W. Benoy Joseph, "The Credibility of Physically Attractive Communicators: A Review," *Journal of Advertising* 11 (Summer 1982):15–24.

7

Humor and Voices

The three preceeding chapters in the second part of this book have demonstrated that a major research stream in the area of sex stereotyping and advertising effectiveness has evolved during the last decade. Two research issues which have begun to receive specialized attention are: the effectiveness of sexual and sexist humor in advertising and the effect of using female voices in broadcast advertising. These areas will be the focus of this chapter. In chapter 5 it was seen that varying the type of humor employed and utilizing female voices have produced findings indicating that the effectiveness of advertising communications to certain target audiences can be increased. But in the studies reported there, many advertising variables were changed simultaneously to measure the preference for traditional versus progressive portrayals, and humor and voice were not manipulated experimentally and tested. In this chapter, however, research is discussed which focuses specifically on humor or voice considerations.

The Effective Use of Humor[1]

In recent years there has been a growing concern among a variety of age, ethnic, religious, and other groups when they have felt that advertising humor was not entertaining, but rather was offensive and demeaning. Sensitivity to humorous portrayals of the sexes, in particular, has been increasing. Because of this growing sensitivity, a commercial found amusing by some people in the audience can be considered to be offensive to others. These differences in peoples' reactions to humor make it extremely difficult for an advertiser, who sincerely wishes to create new humorous copy for a liberated audience, to avoid serious problems.[2] Nevertheless, gender differences in humor appreciation have so far been almost neglected by researchers. This negligence is surprising, given that estimates of the incidence of humor in advertising range from 15 to 42 percent, substantiating the continued popularity of employing humorous copy.[3]

123

The Need for Audience Research on Gender-Related
Humor in Advertising

In 1975 the National Advertising Review Board (NARB) panel, which considered the portrayal of women in advertising, recognized the importance of gender differences in the appreciation of humor when it concluded:

> The Panel feels called on to point out that sometimes meanness is expressed in the guise of humor. In its study of current advertising, the Panel came across some examples of attempted women-related humor which could not have been funny to those who were the butt of the jokes. It is healthy for people to laugh at themselves, but usually this is a luxury only the secure can afford. Effective humor often has a cutting edge, and it requires extraordinary care to ensure that the cut is not made at the expense of women's self-esteem.[4]

The Canadian counterpart to the NARB, the Advertising Advisory Board (AAB), also recognized the problems associated with the portrayal of the sexes in humorous advertising in a 1977 report on women and advertising. The task force recommended that:

> Humor in advertising calls for special skills. It may entertain and yet not sell the product, or it may demean and offend—and this applies to both men and women—instead of creating customer goodwill. One test of a humorous advertisement is the question—"Would it offend me to be portrayed in that way?"[5]

The concern expressed by the NARB and the general advice offered by the AAB are insufficient to serve as the detailed operational guidelines advertisers need to deal with gender differences in humor appreciation. In fact, the advice may be misleading. In a study of advertisers and marketers Courtney and Whipple administered a paper-and-pencil test to a sample of fifty-one male and sixteen female practitioners to obtain their ratings of six television commercials which differed in advertising style.[6] Although the primary purpose of the study was to compare traditional and progressive advertising copy with respect to the portrayal of the sexes in the advertisements, a humor rating also was obtained. One of the commercials showed one woman disparaging another. In this detergent commercial an overbearing mother-in-law puts down her son's frazzled wife because she had failed to use the advertised brand to wash the dishes. The agency which prepared the commercial considered the advertisement's portrayal of the sexes as very traditional and stereotyped.

The detergent advertisement was perceived as more amusing than the other five advertisements by all practitioners. However, when the ratings were analyzed by sex of respondent, the detergent commercial was considered to be significantly more amusing by the male practitioners than by their female counterparts. Although this attitude did not produce gender differences in a composite effectiveness score for the advertisement, it did result in the women rating the advertisement significantly more irritating than did the men. These findings illustrate that male and female practitioners may differ in their reactions to advertising humor. Many female practitioners commented that they did not consider the put-down advertisement to be very funny nor were they very appreciative of humor which showed an antifemale bias. Although these data are limited, they illustrate that it is risky for practitioners to attempt to prejudge responses to humorous copy, and they underscore the necessity to pretest humorous copy with relevant target audiences.

The risks in using humor are illustrated by some recent attempts to create humorous and progressive advertising which have received negative reactions from important market segments. Examples include:

1. An oven cleaner commercial was found by some women to be a demeaning depiction of woman as slave to her husband and kitchen, while others in the target audience considered the advertisement to be a humorous spoof of the same situation.
2. A cosmetic advertisement which stated that "Your Face Isn't Safe in This City" was interpreted by some women as an incitement to violence.
3. A commercial for men's underwear which showed men modeling the product and spoofed similar advertisements for female underwear was interpreted by some men and women as sexually demeaning.

These and other observed differences in humor appreciation have already caused serious problems for some advertisers. Their lack of understanding of gender differences resulted in advertisements which were interpreted as attempts to laugh at, rather than with, men and women in their changing roles.[7]

Creative Factors Affecting the Effectiveness
of Humor Campaigns[8]

A number of comedians and copywriters have accumulated a great deal of experience in humor writing and are acknowledged today as leaders in the field of writing and executing advertising humor. Notable examples are the comedy teams of Dick and Bert, Stiller and Meara, Bob and Ray, Nichols and May, and Barzman and McCormick; individuals such as Artie Johnson, Chuck McCann, Paul Dooley, and Hans Konreid; and copywriters at

Della Femina, Travisano and Partners, and Marsteller advertising agencies. Radio advertisers in increasing numbers have used the services of these humor experts in recent years. Their brand of humor is also popular among some television advertisers and is being promoted by Dick and Bert for direct mail use via Eva-Tone Soundsheets.

Although these experts have produced advertising which is generally judged to be entertaining and creative, success of the campaigns from a marketing and sales viewpoint is mixed. For example, a Blue Nun wine campaign by Stiller and Meara reportedly contributed significantly to an increase in the wine's market share; on the other hand, a Bob and Ray series of commercials for Piel's beer did not retard consistent share loss by the brewer. The difference in opinion about when to use humor in advertising was recently presented by McMahan.[9]

Various creative approaches used by advertisers, agencies, and comedy writer/performer teams may contribute to differences in both the communication effectiveness and the sales performance of humor campaigns. Some advertisers, such as Proctor and Gamble, insist that humorous copy be created according to a formula approach, within their standard message component framework; others set parameters within which to make the copy points with a humorous message. Still other advertisers give the comedy writers virtually free rein to create scripts and produce commercials from scratch, while retaining final authority over script approval and the right to reject the final product.

Another factor which contributes to the differential results of humorous campaigns is the lack of awareness among agency and comedy creative staffs of writings by humor theorists and researchers. Since many comedy-writing creative staff members have performance backgrounds with such troupes as Second City, their expertise is based on creative skills, rather than on research knowledge. In fact neither agency nor comedy writer representatives were: aware of any research ever conducted to measure if there were differential gender responses to their advertisements, able to recall any special considerations given to potential gender differences in appreciation of their advertisements during the creative process, or cognizant of any concerns regarding gender differences in humorous advertising. To them the potential for a gender difference in response to their humorous advertisements was not a relevant issue.

Practitioners claimed to avoid most audience response problems by developing advertisements for neutral products which are appropriate for general audiences. There is evidence that, on occasion, this strategy is not effective. For example, an advertisement which became problematic as a result of regional differences in response was corrected only after the original copy had been aired and deemed ineffective. Potential questions about differential gender responses are dealt with, if at all, on the creative level.

An advertisement making fun of a mother-in-law was reportedly approved when a female member of the creative staff judged the copy to be not too antifeminist. Practitioners also claimed to concentrate on a milder type of humor which theorists classify as nonsensical humor, thus avoiding any potential criticism over the use of sex or aggression in the advertisements. However, examples of campaigns for dictating equipment and salad dressing, cited by the practitioners interviewed, employed put-downs and sexual innuendo.

A final, identified factor which contributes to the mixed success of humorous advertisements is the potential difference between the creative goals of comedy writers and the communication and marketing goals of agencies and advertisers. An exception is noted in a memo by Dick and Bert, who appear to have combined comedy and advertising expertise successfully.[10] They attempt to know their target audience, make believable claims, capture audience attention and interest, produce product awareness, and create an image of being likeable by presenting a zany character or an incongruous situation.

Psychological Evidence of Sex Differences in Humor Appreciation

Evidence from psychological research strongly suggests the likelihood of important gender differences in humor appreciation. For more than fifty years, researchers have used cartoons, jokes, and photos as experimental stimuli to study the moderating effects of audience characteristics on humor appreciation. Psychologists and communication researchers have found that personality and demographic factors affect humor appreciation and that gender of the audience is an especially important determinant of response. Typically, this response is based on funniness ratings, elicited through paper and pencil tests, of the stimuli. Observational techniques, used particularly with children, have corroborated the findings from audience-rating studies and lend support to the contention that sex differences in response begin in early childhood and endure through adult life.[11]

Classification of Humor Types. The most eminent of thinkers and writers from Aristotle to current scholars have wrestled with the complicated subject of humor. Their efforts have resulted in a variety of expressed possibilities as to its nature, as well as discussions about a host of related theoretical issues.[12] The most commonly reported findings concerning sex differences in humor appreciation arise from investigations of different types of humor classified by content. Beginning in the 1920s, researchers isolated three classes of humor and studied individual preferences for the different content. According to Kambouropoulou, the three basic classes are:

1. Hostile humor (humor depicting aggressive drive or intent to ridicule).
2. Sexual humor (humor concerning sexual activity or stimulation).
3. Nonsensical humor (humor of incongruity and nonsense which results from situations associating generally acceptable incompatibilities).[13]

Psychological studies investigating the reaction to these three types of humor have generally concluded that men find hostile humor and sexual humor funnier than do women. Women, on the other hand, generally find humor arising out of nonsensical or incongruous situations to be funnier.[14] Recent in-depth investigations under differing experimental conditions have offered insights into the reasons for differences in humor appreciation.

Hostile Humor. Race, religion, and political affiliation have been shown to affect the way hostile humor is perceived. For example, ". . . people have found jokes in which members of their own group disparage members of other groups more amusing than jokes in which an alien group disparage their own."[15] In general, men have been found to enjoy hostile humor as long as the joke does not disparage members of their own sex. Disparagement of a male is considered funny by men only if the disparaged male can be identified as an enemy. Research has shown, however, that when women are the respondents, the response is much more complex. A number of studies have found that women's reactions to hostile humor are significantly different from men's reactions. In general, women do not find aggressive humor as funny as do men. More specifically, women judge hostile cartoons and jokes to be funniest when their own sex is disparaged. Allen's study of housewives, for example, found that women rated humor involving hostility between the sexes as most funny when men were aggressive toward women.[16] Related research has investigated whether this finding holds under different experimental conditions. The results of studies conducted by Losco and Epstein, and Zellman and Stocking showed that:[17]

1. Both males and females gave higher funniness ratings to stimuli in which females are ridiculed, but females showed the antifemale bias to a greater extent than did males.
2. The antifemale bias applied in responses to different styles of hostile humor including verbal jokes and cartoons showing physical aggression.
3. The sex of the victim was a more important determinant of response than the sex of the aggressor. It was funnier for all respondents to watch a woman be ridiculed, rather than a man, when the dominating person was either a male or female.

4. Females considered self-disparaging humor funnier than did males, and women more than men enjoyed the self-disparagement of a woman.
5. Females perceived the self-disparager, male or female, in a more favorable light than did males, judging him or her to be more intelligent, provocative, and skillful.

The antifemale bias demonstrated in these research findings may reflect attitudes that are undergoing changes. Researchers find that some men and women do not display the traditional patterns of humor appreciation. Contrary to other findings, Priest and Wilhelm found that females judged antimale jokes to be funnier than antifemale jokes.[18] In addition, they determined that high self-actualizers of both sexes, and especially unmarried females, do not enjoy antifemale jokes. Measurement of attitudes toward female liberation has enabled other researchers to corroborate the changing response patterns in humor appreciation. Female supporters of sexual equality were found to side with female protagonists, whereas male supporters of male supremacy sided with male protagonists in jokes.[19] Also, firm advocates of the women's movement laughed less at jokes denigrating women than at nonsense jokes.[20] One effect of ridiculing women was to intensify immediate female support for women's rights.

Sexual Humor. The traditional research finding has been that men find sexual humor funnier than do women. However, there is recent evidence to suggest that women are equally appreciative of sexual humor, as long as it is not sexist. The failure to find sexist humor funny is significantly related to positive attitudes toward women's rights, a relationship found among both women and men.[21] Men enjoy sexual humor more than women do when it is sexist and when the status of men is not under threat. It was found that women dislike sexist humor because of its threatening nature.[22]

Nonsensical Humor. Although nonsensical humor is popular in advertising, as well as in jokes and cartoons, it did not attract the same attention among researchers as hostile and sexual humor did during the 1970s. Traditional findings indicate that women appreciate nonsensical humor more than men do. But, like other humor response patterns, differences in appreciation of absurd humor may be changing in directions which are still unpredictable.

Humor in Advertising

Herold characterized humor in advertising as "... a quiet and sensible and legitimate use of amusing copy/or cartoons, or perhaps amusing illustrations or photographs, to do a job of merchandising—first by attracting attention in *a relevant way,* then by imparting pleasant information and making a soft sell, all in a mixed atmosphere of relaxation and integrity''.[23] The use of humor in an advertising strategy is based on the assumption that humorous copy provides an effective, persuasive vehicle, as well as performing the role as an attention-getter. To date there is no research which documents and compares the relative advertising effectiveness of a humorous and a serious version of the same appeal. However, there is limited evidence that very pleasant messages may be effective in generating attitude change, intention to buy, and product acceptance, while unpleasant but stimulating advertisements may be more effective with respect to comprehension. In terms of communication goals, humorous messages, whether pleasant or unpleasant, appear to attract attention and generate general awareness. Humor used to achieve comprehension, however, may do more harm than good. The perceived effect of humor on attitude change is even less clear because the positive distractive effects of humorous copy are countered by the risk that irritating commercials will impair learning. The combined effectiveness of various types of humor, the pleasantness of the message, and the distractive and irritating effects of copy has not been studied to date.

The word, humor, is often used as if it has a precise, universal meaning to everyone; clearly, this is not the case. According to Sternthal and Craig, humor can be characterized in terms of either: its stimulus properties, the behavioral responses elicited by a stimulus, or audience ratings of the stimulus.[24] Advertisers tend to utilize the third criterion. For example, based on an extensive analysis of consumers' opinions about advertisements, Wells, Leavitt, and McConville showed that humor is one of six dimensions which consistently discriminated among the commercials they tested.[25] The humor factor, defined by a small set of words and phrases (including jolly, merry, playful, humorous, amusing), was successfully used to determine whether a commercial produced the reaction the advertiser intended. However, they found that the humor factor interacted with other important dimensions of responses to the advertisements, particularly the dimension of personal relevance. A commercial which was perceived as humorous, but not personally relevant, was judged to be relatively ineffective.

In addition, Lynch and Hartman have isolated and identified dimensions of humor in both advertising and joke stimuli.[26] Their results showed that a marked similarity existed between the dimensions of humor which consumers used to judge advertising and those used for jokes. These results suggest that some findings from psychological humor research, using joke and cartoon stimuli, may be applicable to the evaluation of possible effects of using humor in advertising copy, and thus relevant to advertisers. Lynch and Hartman's findings also suggest that different types of advertising humor may be more or less effective with different audiences.

*Consumer Research on Gender-Related Humor
in Advertising*

To date, advertising research which addresses the issue of gender differences in response to advertising humor is very limited. Shama and
Coughlin found no significant differences between male and female
respondents attitudes toward three humorous advertisements.[27] Although
the commercials were carefully selected to include three different types of
products (a food, a drug, and a specialty) on two broadcast media (radio
and television), they were all simply classified by the researchers as slapstick
humor. Unfortunately, no attempt was made to classify the commercials
according to the content types commonly used in psychological research.

Taking a considerably different research approach, Madden and Weinberger investigated whether humorous messages attract attention and, if so,
whether gender of the audience confounds the effect of humor.[28] They
utilized syndicated research data to determine if humorous advertising
heightens attention levels. With the cooperation of Starch/Inra/Hooper,
Inc., Madden and Weingberger examined readership scores obtained for
167 humorous liquor and insurance advertisements which appeared in
Starch-audited magazines from 1976 through 1979. The type of humor content was categorized most often as absurd humor. The attention a reader
remembered giving to a particular advertisement was measured by Starch's
aided-recall technique. The data included *noted* scores (percent of readers
who remembered seeing the advertisement), *seen/associated* scores (percent
of readers who remembered reading any part of the advertisement) and
read-most scores (percent of readers who remembered reading more than
half of the advertisement's copy).

Madden and Weinberger concluded that humor improved the overall
performance of the print advertisements measured; their results showed
that a high percentage of the humorous advertisements outscored the Starch
Ad Norms for all three aided-recall measures. When they compared female
and male responses, significant differences were revealed for noted and
read-most scores for the total sample of advertisements. When a subset of
thirty advertisements with matched male and female samples for the same
advertisements were analyzed, significant differences existed for read-most
scores only. In those cases where statistically significant differences were
not obtained, humorous advertisements consistently scored higher among
males than among females. The finding that women reacted less favorably
to humorous advertising for two typically male products could have been
the result of product-interest variations or may have reflected humor-pref-
erence differences between the sexes. The researchers recommended further
work of an experimental nature to isolate gender, product, and humor-type
effects.

A study by Whipple and Courtney did examine gender differences in response to advertising for two products which utilized one type of humor.[29] The design of the research project was based on the psychological research reviewed earlier in this chapter. The main objective of the research was to determine whether humor of incongruity is particularly appropriate for advertising targeted to women.[30] To test the hypothesis that there are no gender differences in response to absurd humor, three magazine advertisements employing the typical use of nonsensical humor in advertising were selected.

Each respondent was given a self-administered questionnaire to complete in a group-administration setting of approximately thirty-five people each. After being exposed to a color slide of an advertisement for thirty seconds, respondents were instructed to rate the advertisement on the basis of how well thirteen criteria described the advertisement. Psychological-research results suggest that the female subjects would more likely find humor arising out of nonsensical or incongruous situations amusing. The data definitely did not support that contention. Instead, the sexes responded similarly when evaluating the funniness of the advertisements.

On the basis of these tentative findings advertising researchers and practitioners could be less concerned that males may not respond as well as females to nonsensical humor. On the contrary, humor of incongruity and nonsense appears to be a likely alternative for advertising targeted to both sexes.

Guidelines for Using Gender-Related Humor Effectively in Advertising

Advertising strategists should carefully reexamine the effectiveness of hostile humor as a copy approach. As expressed by the NARB, humor can be mean, but psychological research shows that people have traditionally found it funny to see an enemy suffer. The way different segments of people define their enemies, however, is very complex and continually changing. Until advertising researchers thoroughly study the communication effectiveness of hostile humor, the best course of action for advertisers is to avoid the use of aggressive or hostile humor. Hostile humor, which in advertising usually takes the form of a put-down, is particularly ineffective with women and liberated men. With male audiences, and with most females as well, showing a put-down of a man by a woman, particularly a low-status woman, is not an effective technique. And even though putting down a friend has been a staple of advertising copy, psychological research shows that neither sex likes that type of humor. In general, both men and women are becoming less tolerant of hostile humor, especially when women are the victims. Self-denigration as a form of humor, however, may be acceptable under certain circumstances. If a female audience perceives that the character in the advertisement is laughing at him/herself in a healthy manner by making light of his/her own foibles, then this technique can be effective. But if females in the audience perceive that the advertiser has set up the character to make fun of him or her, then backlash can be expected from the more liberated women in the audience. Men, on the other hand, do not like self-disparaging humor under any circumstances.

Since most forms of aggression-based humor are not perceived as being particularly funny by either sex and often irritate one or both sexes, advertisers would be wise to employ alternative types of humor. Sexual humor, for example, is appreciated by both men and women as long as it is perceived as nonsexist. Since sexist humor was found to be ineffective with women and with more liberated men, advertisers should guard against creating sexy advertisements which may be misinterpreted as being sexist. Good intentions will not guarantee acceptable copy if advertisers rely on their own judgment to decide what is sexist. Even the best creative efforts in this area require pretesting with the target audience.

The humor of incongruity and nonsense is possibly the most attractive alternative to hostile humor. For advertisers using nonsensical humor care must be taken to ensure that the informational content and the persuasive aspects of the message are not impaired by the absurd humor employed. Pretests of a proposed humorous advertisement should measure whether the communication goals are being achieved and whether certain members of the target audience are offended by the portrayal of either sex in the advertisement. In addition to the moderating effects of gender of the target audience, advertising researchers should be concerned about attitudinal variables which may be of importance in testing the response to humorous copy. Attitudes toward the women's movement are of particular relevance for both sexes, and these attitudes may vary by age, marital status, education, occupation, and other demographic variables. The limited research evidence on the use of absurd humor in advertising does indicate that, if well conceived and implemented, nonsensical humor can be an effective communication technique.

Psychological research also shows that humorous content and techniques which are effective with the target audience may offend others not in the intended segment. Because standards are changing and what is effective varies by segment, attention also should be given to attitudes of those not in the target group. Potential problems posed by people who misunderstand the humor or who have not adjusted to the changing standards suggest that advertisers be particularly cautious in their use of humor in unsegmented media.

The Outlook for Communication with Humor

The psychological-research findings were useful for developing workable guidelines for advertisers who wish to use humorous approaches but who also wish to avoid offensive, ineffective, socially unacceptable copy. Use of those guidelines combined with careful pretesting of advertising should enable advertisers to make practical improvements in the communications effectiveness of their advertisements. To date, research findings indicate that nonsense and nonsexist/sexual humor are preferable to hostile forms of humor with many female and liberated male audiences. Further research should be conducted to confirm or refute the findings. However, studies need to be designed and implemented in a more reliable and valid manner than in the past if they are to make a significant impact on our knowledge of the applicability of humor to specific advertising approaches. A number of research design and measurement issues facing those engaged in gender-related, advertising-humor research are addressed in the next chapter.

Using Female Announcers in Commercials

Another specific issue which has surfaced from the general study of the portrayal of women in advertising is the controversy over the gender of the voice of authority in advertising. There are some changes that have occurred in the last ten years to improve the portrayal of women in advertising, but there is continued male dominance of commercial voice-overs and announcers. Females are used more frequently as product representatives than in the past, yet studies consistently show that approximately 90 percent of the off-camera voices of authority in television commercials are male. The dominance of male voice-overs and announcers in commercials can be accounted for by the belief among advertisers that the male voice is more authoritative and hence more effective.[31] In addition, advertisers claim that there is a lack of trained female announcers. Women have had limited access to this highly lucrative field in which top announcers earn as much as $500,000 yearly playing voice-over roles. The voice-over issue also has more long-term social implications. As discussed in chapter 3 the failure to portray women in authoritative roles may produce undesirable consequences if advertising influences and reinforces perceptions that women cannot exercise authority or make independent decisions.[32]

A managerial consequence of using male voices almost exclusively is that advertisers may not be reaching their target markets as effectively as they might. One example comes from an interview by Seaman with agency president Zal Venet.[33] Venet stated that most supermarket spokespeople are men, even though most customers are women, because there still is a gut feeling in the industry that a woman shopper would rather be talked to by a male. One supermarket chain innovated by using a campaign featuring a female consumer advisor as spokesperson. Chain executives have found her to be an effective spokeswoman for the chain in advertising to traditional female customers and also in appealing to the growing numbers of male shoppers. Other advertising executives interviewed by Seaman agreed that while the sex of the spokesperson often depends on the message the advertiser hopes to convey, the effectiveness of the spokesperson really relates directly to his or her believability.[34] Trying to build a positive image for a retailer, they claim, means giving an impression of trustworthiness.

The belief among most advertisers that a man has automatic credibility and that the authority figure in commercials should be male has not been supported or refuted by published advertising research. In fact, research on the effectiveness of female voices in commercials is extremely limited.

Findings from Psychological and Communications Research

Several research studies in psychology and communications shed some light on the effectiveness of women as authority figures. Psychological studies conducted in the late sixties with female subjects addressed a number of issues relating to the prejudice toward women in areas of professional and intellectual competence. The results from these early studies were inconclusive. Some subjects evaluated professional and intellectual efforts attributed to a man more positively than identical efforts attributed to a woman, whereas other women judged female efforts to be equal to those of males. These differences disappeared, however, when the description of the work evaluated advanced from an effort, attempt, or entry to an actual accomplishment or winning entry.[35]

These studies were replicated in the mid-seventies using both men and women as subjects. This research was designed to determine if the sexes differed in their evaluations, to measure any changes in female prejudice over time, and to investigate the divergent results of the earlier research.[36] The findings indicated that evaluations of male and female professionals by both sexes were more objective than the previous studies had suggested. There were no significant differences in evaluations based on either sex of the subject or of the communicator.

The value of these psychological studies to advertisers is limited by their use of student subjects and their divergent findings and also by their reliance on written and visual-communication materials. Would the results obtained be different if the source of communication was verbal or if the subjects came from a more generalizable group?

Kramer stressed in a 1974 paper that women as speakers have been largely ignored in communication research, but that there is a sizeable amount of information that can be called *folk view:* how people think women speak or how people think women should speak.[37] These folk views support the bias that people do not like to hear the female voice and that the female voice is not authoritative. Key, who documented some of the assumptions and folk views about the male and female voice, noted that they came from outdated books, plays, and poems, and not from empirical studies.[38] Nevertheless, these untested folk views influence decision making. For example, Mannes quoted a broadcaster explaining the reason so few women are employed by television networks, "As a whole, people don't like to hear women's voices telling them serious things."[39] Similarly, a hand-book for announcers published in 1959 gave specific reasons as to why women could not be effective announcers or newscasters.[40] Supposedly, women with high-pitched voices could not hold listeners' attention for any period of time, while low-pitched female voices were perceived as overly polished, ultrasophisticated delivery which sounded phony. Furthermore, the handbook claimed that women's delivery is lacking in the authority necessary for a convincing broadcast. These views also influence adver-tisers. Scott, author of *The Female Consumer,* quoted Joseph Daly, presi-dent of Grey Advertising, who stated "that men are used because the male voice is the voice of authority."[41]

In a recent attempt to examine the validity of such views, Miller and McReynolds examined whether receivers rate a male communicator as more competent than a female communicator when all source qualifications and the message are held constant.[42] Their results showed that the competence ratings of male and female communicators do not differ significantly for male receivers, but that female receivers rate the male source significantly more competent than the female.

In Stone's study on the believability of male versus female newscasters, only 20 percent of the respondents thought that they would be more likely to believe a report just because it was reported by a man rather than by a woman.[43] Of those respondents who did believe that men are more authori-tative sounding, many agreed that it might be due to habit rather than to inherent sex differences. In essence, people were saying that they are more likely to accept that with which they are familiar. Stone speculated that as newswomen became more prevalent, preferences for males will become less common.

Results from more recent communications research suggest that atti-tudes toward female communicators have already begun to change. Using an experimental design, Gitter and Coburn examined male and female ratings of the trustworthiness of a communicator.[44] They varied sex, title, and organizational affiliation of the agency spokesperson. A sample of 576 respondents was asked to evaluate the credibility of the spokesperson on the basis of a fifty-word paragraph description that varied according to a total of twenty-four combinations of the three manipulated, independent variables. How much each respondent trusted what the person said as a spokesperson for the organization was recorded on a ten-point scale. Analysis of variance of the ratings showed that the sex of the subject generated statistically significant differences. Female respondents were found to be more trusting than male subjects. When the sex of the spokesperson was examined, significantly higher trust was attributed to a female spokesperson as compared to a male one. Gitter and Coburn claimed that this finding supported the hypothesis that " . . . females are perceived as less jaded by the business ethic and self-serving pecuniary interests." Consequently, females both trusted more and were more trusted.

Berryman, compared male and female subjects' perceptions of communicators who used sex-appropriate language with perceptions of those who used sex-inappropriate language.[45] These stereotypes of sex-appropriate language were derived from the folk views examined by Kramer. For example, female language distinctions are thought to include correct grammar, clear enunciation, high pitch, and emotional speech. The sex-appropriate language variable was manipulated through variations in pronunciations, interruptions, number of words, pitch, and intonation. Subjects' ratings of the speakers produced some surprising results. On the credibility dimension the female speaker was viewed as most credible when she used sex-appropriate language. However, the male speaker was rated as more credible when he used sex-inappropriate language. From these results it was clear to Berryman that female language distinctions consistently contributed to the speaker's credibility, regardless of whether they were used by a male or a female communicator.

The fact that female language contributed to the user's credibility of both male and female speakers raises questions about those beliefs that males are more credible. Berryman showed that communicators are differentially rated as a consequence of linguistic features rather than as a consequence of mere identification of the speaker's gender. This suggests that the ability of a communicator to use female-appropriate language may be more important than the communicator's gender as such. When Whittaker and Whittaker utilized a number of communication-effectiveness measures in their study on the relative effectiveness of male versus female newscasters, again the male voice was not judged to be more authoritative than the female voice.[46] They found no statistically significant difference in the perceived acceptance, believability, or effectiveness between male and female newscasters.

The research of the 1960s began with the question, "Is it possible that male sources are generally more persuasive than female sources, regardless of the issues involved or the media employed?"[47] The answer of the 1980s is no. The superior effectiveness once attributed to the male voice has not been verified by the research just reviewed. Together, these psychological and communications-research findings indicate that the competence, believability, authoritativeness, trustworthiness, credibility, and effectiveness of female communicators are on par with those of their male counterparts. Nevertheless, women are still rarely portrayed as the voice of authority in advertising.

Advertising Effectiveness of Female Voices of Authority

Although women are increasingly portrayed as product representatives for female-related products, such as household, food, and personal-care items, their authority roles have been diluted by the persistent use of male voice-overs. In nine out of ten cases men usually speak the last word and retain the image of final authority. Role preference, communications, and psychological-research findings indicate that advertisers may be making a mistake, but the data specifically examining the advertising-communications effectiveness of male versus female announcers are limited. Student-research papers are the only attempts that we are aware of at isolating and measuring such effects.

Bennie compared female and male voices in radio advertisements on recall, perceived effectiveness, perceived irritation, and behavioral intention.[48] She also considered product relatedness determined by product use classified according to three categories: female, male, and neutral.

A sample of one hundred twenty women from a list of registered voters agreed to participate in the study, purportedly on radio-programming techniques. Demographic information provided in a preliminary questionnaire was used to randomly split the sample into two homogeneous subsamples. Respondents in each subsample listened individually to a twelve-minute radio program interrupted by one of two commercial messages for each of the three products. Two advertisements each for the sewing machine (female related), the electric shaver (male related), and the vacation travel spot (neutral) varied only in the voice of the spokesperson. One subsample of women heard advertisements which used the female voice, while the other subsample heard a male voice in each advertisement.

Bennie was concerned with measuring the relative effectiveness of male versus female voices at the retention and learning level, at the perceptual level, and at the behavioral-intention level. Product category and brand-name recall; advertising effectiveness, irritation, sound of voice, and authoritativeness scores; and intention-to-buy measures were used to examine the effects of the commercials at the three levels. Nonmetric analysis of variance was then used to determine specifically if voice and product differences were significant and to analyze the interaction between product relatedness and the sex of the communicator.

No significant differences were found between the two subsamples on any of the recall, perceptual, or intention-to-buy measures. The same measures revealed no significant interactions between the sex of the communicator and the type of product being advertised. What is clear from this study is that the voice of the product spokesperson did not have a significant effect on effectiveness of any of the commercials.

Based on her findings Bennie argued that female announcers are perceived to be as authoritative as male announcers. Moreover, authoritativeness alone does not determine the effectiveness of a commercial. Bennie contends that advertisers should review some of the recent research available and reconsider their decision to limit the use of female announcers in commercials.

A second student extended Bennie's research: by including both men and women as subjects, by evaluating advertisements for four different products, by manipulating the sex of two different voices per advertisement, and by adding evaluative criteria which specifically measure voice differences.[49] Instead of using radio advertisements, Schoonover used the audio portion of four television commercials to determine if there were variations in perceived effectiveness, believability, irritation, and behavioral intention with respect to voice gender and product type. In addition to advertisements for a male-related product (men's cologne) and a female-related product (perfume), commercials for two neutral products were also evaluated. Schoonover selected one neutral product (shampoo) requiring only an individual purchase decision, and another neutral product (shower spray) which may require a joint or mutual purchase decision. All four products could be purchased by either sex for self-use or as a gift item.

Each commercial was produced, taped, and edited, with audio only, at a radio station. The copy was patterned after television commercials for each product, with one individual playing the role of the product representative and another the role of the off-camera announcer or voice-over. All advertisements were thirty seconds in length and had the same structure: description of product benefits by the product representative followed by a tag-line sales pitch by the announcer. Audio was used exclusively to focus the attention of respondents on the voices and the sales message and to eliminate any mediating effects of the actors' physical appearances. Voices were provided by two men and two women, one man and one woman playing the role of product representative, while the other man and woman took the part of the announcer. Media personnel at the radio station evaluated the final tapes of the advertisements and judged the voice quality of each male-female pair to be similar.

A three-factor experimental design (four product types by two product representative genders by two announcer genders) with repeated measures was utilized. A total of 474 male and female subjects ranging in age from nineteen to sixty-five were randomly assigned to four of the sixteen treatment combinations. Each respondent evaluated only one advertisement for each of the four products on a ten-item rating scale. The tape was stopped after each commercial to allow for evaluation of the advertisements. Total sum scores for effectiveness were used in the analysis of the commercials. Analysis of variance of these scores was conducted for each product separately to determine if there were significant differences in communication effectiveness due to the sex of the product representative or the sex of the announcer.[50]

The findings for female subjects were consistent with Bennie's results. Women respondents expressed no preference for either male or female product representatives or announcers. Advertisements with female voices were rated equally effective to advertisements with male voices, regardless of the product relatedness of the product. Male respondents agreed with the females' judgments for the female-related product (perfume), but they disagreed somewhat when it came to evaluating the advertisements for the other three products. For the male-related product (cologne), men significantly preferred the male announcer's voice, but they were indifferent with respect to the voice of the product representative. Advertisements for the shampoo and the shower spray, both sex-neutral products, however, were rated significantly higher by men when females were featured. The shampoo advertisement received higher scores when a woman played the role of product representative, regardless of the sex of the voice-over. The only significant interaction effect between sex of the product representative and sex of the announcer occurred for the shower-spray commercial. In comparison to any other communicator combinations male subjects preferred females in both roles. Except for these three significant findings, all other main and interaction effects were nonsignificant. Consequently, men were not so different from women in their advertising evaluations. When the male subjects disagreed with their female counterparts, two out of three times they selected women's voices over those of men.

The results of the study corraborate Bennie's findings and those from psychology and communications. Although further research is certainly warranted, all the results suggest that women can be as effective as men in the role of voice of authority in advertising.

Implications for the Advertising Industry

Research in psychology, communications, and advertising has demonstrated that both men and women perceive female voices as equally effective to male voices. The fact that no consistent preference has been found for the male voice of authority has important managerial implications. If women's voices are used more often in the future, perhaps female announcers may become more widely accepted, and possibly even preferred, to male voices. Such a trend has been taking place over the last decade with respect to female newscasters. By altering the present approach, advertisers may find that they can communicate more effectively with certain target markets. Further research with various consumer audiences and types of products is necessary to determine the most effective communication method for specific advertising campaigns. Learning more about consumers' voice preferences through practitioner-sponsored research should facilitate the efforts of advertisers to communicate more effectively and to better accomplish advertising objectives.

Notes

1. Excerpted and adapted from Thomas W. Whipple and Alice E. Courtney, "How Men and Women Judge Humor: Advertising Guidelines for Action and Research," in *Current Issues and Research in Advertising,* ed. J.H. Leigh and C.R. Martin, Jr. (Ann Arbor: The University of Michigan, 1981), pp. 43–56 and reprinted with permission.

2. Alice E. Courtney and Thomas W. Whipple, *Canadian Perspectives on Sex Stereotyping in Advertising* (Ottawa: Advisory Council on the Status of Women, 1978), p. 39.

3. Patrick J. Kelly and Paul J. Solomon, "Humor in Television Advertising," *Journal of Advertising* 4 (Summer 1975):31–35; and Dorothy Markiewicz, "Effects of Humor on Persuasion," *Sociometry* 37 (1974): 407–422.

4. *Advertising and Women: A Report on Advertising Portraying or Directed to Women* (New York: National Advertising Review Board, 1975), p. 20.

5. Task Force on Women and Advertising, *Women and Advertising: Today's Messages—Yesterday's Images?* (Toronto: Advertising Advisory Board, 1977), p. 19.

6. Alice E. Courtney and Thomas W. Whipple, "Advertising Implications of Gender Differences in the Appreciation of Humor," in *Advances in Advertising Research and Management,* ed. S.E. Permut (East Lansing, Michigan: American Academy of Advertising, 1979), pp. 103–106.

7. Brian Sternthal and Samuel C. Craig, "Humor in Advertising," *Journal of Marketing* 37 (October 1973):12–18.

8. This section is based on telephone interviews conducted in 1980 with representatives from Marsteller Advertising Agency; Dick and Bert, Inc.; Stiller and Meara; Barzman and Company; and Allover Creations.

9. Harry W. McMahan, "No Joking; Humor Sells!", *Advertising Age,* 29 December 1980, p. 19.

10. Dick Orkin and Bert Berdis, "The Funny Thing About Some Commercials," *Broadcasting,* 20 June 1977, p. 16.

11. Paul E. McGhee, "Sex Differences in Children's Humor," *Journal of Communication* 26 (1976):176–189; and Alice S. Groch, "Joking and Appreciation of Humor in Nursery School Children," *Child Development* 45 (1974):1098–1102.

12. Patricia Keith-Spiegal, "Early Conceptions of Humor: Varieties and Issues," in *Psychology of Humor: Theoretical Perspectives and Empirical Issues,* ed. J.H. Goldstein and P.E. McGhee (New York: Academic Press, 1972), pp. 3–41.

13. P. Kambouropoulou, "Individual Differences in the Sense of Humor," *American Journal of Psychology* 37 (1926):268–278.

14. Carney Landis and John W.H. Ross, "Humor and Its Relation to Other Personality Traits," *The Journal of Social Psychology* 4 (1933): 156–175; and Roger L. Terry and Sarah L. Ertel, "Exploration of Individual Differences in Preferences for Humor," *Psychological Reports* 34 (1974):1031–1037.

15. Joanne R. Cantor, "What is Funny to Whom? The Role of Gender," *Journal of Communication* 26 (Summer 1976):169–176.

16. M. Allen, "Appreciation of 'Male Derisive', 'Female Derisive', and 'Sexual' Cartoons in Frustrated and 'Fulfilled' Housewives—The Use of Humor as a Coping Mechanism" (Paper delivered at the Western Psychological Association Meeting, Vancouver, B.C., 1969).

17. Jean Losco and Seymour Epstein, "Humor Preference as a Subtle Measure of Attitudes toward the Same and the Opposite Sex," *Journal of Personality* 43 (1975):321–334; and Dolf Zillman and S. Holly Stocking, "Putdown Humor," *Journal of Communication* 26 (Summer 1976): 154–163.

18. Robert F. Priest and Paul G. Wilhelm, "Sex, Marital Status and Self-Actualization as Factors in Appreciation of Sexist Jokes," *The Journal of Social Psychology* 92 (1974):245–249.

19. Barbara Grote and George Cvetkovich, "Humor Appreciation and Issue Involvement," *Psychoanalytic Science* 37 (1972):199–200.

20. Lawrence LaFave, "Humor Judgments as a Function of Reference Groups and Identification Classes," in *The Psychology of Humor: Theoretical Perspectives and Empirical Issues,* ed. J.H. Goldstein and P.E. McGhee (New York: Academic Press, 1972), pp. 195–211.

21. Anthony J. Chapman and Nicholas J. Gadfield, "Is Sexual Humor Sexist?" *Journal of Communication* 26 (Summer 1976):141–153.

22. William J. Burns and John D. Tyler, "Appreciation of Risque Humor in Male and Female Repressors and Sensitizers, *Journal of Clinical Psychology* 32 (April 1976):315–321.

23. Don Herold, *Humor in Advertising and How to Make It Pay* (New York: McGraw-Hill, 1963).

24. Sternthal and Craig, "Humor in Advertising."

25. William D. Wells, Clark Leavitt and Maureen McConville, "A Reaction Profile for TV Commercials," *Journal of Advertising Research* 11 (December 1971):11–17.

26. Mervin D. Lynch and Richard C. Hartman, "Dimensions of Humor in Advertising," *Journal of Advertising Research* 8 (August 1968):39–45.

27. Avraham Shama and Maureen Coughlin, "An Experimental Study of the Effectiveness of Humor in Advertising," in *1979 Educators' Conference Proceedings,* ed. N. Beckwith et al. (Chicago: American Marketing Association, 1979), pp. 249–252.

28. Thomas J. Madden and Marc G. Weinberger, "The Effects of Humor on Attention in Magazine Adertising," working paper WP 89–19 (Amherst, Mass.: University of Massachusetts, 1981).

29. Thomas W. Whipple and Alice E. Courtney, "Male and Female Differences in Response to Nonsensical Humor in Advertising," in *Advertising 1980: Voice of a Nation at Work,* ed. S.E. Permut (East Lansing, Michigan: American Academy of Advertising, 1980), pp. 71–74.

30. Courtney and Whipple, "Advertising Implications of Gender Differences in the Appreciation of Humor."

31. Courtney and Whipple, *Canadian Perspectives on Sex Stereotyping in Advertising,* p. 41.

32. Thomas W. Whipple and Alice E. Courtney, "Social Consequences of Sex Stereotyping in Advertising," in *Future Directions for Marketing,* ed. G. Fisk et al. (Cambridge, Mass.: Marketing Science Institute, 1978), pp. 332–350.

33. Debbie Seaman, "Spokesmen Spread the Retailers' Word," *Advertising Age,* 27 April 1981, p. S–35.

34. Ibid., p. S–34.

35. P.A. Goldberg, "Are Women Prejudiced Against Women?", *Trans-Action* 5 (1968):28–30; G.I. Pheterson, S.B. Kiesler, and P.A. Goldberg, "Evaluation of the Performance of Women as a Function of their Sex Achievement, and Personal History," *Journal of Personality and Social Psychology* 19 (1971):114–118.

36. H. Levenson et al., "Are Women Still Prejudiced Against Women?", *Journal of Psychology* 89 (1975):67–71.

37. Cheris Kramer, "Women's Speech: Separate But Unequal?", *Quarterly Journal of Speech* 60 (1974):14–20.

38. Mary Ritchie Key, "Linguistic Behavior of Male and Female," *Linguistics* 88 (1972):15–21.

39. M. Mannes, "Women are Equal, But . . . ," in *Current Thinking and Writing,* ed. J. Bachelor, R. Henry, and R. Salisburg (New York: Appleton-Century-Crofts, 1969).

40. B.G. Henneke and E.S. Dummit, *The Announcers Handbook* (New York: Holt, Rinehart and Winston, 1959).

41. Rosemary Scott, *The Female Consumer* (New York: John Wiley, 1976).

42. G.R. Miller and M. McReynolds, "Male Chauvinism and Source Competence: A Research Note," *Speech Monopraphs* 40 (1973):154–155.

43. Vernon A. Stone, "Attitudes Toward Television Newswomen," *Journal of Broadcasting* (Winter 1973–1974):49–61.

44. A. George Gitter and B. Casey Coburn, "Trustworthiness: The Effects of Respondent's Sex, and Communicator's Occupational Title, Organizational Affiliation, and Sex," *CRC Report No. 82* (Boston: Boston University, 1981).

45. Cynthia L. Berryman, "Attitudes Toward Male and Female Sex-Appropriate and Sex-Inappropriate Language," in *Communication Language and Sex,* ed. C.L. Berryman and V.A. Eman (Rowley, Mass.: Newbury House Publishers, Inc., 1980), pp. 195–216.

46. Susan and Ron Whittaker, "Relative Effectiveness of Male and Female Newscasters," *Journal of Broadcasting* 20 Spring 1976):177–183.

47. J. Whittaker, "Sex Differences and Susceptibility to Interpersonal Persuasion," *Journal of Social Psychology* 66 (1965):91–94.

48. Fay Bennie, "Difference of Recall, Perceived Effectiveness, Irritation, and Behavioral Intention Measures of Radio Commercials with Respect to Male and Female Voice and Product Relatedness" (Master's thesis, Guelph, Ontario: University of Guelph, 1979).

49. Sandra L. Schoonover, "Voice-Over Effectiveness: An Examination of Gender Differences" (Master's thesis, Cleveland State University, 1979).

50. Alicia Mathias, "Examination of Gender Differences in the Ad Effectiveness of Product Representatives and Announcers" (Research paper, Cleveland State University, 1982).

**Part III
Strategies for Change**

The Role of Research

The question of how effectively and responsibly to portray the sexes in advertising has been considered from a number of research and action perspectives in the preceeding chapters. Although published research is available in many decision areas, some data are inconclusive or contradictory. Additional valid and reliable information is required to generate the detailed guidelines the advertising strategists need. Research issues are raised in this chapter to stimulate thinking about the unanswered questions and to provide useful directions for further research.

Monitoring the Problem Areas

Sex stereotyping in advertising has been shown to have direct impacts on individuals and society, and, together with other sources of stereotyping, to contribute to longer-range societal effects. Effective monitoring of strategies to reduce sex stereotyping requires the development of performance-evaluation measures for the content and impacts of stereotyping.

The Existence of Sex-Stereotyped Content

Studies documenting the existence of sex stereotyping in advertising provide bench-mark measures for some components of stereotyping. The matter of stereotyped portrayal has been documented and monitored by counting the roles portrayed, tasks performed, settings, product representatives, and voice-overs. However, manner has been only superficially studied. Standard measures for acting styles, body language, tone of voice, and other sources of manner stereotyping are lacking. In addition to documenting the imagery used to portray the sexes, the relationship between visual and verbal imagery needs to be studied further.

It should be recognized that content-analysis studies often imply implicit evaluations of value and taste. The way a researcher assesses sexual innuendo, compares the depiction of a doctor versus a nurse, and evaluates the personality characteristics of the sexes, are such cases. Research needs to be more explicit about the way these judgments are made.

Another aspect of content analysis which is in need of further consideration is the area of male roles. In 1967 Bardwick and Schumann suggested that researchers might gain a greater understanding of sex roles by paying particular attention to male roles. Television commercials portray the U.S. man as:

> . . . muscular, knowledgeable, dominating, independent, sexy, cosmopolitan, athletic, authoritative and aggressive . . . only when he is seen away from his family. In embarrassing contrast the American father and husband is portrayed as passive, stupid, infantile, and emasculated . . . But outside the house trouble is what he's looking for.[1]

Additional analysis of the male portrayal in advertising is long overdue.

The portrayal of both men and women in advertising needs to be documented in media other than magazines and television. Few studies have dealt with images of the sexes in such print media as newspapers, direct mailers, catalogues, billboards, and point-of-sale materials. More studies of special interest consumer magazine advertising also are warranted, especially now that new limited publication magazines are gaining in popularity. As publishers continually attempt to launch successful entries to targeted audience segments, a comparative study of the advertising specifically addressed to these consumers would be most interesting.

Another print medium which has been neglected is the trade press, including professional journals, trade magazines, and other industrial publications. Medical-journal advertising has received some attention from researchers and has revealed very stereotyped portrayals of the sexes. Documentation of the relationship between how women are portrayed in medical advertisements and doctors' prescription behavior suggests that further content analysis of medical-journal advertising is necessary to monitor any changes in these portrayals and to isolate other instances of sex stereotyping. Publications geared to specific industries or trades also have been criticized for the portrayal of women, yet few studies have documented these complaints. The dominant criticism has centered around the use of decorative females as sex objects solely to attract the attention of a male audience. While there is evidence that advertising in consumer magazines has improved somewhat, no such evidence exists for industrial advertising.

In the broadcast media the focus on television commercials has been at the expense and total exclusion of studies of radio advertising. The increasing use of radio for advertising to specialized markets provides opportunities to examine what currently is being done and in what areas improvements are needed. Cable-television advertising also offers new areas for content analysis. Otherwise, occasional studies of television advertising to monitor trends are warranted. Documentation of any changes in voiceovers, sexist language, intonation, acting styles, and body language is especially relevant for the 1980s. Other potentially fruitful areas for investigation are product-category relationships and day-part differences.

Attitudes of Concerned Constituencies

Opinion polls of a variety of advertising have generated a list of complaints regarding how the sexes are portrayed in advertising. At this point no major research is required to further identify the main areas of concern. What is needed, however, are studies which utilize consistent research procedures to provide trend analyses of audience attitudes. In addition to tracking general criticisms, attitudes toward specific areas of concern should be monitored. For example, opinions of feminine-hygiene advertising, new-women advertisements, and advertisements employing sexual portrayals are candidates for close scrutiny. Attitude research also should try to be more precise regarding the identification of segment differences. Attitudes toward sexuality, the women's movement, and measures of women's self-image may provide useful segmenting variables.

A further area which merits continuing effort is the monitoring of marketing and advertising executives' opinions toward reflecting changing life-styles, roles, and attitudes in their advertising. Attitude changes on the part of these executives are necessary precursors to noticeable improvements in the advertising they produce.

Social Consequences of Sex Stereotyping

Busby argues that the research on the effects of sex roles in the mass media has been limited because of the difficulty of isolating mass-media effects on sex-role development from the other socializing effects of home, school, church, friends, and society in general.[2] Separating out advertising impacts from programming or editorial effects further complicates the research problems. She recommends that in addition to analyzing the direct effects of sex role in the mass media, cultural, audience, and media analyses are required to gain a fuller understanding of the impacts sex-role imagery have in our society.[3]

Socialization of Children. Effects of sex stereotyping on children is an important and exciting area for further research and offers great possibilities if difficult methodological problems can be overcome. Further research is needed to document that traditional, sexist portrayals cause or contribute significantly to negative social consequences. Instead of focusing only on negative effects, researchers also must continue to examine the prosocial effects of more progressive sex-role portrayals. Of course, in attempting to show causation, the relation of advertising to other sources of stereotyping must be determined. Many of the correlational studies conducted to date have erred by inferring causation.

Experimental research, too, has been plagued with methodological problems. Nonrepresentative samples, small sample sizes, unrealistic exposure conditions for advertisements, unrealistic effect measures, and the measurement of only short-term effects have reduced the reliability and validity of the experiments. Finding appropriate nontraditional advertisements to test has posed further problems for some researchers.

Perloff, Brown, and Miller, in a recent article, contend that researchers have almost ignored the impact of cognitive-developmental mechanisms in their studies.[4] They suggest, for example, that research focus on the influences of gender constancy on children of varying ages who identify with and imitate same-sex characters they see in the media. According to Perloff and his colleagues, researchers interested in media content also might usefully concentrate on the relative emphasis to be placed on physical versus concrete dimensions of nontraditional sex-role portrayals when advertising to children of different ages.

Effects on Adults. Many complaints by critics of the effects of sex stereotyping have not been researched yet. The contention that a traditional, stereotyped depiction of housewives contributes to the belief that they are low in intelligence, unable to make decisions, dependent on men, superservants, competitive with women, neurotic about cleanliness, and acquisitive for material things certainly should be studied. Contentions by critics that portraying women as sex objects results in depersonalization, which leads to sexual violence, require a significant research effort to verify or refute. Much of the work ahead depends upon the development and refinement of measures to assess the immediate, as well as the far-reaching effects of sex stereotyping. In studies with adults as with children, further examination of prosocial effects would be warranted.

Performance Evaluation. Various sex-stereotyping side effects of social externalities were identified in chapter 3. Measures still need to be developed for many such areas of concern to assess their potential impacts. To effectively monitor the progress of strategies to reduce the negative impacts of sex stereotyping in advertising, performance evaluation measures which extend beyond economic indexes are needed. Social and environmental consequences also must be considered and measured.[5]

Social indicators serve as excellent measures of social-welfare impacts and may be the easiest and most straightforward measures to obtain.[6] Because of the difficulty associated with isolating advertising effects, controlled experimentation may be necessary to examine the degree of advertising contribution. To measure accurately the social and environmental consequences of reducing sex stereotyping in advertising, further work in the development of standardized measures of content and impact is still required.

Measuring Communication Effectiveness

Further research effort is needed to measure the communication effectiveness of more progressive, less sex-stereotyped advertising in comparison to the traditional, stereotyped ones. Academic researchers have begun this effort with a number of pilot studies which, although useful, are limited by their samples, products, advertising copy, and methods of evaluating effectiveness.

The Changing Consumer

Critical to effective marketing today is the continual study of and comprehension of demographic, attitudinal, and behavioral changes taking place among both males and females. The research focus to date has been on documenting the significant changes in the female consumer. Continued monitoring of these changes is recommended as one of the essential efforts in marketing to keep up with the new-woman markets. However, rather than concentrate on the demographic changes, researchers should switch their focus to attitudinal and behavioral changes. For example, trends in attitudes toward sex roles have already been mentioned as important influences in the perceptions of and opinions toward advertising. They also are very likely to impact buyer behavior.

Concentrating on differences in buying behavior across women consumers, over time, will allow researchers to derive behavioral segments of importance to marketers. Rather than defining segments of women on the basis of age, employment, and marital status as other researchers have done, future research may find it more meaningful to describe segments in demographic terms after they have been derived on an attitudinal or behavioral basis. Since these changes impact product development, message content, media planning, and retailing, to mention a few, analysis of the motivations and behaviors of women's segments are essential for any marketer interested in the female consumer today.

While researchers have concentrated on changes in women's markets, the male perspective has been relatively neglected. In this area researchers have a full range of topics to choose from. For example, household task and child-care sharing appear to have changed in the last few years, but the research studies that document these changes and their effects on buying behavior are lacking. Also, changes in household decision making, time management, media habits, and shopping behavior offer the marketer new research opportunities.

Preferences for Sex Roles

Role-preference research has been limited by the availability of advertisements with differing degrees of liberated life-styles. Consequently, the print-oriented research has either relied upon the create-an-ad technique and been criticized for unrealistic copy, or used actual advertisements, only to be faulted for not controlling the many elements in the advertising stimuli selected for testing. The added complexity associated with evaluating preferences for television commercials has significantly reduced the number of such studies.

Buchanan and Reid suggest that to design more effective copy, research should be directed toward determining which cues are picked up from various models appearing in advertisements.[7] The perception of a stereotype, for example, may be a function of the degree to which that stereotype is a focal element of the advertisement. As already suggested, it is also likely to vary among respondents, differing according to their sex and their attitude toward sex roles. Preliminary findings, that product/model congruency in image is important in affecting preferences for advertisements containing models, need to be validated for different products. Gaining a better understanding of the influencing effect of the role portrayed by the model, as differentiated from the presence of the model, is essential.

Further research is required to relate role preference to audience characteristics, including demographic descriptors and psychological variables. Past attempts to develop such relationships have not been successful. Except for working status of women, other variables produced inconsistent findings. These results are partially due to the types of respondents who volunteer for these studies. Instead of college students, randomly selected respondents from target market populations are needed to meaningfully segment the audience on the basis of role preference. However, the greatest hindrance to deriving significant relationships is the measurement problem. Better measures of feminist orientation, independence of judgment, and self-confidence are needed. For example, to date researchers have utilized at least six different women's liberation scales, but none have been validated as sensitive measures of profeminist orientation or behavior. Even standard demographic measures require rethinking before applying them in role-preference studies. Particularly, marital status and employment status measures need to be updated to reflect current classifications as they relate to women and men in a modern society.

Probably the greatest advances will be made in sex-role preference research when advertising practitioners regularly conduct their own research. A commitment is required to create and evaluate progressive portrayals and to test more liberated approaches in test-market environments. Some areas of sex-role preference require more in-depth research to isolate specific factors and to evaluate their effectiveness. Sexual portrayals, humorous appeals, and voices of authority fit this category.

Sexual Portrayals

Most studies of the effectiveness of sexual portrayals in advertising have relied on student subjects, usually male, evaluating female models in laboratory settings. Joseph suggests that future research be designed to avoid these limitations by including field investigations and by employing subjects from nonstudent populations.[8] Research which assesses decorative, attractive, and sexy models must begin by clearly defining and differentiating the terms. Currently there is considerable disagreement among researchers as to what constitutes attractiveness and sexiness. Ultimately, research definitions must correspond with consumer perceptions before these terms can be meaningfully and universally applied to models in advertising.

Researchers also need to be less concerned about simply the presence or absence of a model and consider degrees of a model's attractiveness and sexiness. In doing so, they should measure the impact of more than two levels of the experimental variable. Optimal levels of model attractiveness and sexiness may not be at the extremes but at intermediate levels. The type of product being advertised should be of greater concern in future research as well. Advertisers need to know how attractiveness and sexiness interact with other characteristics to produce favorable advertising ratings. As Baker and Churchill demonstrated in their study, marketers cannot assume that using an attractive model is always better.[9] They must determine the appropriate model for the particular product. For example, an unattractive model may be more effective in appealing for charitable donations and in attracting attention to a new product or service.

Another important relationship to assess is the interaction between the sex of the model and the subject's sex. Since the number of studies testing same-sex response is limited, tentative findings that opposite-sex models attract more attention and receive more favorable evaluations must be validated. A logical extension of this investigation is to examine the combined impact of using male and female models together in an advertisement.

Studies could be designed to determine what degree of attractiveness of each model produces the most favorable responses.

Research on sexual portrayals should be expanded to include verbal and verbal/visual relationships. Reid and Soley have conducted one study which only begins to establish a better understanding of the differential effects of verbal and visual advertising components.[10] They suggest that in follow-up studies the illustration and body-copy sizes be varied to determine the effects on recognition with and without a model. Varying the sexiness of the model and the eroticism of the theme are further extensions which may produce differing results, depending upon the explicitness of the appeal.

Future research efforts should be designed to use criterion measures of advertising effectiveness which are consistent from study to study. Past studies have measured cognitive, affective, and conative attitude dimensions, using a variety of variables. Advertisement, product, and company images also have been assessed. While some researchers have focused on recognition, recall, and content memorability, others have been more concerned with the resulting images left by the advertisement and intentions toward the advertised product. Patzer made several observations during an experiment he conducted which suggest that additional measures also may be appropriate.[11] Observations dealing mainly with male versus female differences in their eagerness to evaluate sexy advertisements and the number of questions asked during the evaluation process led Patzer to recommend that measures be developed to assess the subjective responses. To more fully understand consumer behavior in response to marketing communications, he also suggested that objective measures, including the time spent looking at the advertisement and the time spent completing the questionnaire, be added to future research studies.

A number of researchers also call for future research of sexually oriented advertising communications to be conducted within a theoretical framework. Most of the research to date has not been oriented to theory testing. And, as noted by Alpert, the few studies that have included a theoretical discussion are written mainly from the viewpoint of males' perceptions of sexy women in advertisements and place little emphasis on women's perceptions of sexy males.[12]

Researchers who specifically studied the effect of using nude models in advertising have focused on their attention-getting value and respondents' ability to recall the advertised brand names. While this research has been more simplistic and straightforward in design, the studies have suffered from some of the same methodological problems. The testing of mock-up ads, the inability to generalize to other products, the use of male students as subjects, and criterion-variable measurements have been criticized. In reviewing many of these studies Wilson and Moore make three recommendations for future research: multiple measures of advertising effectiveness

are essential; a realistic experimental setting is of great importance, especially for studies of brand recall; and care must be taken to make realistic,
high quality advertisements without introducing confounding factors.[13] To
enhance the managerial value of research on sexually oriented advertising,
realism is the goal.

Gender-Related Humor[14]

The research completed to date concerning gender-related humor is only a
beginning effort at confirming or refuting the findings from many psychological studies. This research, which is based on forced exposure of a student sample to one set of advertising stimuli, suffers from a number of
reliability and validity problems. Research on advertising humor indicates
that a variety of demographic, personality, and segmentation measures are
relevant to response. These findings, in turn, suggest the need to use more
representative groups as target audiences in future research.

Given the number of measures that are relevant to understanding the
communication effects of humor, larger probability samples often will be
required, despite the significant addition to research costs which is involved.
Field-work control procedures, which make possible nonforced exposure
settings and which minimize frame, selection, and nonresponse errors, will
add further to the credibility of research findings. For example, the
generalizability of results can be increased significantly if respondent-selec-
tion procedures are improved, and if the artificiality of the viewing and
evaluation process is reduced. It is suggested that repondents also be
allocated randomly to test and control groups. Ideally, split-run testing could be used to allow comparisons between alternative humorous
approaches.

The psychological research on gender-related humor appreciation
indicates that demographic, attitudinal, and personality variables have
moderating effects. Relevant advertising-related segment descriptors, such
as respondents' initial awareness of, attitudes toward, and usage of the
advertised product categories and brands should be measured. In addition,
audience and personality characteristics, including sex, age, race, marital
status, attitudes toward the women's movement, and degree of self-actualization should be included to allow humor-appreciation differences to be
related to target market definitions.

Advertising-research findings indicate that the degree of distraction,
argumentation, and irritation produced by a humorous advertisement may
influence its effectiveness. Consequently, it is important to include in the
measuring instrument variables which will obtain these measures, as well
as measures of respondents' perceptions of the humor of the advertising

stimuli. Finally, measures which relate to the communication objectives of the humorous copy (for example, liking for, interest in, identification with the people in the advertisement) should be included. While humor research indicates that humor is likely to have its strongest effects in the areas of attention and affective response, nevertheless such research must consider the full range of advertising-effectiveness measures.

Implementation of these suggestions for improving research design and measurement when developing and testing humorous copy can be an important step toward eliminating offensive ads. Those advertisers who adhere to the suggested guidelines and incorporate the above recommendations when pretesting humorous advertisements will avoid some of the common pitfalls and should produce more effective, yet funny advertisements.

Beyond the issues of research design and measurement involved in pretesting of humorous copy, there are additional issues to be considered by those who might wish to develop more generalizable guidelines for gender-related humorous advertising. The most difficult issue involves selection of stimuli for testing. Although there are indications that the categories of humor studied by psychologists are relevant to advertising humor, advertising humor tends to take a much more complex and ambiguous form than the jokes, cartoons, and other stimuli commonly studied by psychologists. For example, the Blue Nun commercial mentioned in chapter 7 contains light-hearted put-downs of both sexes, combined with humor of the absurd. The need exists, therefore, for more thorough basic research into the ways in which the hostile, sexual, sexist, and absurd approaches are actually utilized by advertisers, and for examination of the variety of humor techniques commonly utilized (for example, pun, slapstick). Content analysis and expert judging can be utilized to develop categories for classification and analysis. Once workable categories have been developed, expert judges can be used to choose advertisements for each humor-treatment category under investigation and match appropriate alternative approaches to the same product category, brand, and program environment.

Voices of Authority

Research on voices of authority in marketing communications has only recently begun to develop. Specifically, additional research on the gender of voice-overs and announcers in commercials is warranted. As a starting point academics and advertising practitioners need to improve upon the student-conducted studies reported in chapter 7. The students' research projects were limited in a number of ways: commercials were developed for only a few products; the commercials were not written by professionals; the voices used were not those of professional actors; the experimental setting was less than realistic; and the measuring instruments could be improved. Future research should overcome these limitations.

Additional research is needed to determine which products are more effectively advertised by a female than by a male announcer. For some products, the combined effect of the genders of both the product representative and the voice-over may be significant in the overall evaluation of an advertisement.

A crucial question which requires additional research evidence is what constitutes sex-appropriate and sex-inappropriate communication.[15] Researchers should investigate the perceptions of voices of authority who use communication styles traditionally associated with the other sex. Such research may show that past expectations of sex-appropriate communications behavior are giving way to the freedom for both sexes to employ situationally appropriate communication styles.

Further research is necessary to determine the most effective combination of voices to use with different target groups. Researchers also need to investigate the gender variable as it interacts with demographic, psychological, and situational variables. Although academics can conduct much of this needed research, advertising practitioners are in the best position to develop and test specific campaign alternatives while taking into consideration product category and target segment differences.

Achieving Changes in Portrayals

Marketing and advertising language traditionally uses military analogies. A marketer or advertiser speaks of a target audience of consumers to be researched, of marketing strategy and tactics, of attacking markets, and of fighting for share of market against competition. Thus, it seems appropriate to discuss the role of research as ammunition in a series of battles in the war to reduce sex stereotyping in advertising.

Influencing Regulation

Research has made an important input to the changes that have been achieved during the last few years. Feminist groups and academics over more than ten years provided the ammunition for the battle in the form of empirical work to document the existence of the problem, its importance, and that effective advertising does not have to be sexist. Such research gave the Canadian government legitimization of its cause in setting up a special task force to investigate the issues involved and to recommend industry guidelines. A position paper reviewing this research for the Federal Advisory Council on the status of Women was a critical input in the decision to establish the task force. Research should continue to play a significant role if similar gains are to be made in other countries.

Advertiser Research

Research within the advertising industry itself can serve to aid in the development of messages which are both more effective and more responsible. For example, as reported in chapter 5, Bartos's research has made a significant contribution to industry practice in showing that advertisements need to be evaluated on a like/dislike dimension during pretesting. Bartos found that if you do not ask the evaluators the proper questions regarding sex-role portrayals, it is difficult to determine whether the target group will react positively or negatively to a new advertisement. Advertisers also have to be aware of the potential for negative reactions to advertisements from non-target audience members. Where it is appropriate, they need to test out-of-target response as well.

This book has discussed newer issues which require further research by advertisers. They include the effects of and preferences for sex-role portrayals; the effectiveness of sexually oriented ads; and the use of models, humor, and voices of authority. To insure maximum communication effectiveness, advertisers need to submit more progressive advertising for testing versus the standard, traditional type.

Focus-group research can be a useful first tool in this process, but more formal pretesting methods, such as day-after-recall and portfolio tests, must be employed to develop actionable information for advertisers. Monitoring of sales results for alternative approaches can then provide a market evaluation of the use of progressive advertising.

Notes

1. Judith M. Bardwick and Suzanne J. Schumann, "Portrait of American Men and Women in TV Commercials," *Psychology* 4 (1967): 18–23.

2. Linda J. Busby, "Sex-role Research on the Mass Media," *Journal of Communication* 25 (Autumn 1975):107–131.

3. Linda J. Busby, "Mass Media Research Needs: A Media Target for Feminists," in *The University of Michigan Papers in Women's Studies* 1 (Ann Arbor, University of Michigan, 1974), pp. 9–29.

4. Richard M. Perloff, Jane Delano Brown, and M. Mark Miller,

"Mass-Media and Sex-typing: Research Perspectives and Policy Implications," *International Journal of Women's Studies* 5 no. 3 (1982):265–273.

5. Alice E. Courtney and Thomas W. Whipple, *Canadian Perspectives on Sex Stereotyping in Advertising* (Ottawa: Advisory Council on the Status of Women, 1978).

6. Thomas W. Whipple and Alice E. Courtney, "Social Externalities of Sex Stereotyping of Women in Advertising" (Paper delivered at the Colloquim on Managing the Social Externalities of Marketing, Brussels, Belgium, May 16–17, 1977).

7. Lauranne Buchanan and Leonard N. Reid, "Woman Role Portrayals in Advertising Messages as Stimulus Cues: A Preliminary Investigation," in *Sharing for Understanding,* ed. G.E. Miracle (East Lansing, Mich.: American Academy of Advertising, 1977), pp. 99–104.

8. W. Benoy Joseph, "The Credibility of Physically Attractive Communicators: A Review," *Journal of Advertising* 11 (Summer 1982):15–24.

9. Michael J. Baker and Gilbert A. Churchill, Jr., "The Impact of Physically Attractive Models on Advertising Evaluations," *Journal of Marketing Research* 14 (November 1977):538–555.

10. Leonard N. Reid and Lawrence C. Soley, "Another Look at the 'Decorative' Female Model: The Recognition of Visual and Verbal Ad Components," in *Current Issues and Research in Advertising,* ed. J.H. Leigh and C.R. Martin, Jr. (Ann Arbor: The University of Michigan, 1981).

11. Gordon L. Patzer, "A Comparison of Advertisement Effects: Sexy Female Communicator vs. Non-Sexy Female Communicator," in *Advances in Consumer Research,* ed. J.C. Olson (Ann Arbor: Association for Consumer Research, 1980), pp. 359–364.

12. Mark J. Alpert, "Sex Roles, Sex, and Stereotyping in Advertising: More Questions Than Answers," in *Advances in Consumer Research,* ed. W. Wilkie (Ann Arbor: Association for Consumer Research, 1979), pp. 73–77.

13. R. Dale Wilson and Noreen K. Moore, "The Role of Sexually-Oriented Stimuli in Advertising: Theory and Literature Review," in *Advances in Consumer Research,* ed. W. Wilkie (Ann Arbor: Association for Consumer Research, 1979), pp. 55–61.

14. Thomas W. Whipple and Alice E. Courtney, "How Men and Women Judge Humor: Advertising Guidelines for Action and Research," in *Current Issues and Research in Advertising,* ed. J.H. Leigh and C.R. Marlin, Jr. (Ann Arbor: The University of Michigan, 1981), pp. 43–57.

15. Cynthia L. Berryman, "Attitudes Toward Male and Female Sex-appropriate and Sex-Inappropriate Language," in *Communication Language and Sex,* ed. C.L. Berryman and V.A. Eman (Rowley, Mass.: Newbury House Publishers, Inc., 1980), pp. 195–216.

16. Mary Lou Roberts and Perri B. Koggan, "How Should Women Be Portrayed in Advertisements?—A Call for Research," in *Advances in Consumer Research,* ed. W. Wilkie (Ann Arbor: Association for Consumer Research, 1979), pp. 66–72.

Regulation and Self-Regulation

This chapter discusses the historical circumstances which led advertisers to develop self-regulatory codes dealing with sex stereotyping and the effectiveness of these efforts in altering the portrayal of the sexes in advertising. When self-regulation is discussed, it refers to codes developed and enforced by advertising-industry groups. In the United States the National Advertising Review Board hears cases concerning false and misleading advertising. In addition, advertisers are responsible to adhere to the codes of the National Association of Broadcasters and the Better Business Bureau. Similar codes exist in Canada, the United Kingdom, and many other countries. In addition, in many countries, major television stations and newspapers have developed their own standards of advertising practice which amplify the more general codes. In some cases specialized codes also exist. For example, in Canada, there are special self-regulatory codes which cover such matters as broadcast advertising to children and the advertising of feminine-hygiene products.

When regulation or legislation are mentioned, they include the restrictions on advertising which come from the legal system of the country involved, whether that be at federal, state, or local level. Such legislation typically deals with issues such as false and misleading advertising, but issues related to sex stereotyping are sometimes included. In some countries government legislation regulates the product categories which may or may not be advertised (for example, advertising of feminine-hygiene products is restricted in some countries). Sometimes government regulation may provide for preclearance by regulatory agencies of certain categories of advertisements. In Canada, for example, most food-product advertising is precleared by the federal department of health and welfare.

This chapter begins by reviewing the history of protest against the portrayal of women in advertising in the United States and the way in which those protests influenced regulatory and self-regulatory action. Later sections of the chapter review the British and Canadian situations and contrast those to the world picture. The chapter concludes with a discussion of the limits of, and future prospects for, self-regulation and regulation of sex stereotyping in advertising.

Protests in the United States and the Beginning of Change

The impetus for change came from the protests staged by feminist groups in the late 1960s. The first protests centered around three topics: classified advertising, the "Fly Me" campaign launched by National Airlines, and other specific advertisements that the protesters identified as being particularly offensive to women.

The classified advertising issue was important for several reasons. It was a clear case where equal opportunity and access to work for women and men was not occurring. The protests, some of which took the form of lawsuits, were generally successful.[1] On that basis help-wanted advertising throughout much of the United States and Canada was changed. The classified-advertising protest was part of the most successful aspect of the women's movement because it achieved equal access to work. In terms of protests against sex stereotyping in advertising, it acted as a spur and an encouragement: if success could be achieved by protesting in this area, then it made sense for feminists to follow up with action against other forms of advertising.

In the late 1960s and the early 1970s, many groups were beginning to organize protests against disparaging stereotypes in advertising. In 1967 a campaign against the Frito Bandito was launched by Mexican-American groups.[2] They viewed this character as a resurrection of the disparaging Hollywood film stereotype of the Mexican bandit. The Chicano community regarded the gunslinging Bandito as an insidious form of racism, but many industry observers wondered why the Mexican-American community could not take a harmless joke. The advertisement was finally taken off the air in 1971.

The first large-scale feminist protest, which focused on the "Fly Me" advertising campaign, emerged in this context. National Airlines began the campaign in 1971. The advertisements depicted attractive women dressed as stewardesses saying such things as "I'm Cheryl, Fly Me." In addition, National stewardesses were required to wear buttons saying "Fly Me" and "We make you feel good all over." This campaign roused the anger of the stewardess organizations which charged that the campaign was degrading to women and their job function.

The advertisers' justification of this campaign was reported as follows:

> A spokesman for the advertising agency that created the campaign noted (that women were used) because ". . . girls *are* the product. Ninety percent of a passenger's time is spent with the stewardess."[3]

Members of the National Organization for Women (NOW) formed picket lines at the agency that created the advertising and at the ticket offices of

National Airlines, carrying signs with such slogans as "Haven't you heard, I'm not a bird." The NOW campaign received support from Presidential candidate George McGovern, who said the "Fly Me" campaign was "inappropriate to the legitimate function of providing transportation."[4]

The "Fly Me" commercials eventually disappeared, but it was never clear whether NOW's protest had shortened the advertising campaign's natural life or not. The feminist protest may have had minimal impact because three years later, in 1974, the approach was imitated by a Continental Airlines advertisement which boasted, "We really move our tail for you."

In March 1970 NOW held a national convention at which they developed another type of protest: "Barefoot and Pregnant Award of the Week for Advertising Degrading to Women." They also printed and distributed thousands of stickers proclaiming, "This Ad Insults Women." Throughout the early 1970s, similar protests against specific advertisements, letter-writing campaigns, and product boycotts were organized by NOW and other feminist groups. In August 1970 a national "girlcott" was launched against products feminists believed were the epitome of female-role stereotyping. Ivory Soap was objected to because of its identification in advertising with motherhood and purity. Pristeen, a feminine hygiene-deodorant spray, was also targeted. By 1972 NOW extended the protest to all feminine-hygiene sprays, both because the product was thought to be potentially harmful physically, and because the advertising was believed to be extremely offensive to women. Another form of protest was against the advertising media: for example, *Cosmopolitan Magazine,* which was alleged to have as its general purpose the encouragement of women to seduce and manipulate men.[5]

Throughout the 1970s women also expressed their opposition to stereotypical portrayals by meeting with advertisers, agencies, and the media. These meetings generally received good coverage in the advertising trade press. The Los Angeles Women's Coalition for Better Broadcasting, for example, reached an agreement with a local television station which provided them with the opportunity to meet the station's major advertisers.[6]

During International Women's Year (IWY) the IWY Commission published a report entitled, *Mass Media: Friend or Foe.*[7] The report recommended vigorous enforcement of communication laws and adopted the "Ten Guidelines to the Media" on the portrayal and treatment of women (for example, women's bodies should not be used in an exploitive way to add irrelevant sexual interest in media). The commission also recommended that the Department of Health, Education, and Welfare undertake a major study to determine the impact of sex-role stereotyping and to measure the extent to which television causes and reinforces sexism. A sixteen-point checklist was drawn up for use in developing entertainment programming and commercials. Advertisers were requested to ask themselves, as one example, "Are homemakers portrayed with dignity?"

In recent years most of the protests against advertising perceived to be offensive to women have been less formally organized. The exceptions are the protests that have emerged from organizations associated with the Moral Majority. Complaints of these groups generally focus on overly sexual portrayals. When the explicit sexual content of a television series is found to offend traditional values held by these groups, they register their protest by encouraging members to boycott the advertised products.

Ms. magazine continues to run its "No Comment" page on which a number of advertisements deemed to be derogatory to women are presented. In its early years the "No Comment" page generally featured advertisements from national brands and manufacturers. More recently, the page tends to feature smaller advertisers, particularly local advertisers. One *Ms.* protest of recent years did meet with success. Heublein developed an advertising campaign for its Club Cocktails with the slogan: "Hit me with a Club." When the advertisement was shown by *Ms.* on the "No Comment" page, it provoked over one-thousand protest letters which decried the advertisement's not too subtle invitation to physical abuse. The company responded to the letter-writing campaign by saying in a letter to *Ms.*, which was printed in the magazine, that it had not occurred to them to interpret the advertisement as a condonement of physical abuse. They found, however, that the arguments presented to them in the protest letters were sufficiently persuasive to convince them to cancel the particular series of advertisements.[8]

Among the other tactics used to protest sex stereotyping during the 1970s were protests at stockholders' meetings. Both Proctor and Gamble and Colgate Palmolive were approached in this manner.[9] Women stockholders protested the companies' advertising portrayal at the stockholders' annual meetings in an effort to raise consciousness about the issue.

Most protests in the last few years have concerned advertising which is considered to be overly sexual. An article appearing in *Time* in December 1980 remarked that, although using sex as an adjunct to selling was not a new practice, "what is new is the prurience of the pitch."[10] The series of Brooke Shields advertisements for Calvin Klein jeans provide ample evidence of this in the eyes of some critics. In one of the television commercials in this series, the camera opens on Brooke Shields squatting on the floor with her jeans-clad legs spread wider than the edges of the television screen. She tells the viewers in a husky tone that nothing comes between her and her Calvin Klein jeans. This advertisement provoked so many complaints from viewers in New York City that NBC removed the commercial. Even before this protest, however, some CBS and ABC affiliates in Los

Angeles and New England had rejected some of the other commercials in the campaign as well.

Regulation and Self-Regulation in the United States

Some of the protests directed at individual advertisers were successful, others were not. The protesting groups, however, became aware that the piecemeal approach was time consuming, expensive, and was not achieving their long-term goals. Consequently, there was a movement toward protest aimed at a bigger target, government regulation.

Government Regulation

One type of action took the form of challenges to television station license renewals by the Federal Communications Commission (FCC). The most famous case took place in Washington, D.C., where NOW challenged the renewal of two licenses.[11] NOW charged that the stations were excluding women from serious programming, and in both advertising and programming were giving a traditional and stereotypical portrayal of the role of women in society. The failure to give women full and fair coverage on the stations, they claimed, was a violation of the *Fairness Doctrine,* the requirement that licensees provide fair coverage of conflicting views on controversial public issues. NOW argued that the role of women in society was both controversial and important, and that by giving full exposure to the sexual and domestic roles of women only, the stations were not fully covering the issues at stake. The FCC rejected this argument, deciding that the portrayal of women was not a one-sided presentation of a controversial issue of public importance. The FCC's refusal to intervene in cases of this sort is understandable in view of the First Amendment prohibition of media censorship. The agencies which regulate the television industry in the United States have been reluctant to interfere with the media's right to determine its own content.

Other legislative recourse in the United States is through the Federal Trade Commission (FTC) which has a mandate to prevent fraud in connection with sale of products. The FTC regulates unfair and false advertising. However, in the Frito Bandito case discussed earlier, the FTC ruled that the Mexican stereotype did not constitute fraud in connection with the sale of the product.[12] Although some critics have contended that the stereotypes of women used in advertising are the very essence of the sales message, this argument would likely be no more successful with the FTC than was the argumentation used in the Frito Bandito case.

In the United States regulative recourse is limited in the case of the FCC by the First Amendment, and for the FTC by the definition of the concept of unfair and false advertising. While the FTC has expressed some concern about advertising which could exploit vulnerable groups (such as children and the elderly), they have so far been unwilling to extend this concern to the portrayal of women. In the current deregulation environment, it is unlikely that there will be federal regulatory action in the United States addressed to reducing sex stereotyping in advertising.

Industry Self-Regulation

Self-regulation of advertising would appear to present greater possibilities for reducing sex stereotyping. The industry bodies involved have already indicated some concern for the subject. The National Advertising Review Board (NARB) was the first industry group to take an active role on the question of advertising and women. The NARB's mandate is to deal with truth and accuracy in advertising. (Truth and accuracy with respect to the presentation of women is not considered a relevant concern.) Despite this limited mandate, the NARB had been under pressure in the last decade to give active consideration to matters of taste and social responsibility in advertising. As a result, the NARB had appointed several consultative panels from its membership which review various areas of public concern and release position papers. In 1975 one such panel produced a report on women and advertising.

The report, *Advertising and Women,* is noteworthy because it was an early (by industry standards) statement explicitly recognizing that there is justification in complaints about the portrayal of women in advertising.[13] The report admits that a problem exists, saying that to dispute this is to deny the basis of the critics' arguments—that advertising, while selling products, also sells a supplementary image. When advertisements present a negative image of women, the NARB report goes on to say, people may accept this portrayal as an accurate depiction of women in our society. The report goes so far as to say that by reinforcing outmoded and traditional stereotypes of men and women, advertisers are derelict in their duty to give the public a fair, accurate, and truthful presentation.

In this statement of the reality of the problem and of advertising's responsibility, the NARB report represents a major step forward by the U.S. advertising industry. In addition, the report attempts to educate agencies and advertisers by offering some creative guidelines that might be followed in the development and approval of advertisements. Those guidelines, reproduced in table 9-1, describe portrayals that might be considered to be destructive and negative versus constructive and positive. For example, a destructive portrayal would be one which depicted women as silly and weak; a constructive portrayal, one which reflected the fact that girls may aspire to careers in business and the professions.

However, the NARB report is simply a position paper. It does not have the force of self-regulation, and the guidelines produced are in no way binding on the advertising industry. Publication of the report did not result in extension of the NARB's mandate to include truth in presentation of the sexes, nor did the report in any other way change self-regulatory practice in the United States. Consequently, in many critical areas the report is impotent. As one example, the report advises against double entendre and the improper use of women's bodies in advertisements. Realistically, such advice does nothing to change the attitudes and practices of those advertisers who are using sexuality to sell such products as jeans, adult films, lingerie, and automotive parts.

The codes of practice under which the U.S. advertising industry operates say little that could be used to control the portrayal of men and women. One such code, the National Association of Broadcasters' (NAB) Radio and Television Code, does not explicitly mention the portrayal of the sexes. However, it does state that "advertisements shall not portray attitudes and practices inconsistent with generally recognized social values and customs."[14] The NAB also rules on the acceptability of certain product types for radio and television advertising. For example, in the early 1970s, advertising of sanitary napkins, tampons, and douche products was. deemed acceptable, and in 1975 the hours during which such advertising could appear were regulated.[15] The presentation of such products on television has proved to be highly controversial and has occasioned serious protests from women's groups.

Table 9–1
What the Panel Recommends: Excerpts from the NARB Report

The Panel offers no hard and fast rules for dealing with advertising appealing to or portraying women. The scene is changing too rapidly. Accordingly, we have not attempted to compile a list of current ads that the Panel thinks merit praise or criticism.

Recognizing that principles are more enduring than specific cases, the Panel has distilled its many months of study into a checklist of questions for advertisers and agency personnel to consider when creating or approving an advertisement. We realize that there will probably be differences of opinion about some of the items on this checklist, but we believe that whatever discussion may be stimulated by the controversial ones will be helpful in clarifying the issues.

Checklist: Destructive Portrayals

Am I implying in my promotional campaign that creative, athletic, and mind-enriching toys and games are not for girls as much as for boys? Does my ad, for example, imply that dolls are for girls and chemistry sets for boys, and that neither could ever become interested in the other category?

Table 9–1 continued.

Are sexual stereotypes perpetuated in my ad? That is, does it portray women as weak, silly, and overemotional? Or does it picture both sexes as intelligent, physically able, and attractive?

Are the women portrayed in my ad stupid? For example, am I reinforcing the "dumb blonde" cliche? Does my ad portray women who are unable to balance their checkbooks? Women who are unable to manage a household without the help of outside experts, particularly male ones?

Does my ad use belittling language? For example, "gal Friday" or "lady professor?" Or "her kitchen" but "his car?" Or "women's chatter" but "men's discussions?"

Does my ad make use of contemptuous phrases? Such as "the weaker sex," "the little woman," "the ball and chain," or "the war department."

Do my ads consistently show women waiting on men? Even in occupational situations, for example, are women nurses or secretaries serving coffee, etc., to male bosses or colleagues? And never vice versa?

Is there a gratuitous message in my ads that a woman's most important role in life is a supportive one, to cater to and coddle men and children? Is it a "big deal" when the reverse is shown, that is, very unusual and special—something for which the women must show gratitude?

Do my ads portray women as more neurotic than men? For example, as ecstatically happy over household cleanliness or deeply depressed because of their failure to achieve near perfection in household tasks?

(A note is needed here, perhaps. It is not the Panel's intention to suggest that women never be portrayed in the traditional role of homemaker and mother. We suggest instead that the role of homemaker be depicted not in a grotesque or stereotyped manner, but be treated with the same degree of respect accorded to other important occupations.)

Do my ads feature women who appear to be basically unpleasant? For example, women nagging their husbands or children? Women being condescending to other women? Women being envious or arousing envy? Women playing the "one-upmanship" game (with a sly wink at the camera)?

Do my ads portray women in situations that tend to confirm the view that women are the property of men or are less important than men?

Is there double entendre in my ads? Particularly about sex or women's bodies?

Checklist: Negative Appeals

Do my ads try to arouse or play upon stereotyped insecurities? Are women shown as fearful of not being attractive to men or to other women, fearful of not being able to keep their husbands or lovers, fearful of an in-law's disapproval, or, for example, of not being able to cope with a husband's boss coming for dinner?

Does my copy promise unrealistic psychological rewards for using the product? For example, that a perfume can lead to instant romance.

Does my ad blatantly or subtly suggest that the product possesses supernatural powers? If believed literally, is the advertiser unfairly taking advantage of ignorance? Even if understood as hyperbole, does it insult the intelligence of women?

Table 9–1, continued

Checklist: Constructive Portrayals

Are the attitudes and behavior of the women in my ads suitable models for my own daughter to copy? Will I be happy if my own female children grow up to act and react the way the women in my ads act and react?

Do my ads reflect the fact that girls may aspire to careers in business and the professions? Do they show, for example, female doctors and female executives? Some women with both male and female assistants?

Do my ads portray women and men (and children) sharing in the chores of family living? For example, grocery shopping, doing laundry, cooking (not just outdoor barbecueing), washing dishes, cleaning house, taking care of children, mowing the lawn, and other house and yard work?

Do the women in my ads make decisions (or help make them) about the purchase of high-priced items and major family investments? Do they take an informed interest, for example, in insurance and financial matters?

Do my ads portray women actually driving cars and showing an intelligent interest in mechanical features, not just in the color and upholstery?

Are two-income families portrayed in my ads? For example, husband and wife leaving home or returning from work together?

Are the women in my ads doing creative or exciting things? Older women, too? In social and occupational environments? For example, making a speech, in a laboratory, or approving an ad?

Checklist: Positive Appeals

Is the product presented as a means for a woman to enhance her own self-esteem, to be a beautiful human being, to realize her full potential?

Does my advertisement promise women realistic rewards for using the product? Does it assume intelligence on the part of women?

Humor

The Panel is not so sober sided as to suggest that humor has no place in women-related advertising. At the same time, the Panel feels called on to point out that sometimes meanness is expressed in the guise of humor. In its study of current advertising, the Panel came across some examples of attempted women-related humor which could not have been funny to those who were the butt of the jokes. It is healthy for people to laugh at themselves, but usually this is a luxury only the secure can afford. Effective humor often has a cutting edge, and it requires extra ordinary care to insure that the cut is not made at the expense of women's self-esteem.

In the present context, for example, the Panel suggests extreme caution in making fun of efforts to improve the status of women and the opportunities available to them.

Source: *Advertising and Women: A Report on Advertising Portraying or Directed to Women* (New York: National Advertising Review Board, 1975). Reprinted with permission of the National Advertising Review Board.

Another self-regulatory group, the National Advertising Division (NAD) of the Council of Better Business Bureaus, has a more detailed set of criteria for the acceptability of social and sexual portrayals in advertisements. The NAD code prohibits "unacceptable reflections of social, legal, moral, institutional or family values; disdain for parents and other sources of child guidance; undesirable living habits and manners; and poor (other than informal) use of language."[16] However, neither the NAD code nor the NAB code has, to date, been applied to such presentations when they involve sex-stereotyping issues.

As a result, there has been little attention paid in the United States to sex-stereotyping issues either by regulatory or self-regulatory agencies. While the NARB has very forceably expressed its concern, compliance with their guidelines is strictly voluntary and problems persist. The situation is similar in the United Kingdom.

Regulation and Self-Regulation in the United Kingdom

The Advertising Standards Authority (ASA) is Britain's self-regulatory agency. Despite high level of protest about sex stereotyping in advertising in The United Kingdom, the ASA has taken little action to develop regulations or to hear complaints concerning women and advertising. The situation may, however, be in the process of change.

In its 1974–1975 annual report, the ASA published its views concerning the question.[17] That report argued that if advertising failed to achieve a rapport with its audience, it would be ineffective. The ASA contended that advertising is unsuitable for use as a lever to achieve social change because in this capacity advertisements would, no doubt, fail to be relevant to consumers and thus fail to sell products. Advertising depicts women in traditional roles and settings, the ASA argued, because the majority of consumers see themselves in these roles. When the public no longer wishes to see itself in traditional, stereotypical roles, then advertising will reflect this attitudinal change.

In December 1975 a sex-discrimination law came into effect in England, requiring nearly all recruitment advertising to be sexually nondiscriminatory. However, this did not affect the ASA's position on other forms of advertising. In 1978 the ASA again reported its point of view about the depiction of the sexes in advertising. In a document entitled, *Women in Advertising,* the council reiterated its belief that it was proper to represent women as housewives and that advertising should not attempt to change traditional ideas of women's role in society.[18]

However, under the British Code of Advertising Practice, the ASA does rule on matters of public decency in advertising, and many of the cases covered under this category concern the sexual portrayal of women. In ruling on such complaints the ASA considers both advertising-media context and the degree of offensiveness. For example, in the authority's case report of September 1981, eight decency complaints were reported, and three had been ruled to be in breach of the code.[19] A complaint concerning a computer advertisement which included an illustration of a woman with her knickers around her knees and a vulgar headline was found to be in bad taste, but the complaint was not upheld since the advertisement was considered unlikely to cause grave and widespread offense. However, a complaint about a boat advertisement appearing in a family magazine and featuring a naked female model was upheld.

Two recent studies conducted in Britain indicate that issues concerning the portrayal of women are still of great concern in that country. In 1981 the Equal Opportunities Commission sponsored a study of the marketing effectiveness of traditional versus modern portrayals of women in advertising.[20] The study examined the relative effectiveness of two alternative treatments, traditional and modern, of the advertisements for each of four products. Television and print advertising were both included, chosen from current advertising in Britain. Personal interviews were conducted with matched samples of female consumers who had viewed either a traditional or modern advertisement for the product. The conclusion of this British study was that the modern portrayals of women resulted in substantially higher effectiveness as measured by intention-to-buy questions. These results were found both among women employed in the labor force and among housewives. The authors concluded that the modern styles of advertisements were more effective because they portray women as "attractive, independent, capable people in roles in and out of home, and they do it in a manner which is realistic and natural."[21]

The continuing concern of the ASA about self-regulation with respect to decency in advertisements is indicated by an ASA-sponsored national survey which was released in.1982.[22] In its rationale for this survey the ASA notes that over six thousand five hundred complaints about decency and taste are received annually and that approximately 40 percent of these deal with the way advertising depicts or refers to women. Along with continued pressure from women's groups to amend the British Code of Advertising Practice to apply more strict standards to the portrayal of women, the complaints occasioned the authority to attempt to learn more about women's attitudes toward nudity and decency in advertising. A sample of almost three thousand adult women was interviewed about advertising in women's magazines and completed a detailed questionnaire about a folder containing twenty-four advertisements selected from the authority's complaint files. The study results offer rich data about the elements in advertising that British women consider to be distasteful and offensive.

The overall conclusion of the authority is that the concerns expressed by feminists are not generally shared by British women. For example, it was found that few women take exception to partially or totally nude depictions of women and that female nudity is accepted to the extent that the woman portrayed is perceived to be beautiful and relevant to the advertised product. Offense was more often related to the nature of the product than to the style of the advertisement.

In its conclusions to the report the ASA contended that "the findings of our inquiry do not suggest wide support. . . . for the assertions about the effects of advertising on the status of women which have become part of the stock-in-trade of some leaders of the campaign for women's liberation."[23] Thus, while public controversy about the portrayal of women in British advertising continues, and the ASA continues to rule on decency issues, there is at present little likelihood of stronger self-regulatory action.

Regulation and Self-Regulation in Canada[24]

Canada has taken one of the world's strongest stances concerning the improvement of the portrayal of the sexes in advertising. In Canada, as the result of public protest, government pressure, and enlightened response by the advertising industry, the self-regulatory agency is acting to try to change the way the sexes are portrayed in advertising.

In 1976 the Advertising Advisory Board (AAB), the Canadian self-regulatory body, established a task force and released its report: *Women and Advertising: Today's Messages—Yesterday's Images.*[25] In many respects this report was softer in tone and content than its U.S. counterpart. The AAB task force implied that Canadian advertisers were responding to the need for change. Although the report indicated that some additional improvements were needed, on the whole it suggested that the changes merely involved more appropriate interpretations in the advertisement production state—a sort of fine tuning of acting styles. The report noted that the major problems lay in the cumulative impact of all advertisements taking the same approach and being somewhat off in their portrayals of women. Such a cumulative impact effect, it was implied, defied regulatory remedies; no one advertiser was guilty, but all should be encouraged to change.

Although the AAB does have a regulatory arm (the Advertising Standards Council, which administers a self-regulatory code), no new regula-

dards Council, which administers a self-regulatory code), no new regulations were proposed. The report then was just a position paper, and little was done beyond its initial introduction at an annual meeting of the AAB to promulgate the report or to promote industry attention and response.

A major stumbling block to further action was the stand of the AAB that issues concerning the portrayal of women fall into the category of taste and opinion. In this category the AAB also included such concerns as the display of violence, the encouragement of materialism, the parading of sex, the insulting of minorities, and the encouragement of smoking and drinking. The AAB's rationale for the omission of personal-opinion matters is contained in a footnote to the Canadian Code of Advertising Standards, the self-regulatory code. The footnote states, "The foregoing Code embraces those areas in which it is possible to make an objective appraisal of advertising content. It avoids entry into the subjective area of taste, which is difficult to pinpoint, and in which personal judgment plays an important part."[26]

During this period the advertising on television of feminine-hygiene products became an issue of particular concern. The Advertising Standards Council records for 1978 and 1979 list this product category as the one with the largest number of complaints, a response by women to the beginning of the practice of airing advertisements for such products on television. In the fall of 1978 several newspaper stories by consumer columnists ran in Vancouver, Winnipeg, and Toronto criticizing the existence, style, and tone of the television commercials. The articles urged readers with similar views to complain to the Canadian Radio-Television and Telecommunications Commission (CRTC), the federal government's regulatory body responsible for broadcasting. Within two months over one thousand two hundred petitions and letters from individuals and groups were sent to the ASC and to the CRTC.

Industry representatives had mixed feelings about the protests. Many were unsure they should be advertising on television but were engaged in the practice because their competitors were. Others felt that only a very small minority of women objected to such advertising. In response to the protest and to ease the pressure from the government, the Canadian Association of Broadcasters (CAB) developed a self-regulatory code for advertising of feminine-hygiene products on television. The code requires preclearance by the CAB of all such advertisements, but its main clauses deal with standards for the use of certain words and product depictions within the advertisements (see table 9-2). From the start some industry representatives were sceptical that such a code really addressed the problems and would be effective. The new code was introduced in June 1979, with December 31, 1979, as the expiry time for existing commercials. One year later the ASC had noticed no change in consumer-complaint levels.

Table 9-2

Excerpts from the Television Code of Standards for the Advertising of Feminine-Sanitary-Protection Products

Published by the

Canadian Association of Broadcasters

June 1, 1979

Background

This Code has been created by the Canadian Association of Broadcasters in cooperation with advertisers, their advertising agencies, the Telecaster Committee, and the Advertising Standards Council which will administer the Code.

In this Code the words "advertising" and "commercials" refer to those messages broadcast on Canadian television stations or on behalf of Canadian advertisers promoting such menstrual-related products as sanitary pads or napkins, tampons, or their equivalent. Commercials coming in from U.S. stations, either directly or by cable, are of course beyond the Council's jurisdiction.

The Code is complementary to the Canadian Code of Advertising Standards which applies to advertising in all media.

Advertising is essentially a communications process, presenting consumers with an array of choices. Sometimes these choices concern products related to basic bodily functions that are a natural part of everyday living but that in our time and culture are also regarded by many as personal and private.

Advertising for this category poses a special responsibility on advertisers, their agencies and media for observing the canons of good taste. As the Canadian Code of Advertising Standards notes, taste inevitably falls within a very subjective area, varying widely from person to person, from region to region and from time to time. Many informed, intelligent and responsible citizens, for example, hold widely-conflicting views on whether certain "facts of life" should ever be publicly explored or discussed. It is not the function of advertising to resolve such conflicts. Indeed, in a democratic environment, mass communication by its very nature will reflect the diversity of interests and opinions in the marketplace.

Both broadcasters and advertisers, however, recognize their obligation to be sensitive to the attitudes of their audience. They have therefore adopted this Code as a set of basic standards for all sectors of advertising involved in one area that is of evident public concern—the televised advertising of feminine sanitary protection products.

Code Clauses

1. (a) All commercials must conform to this Code and be pre-cleared through the Advertising Standards Council.

   (b) All authorized commercials must carry an ASC number (e.g. ASC 9-79), indicating the month and year of approval. This approval number should appear on the Broadcast Order, as with CRTC numbers. *Stations must not accept advertising in this category unless it carries such a number.*

2. Because of the personal nature of this product category, all commercials should be treated with the sensitivities of viewers in mind.

3. (a) Commercials must not play upon fears or draw parallels between the use of the product and femininity. Generalized statements relating to femininity, freshness, etc., are, depending upon context, acceptable.

   (b) The audio-visual presentation must not employ graphic details of the product or product capabilities, and considerate care should be exercised in the use of language. For example, the use of personal references such as "accidents", "surprises" is prohibited, whereas product terms such as "absorbency", "comfort" are permissible.

   (c) The foregoing does not in any way preclude the use of a product brand name in commercials.

4. Commercials must be scheduled only within the following times:

   (i) School days: adult viewing time (9 a.m. to 4 p.m.) and after 9 p.m.

   (ii) Weekends and recognized school holidays: after 9 p.m.

This Code has been adopted by our English-language member stations. We recommend that French-language member stations use Clauses 2 and 3 as good taste guidelines.

Source: *Television Code of Standards for the Advertising of Feminine Sanitary Protection Products* (Toronto: Canadian Association of Broadcasters, 1979). Reprinted with permission of the Canadian Association of Broadcasters/Advertising Standards Council.

Government Intervention—1979 and 1980

Protests of advertising abuses and complaints about the misrepresentation of women continued. Direct appeals for government intervention were launched by federal and provincial status of women councils. Most notably, in 1978, the Federal Advisory Council on the Status of Women published a lengthy position paper on the issue, reviewing relevant research data and the history of the controversy, and recommended government intervention if industry did not respond more favorably.[27]

Despite such effort, government responses were not rapid. Probably the major reason lay in the difficulty of determining what would be an effective response. Canadian governments have long favored a self-regulatory approach as opposed to direct controls over the advertising industry. In addition, there are difficult questions of federal versus provincial jurisdiction.

The Quebec government, however, did act in 1978. In August of that year it established a twelve-member committee to probe sexism in advertising, and in 1979 the committee produced guidelines that had been developed in consultation with industry and women's groups. The Quebec Status of Women Council developed a series of four television commercials that attacked sex stereotyping in several dimensions of society, including advertising. In addition, advertisements designed to sensitize advertisers and their agencies to the issues were run in the advertising trade press.

The CRTC Task Force

In 1979 the Federal Minister of Communications suggested that some action should be taken on sex stereotyping in all aspects of the media, presumably including advertising. A task force was established by the CRTC and was specifically charged with developing guidelines for advertising on television:

> . . . the CRTC is setting up a Task Force composed of representation from the advertising and broadcast industries, from the public and from the CRTC. The public representatives will be women who have done much work in the area of sex stereotyping . . . [The purpose of the Task Force] will be to delineate guidelines for a more positive and realistic portrayal of women in radio and television in both programming and commercials and to make policy recommendations for consideration by the commission in the broadcast industry.[28]

From the first the CRTC Task Force had a stormy history. Unlike the more understanding atmosphere of the self-regulatory group, the government-established committee was composed of few industry people and was dominated by strong feminists unsympathetic to the advertising-effectiveness issues that concerned industry. The difference in perspective was highlighted during a meeting in February 1980 when the industry submitted thirty-three commercials, considered by them to be good, to be viewed by the task force. In the face of criticism of these commercials by feminist members of the task force, a prominent advertising-industry representative withdrew from the committee amid a flurry of protest and publicity.

Nevertheless, in March 1980 feminist members of the task force submitted a position paper entitled "Sex-Role Stereotyping in Advertising: A Summary of Concerns." This three-page document summarized some major issues: Images, language, roles, family, and interpersonal relationships, personality, women as buyers, women as sellers. A sample section is shown below.

II. *Language*
A. Language should be inclusive and non-sexist. For example, when all persons are meant to be included, do not use the so-called "generic 'man'." Diminutive terms should not be used to label women.
B. Ads should not demean or degrade women through language.[29]

The Battle

By this time the CRTC Task Force and the industry response to it had become big news within the advertising community. It appeared that the industry would make one final attempt to block the efforts of the task force to impose legislative change. In an effort to promote a full airing of views leading to nonregulatory action, the Association of Canadian Advertisers (ACA) decided it was necessary to stage a typical industry/feminist confrontation on the issue at its May 1980 annual meeting.

In order to spark controversy, John Foss, president of ACA, arranged a presentation of the large industry audience with Lynne Gordon, chairperson of the Ontario Council on the Status of Women, and the ACA representative on the CRTC Task Force, Michael Kennerley, as the speakers. To set the stage for Lynne Gordon, Foss led off by enunciating a point of view, not his own, but still held by a substantial number of advertisers:

> Persons in skirt and persons in shirt: it is my pleasure to talk to you today of the work that is taking place to reduce sex-role stereotyping by addressing you as "in skirt" or "in shirt"; which is not hidden sexism implying that only a skirt is being worn, i.e., that you are topless, or only a shirt is being worn—which would mean the end was in sight—before I have even begun.[30]

Foss's talk went on in the same tone, using the defenses characteristically offered by some industry members in order to provide the cue for a dramatic interruption from the audience:

> A commercial costs a lot of money and every sex role may not be portrayed, only those representing a majority. As an aside, sex and money have many similarities in this regard; it is not enough to go around—and somebody else has got most of it. Anyway, as you can see, the ACA position is that there is no serious problem with sex-role stereotyping. There is no cause for great concern . . . . There is nothing here that alert advertisers cannot take care of . . . .[31]

At this point there was a shout of protest from the floor as Lynne Gordon jumped up and came to the podium. With one final staged objection, "What in blazes is going on here?" John Foss yielded the floor to Gordon, who presented the feminists' position at length, concluding:

> The Honorable Dr. Lloyd Axworthy recently stated that the decade of the 1970's was one in which the principles recognizing the right of women to have equal status with men were established. The 1980's should be a decade of action geared towards the implementation of these principles. If anyone does not agree, please stand up and be counted![32]

But Gordon's call for action was not the last word. It was indeed a cue for the Association of Canadian Advertisers' representative on the CRTC Task Force, Michael Kennerley, who spoke, in part, as follows:

Pardon, Lynne Gordon, but I would like to accept your invitation to stand up and be heard. You see, you are making an assumption that not only are advertisers guilty of using stereotypes on television and of demeaning women, but we are also guilty of not doing anything about it, not taking any corrective action . . . . Advertisers have recognized the problem and are, in fact, taking steps to seek a solution . . . .

Since October of last year when the CRTC Task Force began to hold meetings, *Marketing Magazine* and other papers and magazines have carried stories about the battles and the controversies. They have all served a purpose in putting a spotlight on the problem and allowing us to vent some of our frustrations over the intrusion in our business . . . .

It has been extremely difficult to convince feminists on the Task Force of the legitimacy of using stereotypes in a television commercial. Stereotypes don't necessarily have to be negative, many of them are not only legitimate but are, in fact, the only reason why we can put in a commercial 30 seconds in length some of the things we put in and still have an effective selling message . . . . Another side of our argument, of course, was the fact that the role of the housewife is legitimate. Canada has many of them and they like what they do and they are proud of their accomplishments . . . .[33]

Kennerley went on to say that the industry itself had set up a number of its own committees to investigate the problem and to develop positive-action statements designed to take the place of guidelines. Exactly how such positive-action statements were to be implemented, he did not indicate.

The antiregulation view received strong endorsement in the trade press. For example, a column in the trade magazine *Marketing* was entitled "Fight for the 'Right' to Stereotype," and included such statements as these: "We should not react out of fear of a vocal minority"; "It is disturbing to think that there is a possibility that the government or the advertising industry will legislate the 'correct stereotype' for today's society"; "I submit that many of those who complain about sex stereotyping fail to recognize and respect the freedom and dignity of every Canadian"; . . . "freedom of choice means that women can still choose to be housewives"; "We should not let a vocal minority or government committee use our industry as a tool to reshape society according to its beliefs."[34]

Despite these vocalizations of righteous indignation from the industry, many industry leaders recognized that the CRTC Task Force would not quietly disappear and that, in fact, the task force had government support and evidence it felt would strongly support its case against advertising. Consequently, industry representatives began slowly to revise their positions. Industry associations, led by the Grocery Products Manufacturers of Canada and the Association of Canadian Advertisers, recognized that change of some sort was inevitable. Rather than allow that change to be imposed by government, proposals were developed for industry self-regulation to help alleviate the problem. In July 1980 the industry presented its own brief to the CRTC Task Force.[35] The brief admitted the existence of a problem and the necessity for reform, but recommended that the responsibility for reform be left in the self-regulatory hands of the industry itself. The brief stated, in part:

> Industry had made a commitment to deal with these concerns. However, industry believes that the very nature of the issue touches on judgment of the role of women in contemporary society; judgments which vary in accordance with individuals' perceptions, tastes and opinions . . . . the process is one of evolution rather than revolution.
>
> The advertising industry believes that more can be accomplished if the industry itself recognizes the problem and takes on the task of dealing with it in a positive manner. Recognizing that self-imposed regulation is a difficult and serious matter, the associations submitting this brief have undertaken:
>
>> To communicate to advertisers and the agencies preparing advertising, concerns over the portrayal of women in broadcast advertising.
>>
>> To develop guidelines to help the industry present a more realistic portrayal of women in broadcast advertising.

While the task force was considering the industry proposal to replace the intended government guidelines with industry self-regulation, the industry view received strong endorsement in an editorial entitled, "Judge Not," in Canada's leading newspaper *The Globe and Mail:*

> Which of us is qualified to identify and denounce the sexist element in advertising? That's easy: you are, we are, the lady next door is and so is the Advisory Council on the Status of Women. Certainly Ontario Liberal Leader Stuart Smith qualifies on the strength of having detected sexism in a recent environment-ministry advertisement.
>
> There is, you will correctly conclude, no shortage of bodies to pass judgment on other bodies. The difficulty arises in attempting to devise a common standard of what is acceptable and what is intolerably offensive. Should we rely on the views of those who have made a specialty of hunting down sexism, and those who have prepared themselves to the point where a glimpse of stocking is looked on as something shocking? This would be as bad as leaving it all to the individual who prides himself on being able to withstand any indignity—as long as it does not touch him personally.
>
> We outline the dilemma because there is—and may always be—pressure for authority over advertising content to be vested in some official body . . . . Not unexpectedly, the advertising industry is resisting this move strenuously—and with sound arguments . . . .
>
> We share the anxiety of the industry over the appointment of official arbiters. Self-regulation may not be the perfect answer, but it stands a better chance of striking a rational balance. Advertising, by its very nature, must concern itself with public taste.[36]

The Compromise

The battle was resolved—if not won by either side—by a series of decisions taken during the summer and autumn of 1980. First, the industry compromised. Despite previous statements that the industry could not and should not attempt to regulate in the areas of taste and opinion, the AAB made an addition to the Canadian Code of Advertising Standards. The addition to the code reads as follows:

> As a public communication process, advertising should not present demeaning or derogatory portrayals of individuals or groups and should not contain anything likely, in the light of generally prevailing standards, to cause deep or widespread offense.

> It is recognized, of course, that standards of taste are subjective and vary widely from person to person, and community to community and are, indeed, subject to constant change.[37]

The task force compromise was to agree to industry self-regulation as the mechanism for dealing with sex-role stereotyping problems. It agreed to accept a carefully redrafted, mutually acceptable version of the industry associations' July brief. The redraft version of the industry-suggested guidelines was accepted by the task force, and the task force conceded that self-regulation, if done properly, could contribute to changed attitudes on the part of advertisers and agencies, which were the real solution to the problem. The following guidelines, to be implemented through the ASC, were adopted in November 1980:

1. Advertising should recognize the changing roles of men and women in today's society and reflect the broad range of occupations for all.

2. Advertising should reflect a contemporary family structure showing men, women, and children as equally supportive participants in home management and household tasks and as equal beneficiaries of the positive attributes of family life.

3. Advertising, in keeping with the nature of the market and the product, should reflect the wide spectrum of Canadian life portraying men and women of various ages, backgrounds, and appearances actively pursuing a wide range of interests—sports, hobbies and business—as well as home-centered activities.

4. Advertising should reflect the realities of life in terms of the intellectual and emotional equality of the sexes by showing men and women as comparably capable, resourceful, self-confident, intelligent, imaginative and independent.

5. Advertising should emphasize the positive, personal benefits derived from products or services and should avoid portraying any excessive dependence and/or need for them.

6. Advertising should not exploit women or men purely for attention-getting purposes. Their presence should be relevant to the advertised product.

7. Advertising should reflect contemporary usage of nonsexist language, e.g., hours or working hours, rather than man hours; synthetic, rather than man-made; business executives, rather than businessmen or businesswomen.

8. Advertising should portray men and women as users, buyers, and decision-makers, both for "big-ticket" items and major services as well as smaller items.

9. Advertising should reflect a realistic balance in the use of women both as voice-overs and as experts and authorities.[38]

In addition, the industry agreed to set up an ongoing educational program for the advertising industry, and to develop an industry committee to serve as a reception point for complaints regarding sex-role stereotyping in advertising in all media (see table 9–3).

Table 9–3
Excerpt from Background on AAB Advisory Committee on Women and Advertising

Background

In 1976 AAB established a Task Force to "examine how women are addressed and portrayed in advertising carried by Canadian media." In its Report the Task Force noted that "woman is typically portrayed in a limited and traditional way in advertising." The Report identified areas of specific concern, recommended several constructive steps that advertisers, their agencies and media could take in response, and included a check list as a guide to positive portrayals of men and women.

But the problem persisted. In September, 1979, the then Minister of Communications and Secretary of State, David MacDonald, announced a restructuring of a Task Force formed earlier in the year by the Canadian Radio-Television and Telecommunications Commission (CRTC) to examine the same issue. This Task Force comprised members of the advertising industry and public sector representatives of recognized feminist organizations. The Task Force determined that its responsibility was to investigate the best method of ensuring that sex-role stereotyping was recognized and to develop some mechanism to correct the problem.

Public Sector Task Force members developed a consensus of concerns based on research studies from the last ten years, which showed that many advertisements are considered insulting to women. These concerns included: manner of portrayal of sexes, presence of sexes, (e.g. predominance of male authority figures), use of sexual innuendos and exclusion of ethnic and older women.

Industry Response

The advertising industry undertook to prepare constructive proposals for responding to these concerns. Past experience has shown that self-regulation, involving industry and public repre-

Table 9–3 continued.

sentatives, has been effective in changing attitudes and, further, is more flexible and less costly to administer than government regulation.

These proposals, endorsed by numerous industry associations, were presented to the Task Force and, after discussion and some modifications, were unanimously adopted.

As part of the industry response, AAB agreed to set up a special Advisory Committee on Sex-Role Stereotyping.

Committee Mandate

1. The Committee is responsible for an on-going information and "sensitizing" program with industry associations and groups, to be conducted by AAB staff and committee members. As part of this educational program, the Committee is supervising the distribution of a film dealing with the issues raised.

2. The Committee will supervise public attitude research on related concerns.

3. (a) Members of the public are encouraged to send to the Committee complaints about advertising which they feel is not in accordance with the Guidelines, and
   (b) Advertisers and advertising agencies are encouraged to seek counsel from AAB when they have any doubts as to whether certain creative concepts might conflict with the Guidelines.

Source: Advertising Advisory Board, Toronto, Ontario. Reprinted with permission of the Advertising Advisory Board.

*Current Activities of the Canadian
Sex-Stereotyping Committee*

The AAB began its efforts under the guidelines with the production of an eighteen-minute film dealing with advertising sex-role stereotyping. Although some women's groups in Canada felt the film was poorly done, the AAB has received many requests from industry and public groups to show it, and this presumably has helped to raise consciousness about the issues. As promised the AAB established a committee comprised of industry and public members to oversee compliance with the guidelines. In recent months the AAB has received over ninety complaints under the guidelines; these deal with eighty-two different products and services. Most complaints come from members of feminist groups who are participating in a national effort to oversee advertising which has been organized by Canadian feminist organizations.

When the committee receives a complaint, members of the staff inform the advertiser of the complaint and of the committee members' deliberations concerning it. Of course, the committee cannot force advertiser compliance with its ruling because it administers guidelines, rather than a self-regulatory code. Nevertheless, the process of informing advertisers about complaints serves as an effective reeducation effort. The committee finds that advertisers informed that the committee has sustained a complaint against them rarely remove the advertisement in question; however, almost invariably the next advertisement produced by the offender is found to be acceptable. Moreover, the AAB staff reports that the advertisements of major, national advertisers rarely come under committee review, since those advertisers are highly aware of and supportive of the guidelines.

It is noteworthy, however, that the cases upheld by the committee invariably deal with the important, but limited, issue of decency and derogatory portrayals. They do not deal with broader issues such as the depiction of occupational roles or portrayals of housewives. For example, the committee has found complaints justified where the advertisement portrays a nude woman, uses double entendre, or uses demeaning sexual language to refer to women. But they have not upheld complaints concerning limited occupational roles. A complaint concerning an advertisement showing engineers, but not representing women engineers, was considered unjustified because committee members felt that advertising should not be required to be ahead of societal trends.

As yet the AAB has not made major efforts to publicize the sex-stereotyping guidelines outside the advertising industry. Thus, public awareness of the guidelines is low, except among organized feminist groups. Despite that, the guidelines exist, and there is growing industry support for them, and that in itself makes the Canadian advertising industry the world leader in attempting to eliminate sex stereotyping in advertising.

Regulation and Self-Regulation in Other Countries

The issue of advertising sex stereotyping has received worldwide attention most notably from the United Nations. Under the auspices of United Nations Educational, Scientific, and Cultural Organization (UNESCO), the United Nations in 1980 held a series of meetings and published a report, *Women in the Media.*[39] The conferees agreed that the images of women in the media (and its advertising) were among the main obstacles to eliminating discrimination against women and to preserving traditional sex-role attitudes and behaviors. Advertising was criticized worldwide for what was viewed as its negative and harmful influence and for its distorted and dishonest images of women. UNESCO reported that Caribbean women were particularly concerned that the image of women in advertising was degrading and sometimes obscene. In Australia a women's organization had prepared a list of recommendations aimed toward improvement of the portrayal of women. These recommendations specifically addressed changing the stereotyping of sex roles and eliminating the use of the woman's body to sell products.

International standards of acceptability and the degree of local concern for sex-stereotyping issues vary widely. In 1979 Boddewyn reported a survey conducted for the International Advertising Association concerning regulation and self-regulation of decency and sexism in advertising throughout the world.[40] Standards vary widely from country to country, but there are several factors identified by Boddewyn which influence those standards.

Boddewyn defines decency in advertising as what is not offensive to the community, and sexism as the exploitation of sexuality in the advertisement. He found that five key factors influence the degree to which regulation or self-regulation are applied to these issues. Those factors are: religion and cultural-value systems; legal systems that reflect the country's moral standards; the strength of concerned religious or feminist groups; media preclearance systems; and the existence of advertising self-regulatory bodies.

In general, industry respondents considered decency and sexism in advertising to be relatively minor concerns compared to other self-regulatory problems. The problem of decency arose generally around whether certain product categories could properly be advertised. Standards of the acceptable advertisement varied widely from country to country. There were also major differences among countries concerning the acceptable use of women in advertising.

Boddewyn presented respondents with four hypothetical situations and asked what kinds of restrictions would be placed on this type of advertising in each country. He found that the use of women as attention-getting devices, when they have no particular relevance to the product, was controlled most strictly in Scandinavian countries and in the Netherlands. This kind of advertising is restricted either by law, self-regulation, or media codes in Denmark, Finland, Greece, Indonesia, Lebanon, Norway, the Philippines, South Africa, Sweden, and Venezuela. The South African restrictions demand that when women are used as attention getters, the advertisements should be tasteful. In Italy and Venezuela there are prohibitions against using women in this way in liquor advertising.

In a second type of situation, when an advertisement presents a woman in a lewd or salacious way, Boddewyn found that almost all countries have restrictions. The strictest codes exist in Hong Kong, Ireland, Italy, Malaysia, South Africa, Taiwan, Thailand, and the United Kingdom.

The third situation is one where the product is shown as conferring the power of seduction on its users. Legal constraints on such advertisements were minimal, but Australia, Greece, Hong Kong, Indonesia, Ireland, Malaysia, Mexico, the Philippines, Turkey, and the United Kingdom had some self-regulatory or media mechanism to restrict such advertisements.

Boddewyn's fourth hypothetical advertisement was one which showed the product which is, in fact, used by both sexes as being used exclusively by one. This case would evoke regulation only in Scandinavian countries, but

Boddewyn believes that advertisers are generally more aware of this type of discrimination and are attempting to limit it themselves.

Despite the major differences among countries, Boddewyn concludes that concerns about decency and sexism in advertising will continue to be a major source of consumer complaint throughout the world. In particular, he concludes that there will be increased efforts to eliminate the more sexy and indecent approaches used in advertisements.

The Limits of Regulation and Self-Regulation as a Change Mechanism

Several factors limit the willingness of government bodies to act to regulate advertising with respect to sex stereotyping. Perhaps the most important is the strong free-speech traditions of most Western countries and the consequent reluctance of governments to intervene in issues where judgments appear to be based on personal taste and opinion. Nevertheless, the Canadian experience shows that when a concerned protesting group is persistent and is able to get the ear of government, the threat of government intervention can prove to be strong enough to ensure changes in industry self-regulatory practices.

In the absence of government pressure, however, advertising-industry self-regulatory groups continue to defend present practice and are reluctant to add women's concerns to the other regulatory issues which burden them. Their usual defense has been that of taste and opinion. The taste and opinion defense, however, does not bear up well against careful scrutiny, because industry self-regulatory codes have for many years dealt with judgmental issues, albeit in different contexts from the portrayal of the sexes. In Canada, where the content of advertising to children and advertising for personal-hygiene products had already been included under industry codes, the argument was made that taste and opinion concerning the portrayal of the sexes could also be regulated. Moyer and Banks, commenting on Canadian self-regulatory practice in the mid-seventies, noted:

> It seems . . . accurate to say that judgments of most advertising must be subjective to some extent, and that some of the issues that the code still sidesteps are no more subjective than others that it already tackles.

> Similarly, it challenges one's sense of relevance to observe that the council is willing to eliminate an ad that "unfairly disparages the products . . . of other advertisers," but is not willing to consider an ad that unfairly disparages women. It seems more reasonable to say that what is covered by the code should be governed by the consumer's concerns rather than by the council's convenience, and that some of the issues that the code still ignores are at least as relevant as others that it already acknowledges.[41]

As Moyer and Banks indicate, issues of decency, obscenity, and unfair sexual disparagement probably could be incorporated into self-regulatory codes if the industry were to consider them sufficiently important. What is needed to make this happen appears to be continued protest, cultural consensus about its validity, and pressure from government agencies to regulate should the industry not act on its own.

The broader and more subtle issues of sex stereotyping in advertising, such as occupational role portrayal, voice-overs, and authority roles, are less susceptible to self-regulatory approaches. Even in Canada, where comprehensive guidelines have been adopted, those aspects of sexual stereotyping get little attention from the self-regulatory agency. The major stumbling block is that the problem does not lie with one advertisement, but rather with the cumulative effect of all the advertisements which reflect outdated stereotypes. One of the Canadian guidelines, for example, states that men, women, and children should be presented as equal participants in running a household. This is a reasonable expectation for all advertising taken together, but it would be entirely inappropriate to use it as a strict rule to prohibit any one advertisement that showed a woman using a washing machine. The manner in which women are depicted within an individual advertisement can be a valid subject for self-regulation when the concern is to prevent an overtly disparaging portrayal, whether that be an indecent sexual portrayal or one which shows a woman as neurotic or dumb. However, regulation is not a valid means for achieving change in the range of roles shown for the sexes.

Another difficult regulatory problem exists when demeaning stereotyping is created through the use of subtle creative techniques. As was noted in chapter 1, the problem of sex stereotyping often does not lie in the script of a commercial, but rather in its executional style. Similarly, in print advertising, the problem often lies not in the picture or headline taken separately, but in their juxtaposition. It is difficult to imagine how guidelines can be effective in eliminating such problems as stereotypical acting styles, body language, and voice inflection.

Advertising regulation and self-regulation do have important potential in helping to eliminate sex stereotyping in advertising. However, that potential lies primarily in the ability to control the worst offenses against public decency and to control instances of flagrant disparagement of the sexes. Increased attention to these issues by self-regulatory groups would appear to be feasible and to be warranted. Self-regulatory groups can make a further contribution by developing guidelines and engaging in other industry-education efforts in an attempt to improve the way the sexes are portrayed in advertising. Such efforts, however, are only the first step to achieving change to eliminate other basic problems of advertising sex stereotyping. Ultimately, real change must come through advertiser reeducation.

Notes

1. Muriel Akamatsu, *Liberating the Media: Advertising,* Freedom of Information Center Report No. 200 (Columbia: University of Missouri, 1978).

2. *Window Dressing on the Set: Women and Minorities in Television* (Washington, D.C.: United States Commission on Civil Rights, 1977).

3. *Window Dressing on the Set,* p. 12.

4. Akamatsu, *Liberating the Media,* p. 5.

5. A useful history of early feminist protests against advertising in the United States can be found in Charlene Ventura, "Ad Liberation: The Feminist Impact," *Sybil-Child* 1 (1975):37–54.

6. Donna Allen, "Testimony Concerning the Socio-Economic Influence of Advertising," in *The Corporate Influence on the Images of Women in Advertising,* transcript of public hearings held by the Interfaith Center on Corporate Responsibility, New York City, October 7 and 8, 1976.

7. *"To Form a More Perfect Union," Justice for American Women* (Washington, D.C.: National Commission on the Observance of International Women's Year, Government Printing Office, 1976).

8. "Backpage," *Ms.,* October 1980, p. 108.

9. *"To Form a More Perfect Union," Justice for American Women,* p. 20; and *The Corporate Influence on the Images of Women in Advertising,* p. 47.

10. "The Bum's Rush in Advertising," *Time,* 1 December 1980, p. 75.

11. The history of NOW's challenge to the FCC is described in *Window Dressing on the Set: Women and Minorities in Television,* 63 ff; *"To Form a More Percent Union," Justice for American Women;* Nancy E. Stanley, "Federal Communications Law and Women's Rights: Women in the Wasteland Fight Back," *Hastings Law Journal* 23 (1971):15–53; and Kay Mills, "Fighting Sexism on the Airwaves," *Journal of Communication* 24 (Spring 1974):150–155.

12. Frank Mankiewicz and Joel Swerdlow, *Remote Control: Television and the American Life* (New York: New York Times Books, Inc., 1978).

13. *Advertising and Women: A Report on Advertising Portraying or Directed to Women* (New York: National Advertising Review Board, 1975).

14. Discussed in John R. Rossiter, "Source Effects and Self-Concept Appeals in Children's Television Advertising," in *The Effects of Television Advertising on Children,* ed. R.P. Adler et al. (Lexington, Mass.: Lexington Books, 1980).

15. "The Code and Personal Products Advertising: A Chronology," *Code News,* Code Authority of the National Association of Broadcasters, 10, no. 4, April 1977.

16. Rossiter, "Source Effects and Self-Concept Appeals," p. 63.

17. *Annual Report 1974–1975* (London: The Advertising Standards Authority, 1975).

18. *Women in Advertisements, ASA Case Report 38* (London: The Advertising Standards Authority, 1978).

19. *ASA Case Report 77* (London: The Advertising Standards Authority, 1981).

20. *Adman & Eve: A Study of the Portrayal of Women in Advertising,* Equal Opportunities Commission and Marketing Consultancy and Research Services of the University of Lancaster Department of Marketing, Manchester, April 1982.

21. *Adman & Eve,* p. 1.

22. *"Herself Appraised,"* The Treatment of Women in Advertisements (London: The Advertising Standards Authority, 1982).

23. *"Herself Appraised,"* The Treatment of Women in Advertisements.

24. Excerpted and adapted from Louise A. Heslop and Alice E. Courtney, "Advertising and Women," in *Marketplace Canada: Some Controversial Dimensions,* ed. S.J. Shapiro and L.A. Heslop (Toronto: McGraw-Hill Ryerson, 1982), pp. 59–86.

25. Task Force on Women and Advertising, *Women and Advertising: Today's Messages—Yesterday's Images?* (Toronto: Advertising Advisory Board, 1977).

26. *Canadian Code of Advertising Standards* (Toronto: Advertising Advisory Board, 1980).

27. Alice E. Courtney and Thomas W. Whipple, *Canadian Perspectives on Sex Stereotyping in Advertising* (Ottawa: Advisory Council on The Status of Women, 1978).

28. "Speech Notes," Association of Canadian Advertisers, Notes for Seminar Presentation, Toronto, 1980.

29. *Sex-Role Stereotyping in Advertising:* A Summary of Concerns (Toronto: Canadian Radio-Television and Telecommunications Commission, 1980).

30. John Foss, "Speech Notes," Notes for Seminar Presentation (Toronto: Association of Canadian Advertisers, 1980).

31. John Foss, "Speech Notes."

32. Lynne Gordon, "Speech Notes," Notes for Seminar Presentation (Toronto: Association of Canadian Advertisers, 1980).

33. Michael Kennerley, "Speech Notes," Notes for Seminar Presentation (Toronto: Association of Canadian Advertisers, 1980).

34. Bill Curley, "Fight for the 'right' to stereotype," *Marketing,* 4 August 1980.

35. "Brief to the CRTC Task Force on Sex-Role Stereotyping," Advertising Industry, Toronto, 23 June 1980.

36. "Judge Not," *Globe and Mail,* 11 August 1980, p. 6.

37. *Canadian Code of Advertising Standards.*

38. Advertising Advisory Board, Annual Meeting/Survival Seminar news media briefing material, Toronto, 26 November 1980.

39. *Women in the Media* (Paris: UNESCO, 1980).

40. J.J. Boddewyn, "Decency and Sexism in Advertising: An International Survey of their Regulation and Self-Regulation" (Report prepared for the International Advertising Association, Inc., New York, 1979).

41. Mel S. Moyer and John C. Banks, "Industry Self-Regulation: Some Lessons from the Canadian Advertising Industry," in *Problems in Canadian Marketing,* ed. D.N. Thompson (Chicago: American Marketing Association, 1977), p. 197.

10 Educating the Advertiser

Until recent years, the advertising literature dealing with the development of effective communications strategies for female and male audiences was based largely on opinions and preconceptions; little or no empirical research had actually been done. The recommendations to advertisers about how best to communicate with women were often doubtful in their accuracy. Here is a typical recommendation to advertisers from that literature; its usefulness and accuracy were doubtful when it was written thirty years ago, and today it is even more questionable:

> The experiments of the psychologists indicate definitely that women are more neurotic than men. This means that they are more inclined to be nervous, moody and emotionally unpredictable than are men. . . . the emotional appeal is especially to be preferred in promotional material, either oral or written, designed to motivate women.[1]

Such advice is an outmoded reflection of the attitudes and beliefs of the past, and such blatantly biased statements rarely appear in current literature. But while a large body of empirically based and unbiased research about men and women has begun to appear in the literature, little change in advertising practice has resulted. The underlying biased attitudes about the sexes still persist in the messages produced by the advertising industry.

Sex-stereotyped advertising no longer reflects the roles of the majority of men and women in North American society, it creates consumer irritation and dissatisfaction, and it is increasingly less effective as a communications tool. It is therefore surprising that so little in advertising has changed and that, for the most part, the changes that have taken place result from pressures coming from outside the advertising industry itself.

Advertising's Resistance to Change

Many defenders of the advertising industry's approach to women have asserted that no advertiser consciously sets out to demean or insult the woman consumer. Nevertheless, most advertising remains stereotyped and limited in its portrayal of the sexes, and a substantial portion of it continues to be overtly demeaning and insulting. Despite their stated good intentions, advertisers have made little progress in improving the portrayal. This is particularly surprising in the case of companies who target their products to the modern North American woman. For such advertisers the desire for managerial effectiveness alone would indicate a changed portrayal. These companies presumably want to please and persuade effectively, not to offend. Yet their advertisements too often remain a part of the problem, not a contribution to its solution. The evidence of real and dramatic changes taking place in our society, together with the evidence that advertisers can respond to such changes with effective communications, make it extremely difficult to posit explanations for the continued reliance on outdated stereotypes and sexist approaches.

Industry Defenses of Sex Stereotyping

Many in the industry seem either unaware of the changes that have occurred or, if aware, reluctant to concede to their implications for advertising practice. Instead, they defend the current portrayal of the sexes, using a variety of seemingly valid, but ultimately weak, arguments to bolster their position. In this section some of the more common defenses of advertising's resistance to change are discussed.

Mirror of Society. A common argument made in defense of advertising's portrayal of the sexes is that advertising is a mirror of society. Its purpose, it is argued, is to reflect conditions that already exist, not to induce social change or create new societal attitudes.

Advertisers who defend sexism and sex stereotyping on these grounds are either out of touch with current reality or purposely obstructive. As the National Advertising Review Board pointed out in 1975, by reinforcing outmoded and traditional stereotypes of men and women, advertisers are derelict in their duty to give the public a fair, accurate, and truthful presentation.[2] Indeed, if advertising was truly a mirror of society, the presentation of the sexes would certainly have changed already—dramatically and positively.

Advertising, of course, has never been a mirror of society or seriously attempted to become one. Advertisements represent people's desires and aspirations, not their realities. The beautiful blondes in the cosmetic advertisements, the loving couples in the liquor advertisements, the group at the beach drinking diet soda, the sexy girls in the jeans advertisements—all portray images of our aspirations and dreams. As a recent observer noted, advertisements portray an image that represents the interpretation of those cultural values which are profitable to propagate.[3] The social problem lies in the fact that the advertising reflects only certain aspects of a society's aspirations. Many critics of the portrayal of women in advertising claim that the industry refusal to change its view of women stems, at base, from a desire to keep women in their place, as passive, mindless, and easily manipulated consumers. While such criticism may be, for the most part, an overstatement of the problem, advertisers who refuse to recognize current aspirations of women give continued ammunition to the critics. Some advertiser attitudes make the observer agree, at least in part, with the observation of an advertising executive quoted by Scott:

> Gartner . . . vice president for research at Daniel and Charles . . . suggests that advertising men actually avoid the notion that current images may be stereotyped and demeaning, and that other approaches *could work as well or better,* because the current approach is ultimately a reinforcement of their own prejudices. To change the method would need a counter-change, a reformulation of their own attitudes which would be cognitively discomforting.[4]

While it does seem that advertisers avoid facing the evidence of changes in society because of their own preconditioning, Gartner may be incorrect in putting the burden of this criticism on advertising "men". In the authors' experience many men in the industry are open to change, while many women are not. The ability to overcome prejudice and respond to a changing society is not the exclusive province of either sex.

Stereotyping and Sexism Sell. Much of advertisers' resistance to change likely stems from a continued belief that stereotyping and sexism in advertising are effective as selling methods. While evidence mounts that progressive, nontraditional portrayals are equally or more effective in communicating, many advertising people are reluctant to accept that evidence. As Callan learned when she examined the problems of advertising women who wished to change their agencies' approaches, a majority of agency men still held stock in the old philosophy 'sexism sells.'[5] Bill Huckabee, vice president of Management Horizons agrees with that philosophy. In a report by Baltera in *Advertising Age,* Huckabee is reported to believe that in successful advertising, men act and women appear.[6] He actually urges advertisers to reinforce traditional stereotypes of the sexes, not to try to eliminate them. In a similar vein the Canadian trade magazine, *Marketing,* published an article by Fisher entitled, "Those rotten sex-stereotyped ads sell, dammit!"[7] The article not only denies evidence which shows that progressive, nonstereotyped advertisements communicate effectively, but goes so far as to defend traditional advertisements on the basis that exploitation of women cannot be changed without wrecking the economy.

Many advertisers whose views are substantially more progressive than

Fisher's believe that the sexually stereotyped or sexist portrayal is still the most effective selling tool. These advertisers argue that if women did not like the way they are portrayed, they would immediately react by not buying the product. Because women continue to buy products whose advertising is stereotyped, such advertisers conclude that stereotyped advertising is effective.

The facts, however, do not support this argument. Most advertisers are highly aware that numerous factors influence buyer behavior. They include: product quality, distribution, shelf space, packaging, and pricing. Advertising is only one of the many variables which marketers use to influence sales and, even there, consideration must be given to other elements of the communication decision, including competitive positioning, advertising weight, and media mix. Message content, and even more narrowly, the role played by stereotyping within the message, is only one of the factors of importance.

Women do buy products which employ sex-stereotyped advertising approaches. In some cases the marketing situation may be such that advertising content plays only a minor role in the buying decision. But even when content is an important element, the prevalence of stereotyped portrayals provides women only limited options. Indeed, women may be buying despite the advertising sex stereotyping, not because of it. They have little choice. In many product categories where women are major buyers, it is virtually impossible to find a major brand which does not employ a stereotyped approach. Yet women must buy detergents, household cleaners, and personal-care products. One option for the woman who objects to, or fails to identify with, the stereotyping is to base her purchase decision on factors other than advertising/product experience, distribution, or price, for example. Another option is to buy on the basis of a product claim that can be understood without necessarily accepting the stereotypes with which it is communicated. Or the woman might decide to select that brand whose advertising is least offensive to her. In any of these cases, however, it is not the stereotyped portrayal that is doing the selling, but exactly the opposite.

The important question that advertisers must examine is whether their products would sell as successfully, or even more successfully, if the advertising was to become progressive. While the data indicate that such approaches can improve communication effectiveness, evaluation of sales effects requires controlled market testing of alternative approaches. An advertiser who falls back on the stereotyping-sells argument, without testing alternatives, not only continues to contribute to a serious social problem, but may also be missing opportunities to enhance communications and sales effectiveness. It should be noted that advertisers also may be missing opportunities to communicate more effectively with male markets. Men, too, must buy products that employ sex-stereotyped advertising approaches which offend them. As more men participate in household buying and household tasks, progressive advertising presents opportunities in that market as well.

The advertiser who defends sex stereotyping on the basis that it sells thus typically ignores marketplace realities. In some cases what is denied is the importance of factors other than advertising content in generating sales. In other cases, what is ignored is the possibility that nonstereotyped advertising might sell even more effectively.

While there is reluctance on the part of advertisers to change stereotyped portrayals, they appear to be more amenable to reflect in their advertisements changes in occupational status than they are to reduce sexist, sexual portrayals. Nudity, seminudity, innuendo, double entendre, and explicit sexuality are being used with increasing frequency and intensity in advertising. Sexually explicit approaches are no longer limited to specially targeted products in specialized media, but have been extended to much more widely advertised products and to the mass media. They now are commonly used in fashion, cosmetic, beverage, tourism, and personal-care product advertisements. Apparently, many advertisers continue to believe sex sells, especially if the sex portrayed is a female.

Research shows that an attractive, sexy, or nude female model can increase the attention-getting power of an advertisement, especially among male audiences. Under some complex conditions that model may increase favorable evaluations of the brand and intentions to buy it. However, the evidence suggests that this effect occurs because both sexes prefer to look at people they perceive as attractive and sexy. It is the attraction factor of the model and her appropriateness to the advertised product that creates attention—not the nudity. In fact, as the sexuality of the model becomes more explicit, the risks to the advertiser increase. Sexually explicit portrayals, such as the use of nude models, can result in less favorable brand and manufacturer attitudes and inhibit brand learning. Moreover, the sexual portrayal that is rated favorably by one group is very likely to be considered unacceptable by another: there are significant differences in perception, both between sexes and within same-sex groups. Taken as a whole, the data indicate that attractive and sexy models can aid the advertiser, but the use of explicit, sexual approaches is dangerous and potentially counter-productive. Advertisers who ignore the warning signs and continue to use sexually explicit appeals, without careful research, may be producing advertisements which are ineffective or less than optimally effective.

Advertisers who use the sex-sells defense may be making a serious managerial error. However, the issue is not just managerial, it also has important public-policy implications. Advertising continues to exploit women's sexuality, demean them, objectify them, show violence and aggression against them, and cause widespread offense. Such advertisements should be unacceptable to any advertiser, no matter how effective the advertisement might be with some segment of the market. Healthy sexuality in advertising can be acceptable both from a managerial and societal point of view, but sexism and the exploitation of women cannot be condoned.

Research Does Not Indicate Problems. Another common argument in favor of continued reliance on stereotyped and sexist approaches is that the advertiser did some research on the advertisement, and no problems about role portrayal arose.

The major weakness with such a defense is that typically the research referred to consists of a few focus group sessions and, during those sessions, the moderator made no effort to elicit comments on the role portrayals in the advertisement. Not surprisingly, under those research conditions, the problems are not revealed. Rarely is advertising research designed to measure role-portrayal preferences or even to measure liking and disliking. Practitioners have traditionally considered these dimensions to be irrelevant to effectiveness. Bartos has shown, however, that the like/dislike dimension, as it applies to role portrayal, is an important component of effectiveness. She has concluded that the evidence is so strong that negative attitudes toward the advertisement may affect consumer attitudes toward the brand and company that:

> Until the hypothesis that advertising which consumers say "insults my intelligence" is proved to have no deleterious effect on brand image and credibility, we should proceed with caution.[8]

Unless research is designed to measure men and women's attitudes toward their portrayal, problems and opportunities will not be revealed. Such research, moreover, must be designed in such a way that the consumers' true attitudes are revealed, not merely those the advertiser hopes to find. Scott, who has analyzed the sources of bias in research about female consumers, has concluded that as long as advertising research is designed within a culturally biased view of women:

> Marketers, advertisers, and researchers alike, will receive from research on women results which are mere mirrors of existing marketing and advertising imagery, and reflections of their own cultural expectations.[9]

Until advertisers are willing to develop advertisements with more progressive approaches and submit those to testing alongside the stereotyped advertisements, they will by definition fail to test the real possibilities for new role portrayals. Stereotyped and sexist portrayals will continue simply because they are the only ones ever considered by the advertiser.

Protesters Are Not Typical People. Another common defense of sex stereotyping is to dismiss criticism as coming from an atypical and radical fringe.

An advertiser who thinks his advertising is in tune with the female consumer usually responds with anger and dismay when it becomes the target of criticism. The advertiser does not perceive the advertisement as offensive and does not understand why anyone else should. An alternative to listening to the criticism is to claim that the people objecting are extremists, prudes, or reformists who do not represent the wider public. While it is true that feminists (although not a lunatic fringe) are often among the most critical of advertising, this fact does not negate the validity of their complaints. Moreover, they often express views which have been shown by research to be much more widely shared by society.

Several years ago the female coauthor of this book had a conversation with an executive from a major detergent company about stereotyping in advertisements for laundry products. The executive informed her that, because she was a working, professional woman, her opinions were of no interest to him. He cared only about the attitudes of women who did four or more washes a week. When she protested that she did do that many washes in an average week, the executive seemed unable to deal with such discordant information, stared blankly, and withdrew from the conversation without a word.

A much more serious incident illustrating the unwillingness of some advertisers to listen to criticism occurred recently in Toronto. A feminist group was protesting against an advertisement running in one of the transit media. The advertisement showed a large picture of a partially clothed woman and was attempting to sell stereo equipment. The feminist group claimed that the portrayal of the woman was irrelevant to the advertised product, that the picture showed a great deal more of the woman's breasts than was appropriate in a public medium, and that the sexist headline in the advertisement contributed further to its offensiveness. When they presented their case to the transit group and its agency (who did agree to meet with them), the protesters brought with them a petition signed by two-thousand three-hundred men and women protesting the advertisement. They also brought an opinion from the advertising industry self-regulatory group that the advertisement in question violated the spirit of the Canadian self-regulatory guidelines on sex stereotyping in advertising.

What was striking about the occasion was the unwillingness of the advertising industry and transit groups to recognize that there was significant consumer concern about the advertisement. The petition was dismissed on the grounds that people who sign petitions are, by definition, atypical and not representative of public attitudes. The self-regulatory agency's statement was simply ignored, and the industry spokespeople resolutely took the position that they—the advertisers—saw nothing wrong with the advertisement. It is not the place here to comment on the validity of the protest or on the advertisers' decision to continue the advertisement. It is startling, however, to have observed how easily they were able to dismiss critics as unrepresentative. If meaningful changes are ever to be achieved, some advertisers need continual reminding that their critics are consumers too.

Achieving Change

This book has stressed that the implicit attitudes that produce stereotyped and sexist advertising are not only harmful to our society but are also harmful to advertising practice. In the authors' view this unconscious sexism on the part of advertisers is self-destructive: it produces advertising which is either ineffective or, at best, less than totally effective.

A cartoon which appeared in *Marketing* in January 1981 illustrates current industry attitudes very effectively. The picture shows an advertising agency creative director (male) returning a piece of paper to the copywriter. "Destereotyping the housewife can't be done overnight, Angela," the caption reads, "be a good kid and let her sing to her mop in this one, and I promise next time she can do something else with it."[10]

The challenge facing the advertiser is to respond to change today and to do so in ways which are managerially effective and socially responsible. That requires a willingness to listen to critics, to reexamine traditional advertising philosophies, and to submit new and potentially better advertising to testing. For many this will mean breaking out of old attitudes and beliefs to a new willingness to explore the implications of a changing consumer world. Attitude changes on the part of reluctant advertisers is a first step. The next step is to translate those new attitudes into new advertising concepts that will keep pace with social changes. Such advertising will contain new themes, new twists on old themes, and both new and old images. The following section examines the possible shape, form, and content of new and nonstereotyped advertising.

Sex Stereotyping and Advertising Creativity

Since advertising has defined gender-appropriate behavior and attitudes for decades and continually reinforces them, new creative strategies are needed to significantly change the stereotypes pervasive in the advertising media. Every advertiser, however, will not follow the steps proposed to eliminate sexist advertising. Some advertisers, undoubtedly, will continue to rely on the old defenses just reviewed, rather than change. Therefore, there is good reason for concern about the cumulative effects of sex stereotyping on men, women, and children in society. To approach reality in advertising's portrayal of the sexes, and thus significantly reduce these effects, the great majority of advertisers will have to change their thinking and their creative process.

Traditional and Outdated Stereotypes

The discouraging truth, confirmed by the content analyses which began this book, is that very little has actually changed. Presented here are a sampling of disguised, but nonetheless real, advertisements being shown on television and appearing in print. The advertisers are large and national in the case of the commercials and most of the print advertisements; the retail store advertisement is that of a major outlet in a large metropolitan city. Yet, as will be seen, most of the portrayals in these advertisements are as stereotyped, and in some cases as offensive, as the advertisements which have been provoking protest since the mid-1960s.

> In a recent commerical for a soft drink, a black woman serves her husband a pizza and a soft drink. A male voice-over talks about how well the soft drink goes with pizza.
>
> A woman is shown washing clothes with the advertised detergent. The clothes are those of her husband and son. She talks about how proud she and her whole family are of the way the detergent gets the men's clothes clean. A male voice-over states that the advertised product is best at cleaning tough dirt.
>
> A commercial for a household-cleaning product shows a woman cleaning in the kitchen and bathroom. A female voice-over sings about how wonderful it is to have the advertised product to clean with.

The characteristics of these stereotyped advertisements can be picked out easily. In these commercials what is portrayed is the typical pattern of the wife performing household chores to serve her husband and children (usually her male children). In the second advertisement the woman derives prestige, self-satisfaction, and love from having the cleanest clothes in town. The lack of realism in the rewards and delights of housework is shown even more clearly in the third commercial, where the woman is so happy to have found a good cleaner that she literally sings about it.

> In a commercial for a convenience food, a confused woman is unable to find the meat department in the supermarket. She has to ask the butcher where the meat products are sold. A male voice-over talks about the advertised product.
>
> A famous male comedian and an unidentified woman appear in a commercial for a household disinfectant. As he tells joke after joke and laughs at her strange behavior, she runs around the house with a rubber duck under her arm, spraying with the advertised product.

One woman says to another in an angry, shocked voice, "Are you going to let your daughter go without?" She then discusses with the other woman the advantages of the advertised brand of toothpaste. A male voice-over concludes the commercial.

The first of these recent commercials is the 1980s version of the stupid-housewife stereotype. The woman is too stupid to find the meat department, although she is standing right in front of it. In the second commercial the attempt to be humorous results in the housewife being portrayed as manic and moronic. The toothpaste commercial shows more intelligent women—but women are moved to anger and an almost bitter confrontation—over the choice of a toothpaste. The implication is that the woman who chooses an inadequate brand of toothpaste is failing in her duty to her child. Moreover, the commercial implies that it is perfectly proper for her friend to point out this failing.

A male announcer asks a woman to test the advertised brand of cleaner against her present brand. The woman defends her own brand, but reluctantly agrees to try the test. She discovers how wrong she's been for years, ashamedly confesses this to the announcer, and he lectures her on the advantages of the advertised brand.

This example shows the continued dominance of the male authority figure in commercials addressed to women. The woman discovers with the aid of a male expert that her years of experience cleaning up have all come to naught—she's been using the wrong cleaner all this time! While this is the most obvious of the advertisements in showing the use of the male authority figure, it is worth noting, that with the exception of the woman who sings about the advertised cleaner, all the voices of authority are male, because male voice-overs end every commercial.

A print ad for a woman's clothing chain shows a woman wearing harem pants, her legs spread from one side of the page to the other, with a facial expression as vulgar as one you would expect to find on the cover of a pornographic magazine. The headline announces, between her outspread legs, "We are having a big sale."

This is a vulgar, almost pornographic depiction of the woman as sex object. Curiously, the advertisement is trying to attract women, not men, to shop at the clothing store. Yet, even in advertising targeted to women, denigrating depictions of female sexuality are still employed.

Modifying the Portrayal

This collection of current advertising reinforces the traditional and outdated stereotypes of the past and misses the opportunity to communicate more effectively with the modern consumer. In most of these cases, however, it would be a relatively simple matter to modify the advertisements such that they were both less stereotyped and also better at communicating with the target audience. Many of these advertisements could be modified slightly to produce advertisements that are on target with the audience, faithful to the strategy intended by the advertiser, and at the same time modern and progressive. Generally, only a minor shift in creative emphasis is required.

The advertisements portraying housewives serve as the first examples. While women do most of the housework in our society, there is no need to portray them constantly as the givers of cleaning and cooking services to males. Advertising can serve the same brand strategies while showing women as sharers in, or recipients of, such services. In the soft-drink commercial, for example, it would have been possible for the husband to pour the soft drink while she served the pizza (or vice-versa). Or perhaps the husband could have been shown bringing the pizza home from the store while the wife served the drink. In the detergent advertisement the woman could easily have been washing her own clothing or her daughter's, instead of, or as well as, the clothing of the men in the household. Household cooking and cleaning advertisements might alternatively use a role-sharing or role-reversal approach. Instead of showing the wife performing traditional household tasks alone, commercials could show the husband participating in them or taking the lead in performing them. Research shows that women do not resent advertising that shows husbands cooperating in chores.

The advertisement with the singing housewife is an exaggerated portrayal of women's feeling about housework. Research shows that women are not ecstatic about cleaning: they want their homes to be clean, but the task itself is boring and often arduous. With modifications, in this case fairly major ones, the woman in this commercial could be shown appreciating the benefits of the product, but intelligently and with realistic ardor. Perhaps a less exaggerated portrayal would be even more effective in communicating the product's benefits.

The commercials that portray the woman as silly and stupid probably require major strategic changes. Studies have shown that women find this kind of portrayal insulting; they do not like to see advertisements that show them as personally unintelligent or that criticize their performance of household chores.

The advertisements which show women deferring to male authority could be altered slightly without major strategic changes required. Male announcers or male actors are commonly portrayed as the experts on household work. Research, however, shows that women feel that they do not require male authority to help them in their purchase decisions. Moreover, women consider themselves to be the experts on household matters. The time is therefore opportune to portray women in these authority roles and to use female voice-overs. However, when women (or men) are used as authorities, care should be taken not to portray them as interfering or critical of the housewife, as in the toothpaste advertisement. Women resent that kind of advice—whether given by a man or by a woman.

The print advertisement for the retail store would need an entirely new illustration to eliminate the sexist portrayal and to make it acceptable. This retailer seems to have lost sight of the store's customer. The sexual portrayal is highly inappropriate for a major retailer of clothing that sells to an adult female market. Overtly sexual portrayals of women always elicit controversy. When advertisements portray woman as sex objects, they are likely to cause strong negative reactions. The retailer might, more effectively, use a picture of an attractive female model without the explicit sexuality and innuendo.

These advertisements are similar in several respects. They are out of touch with their target markets; they use outdated and overused creative formulae; they reflect stereotypes which are demeaning and offensive—they are less effective in communicating than advertisements which would more accurately reflect changed societal roles—and most could be substantially improved without any departure from the intended advertising strategy.

Attempts to Change the Portrayal

Advertisements which rise above the outdated stereotypes are still few, although there are many advertisers who are now making attempts to do so. Many of today's advertisements do clearly attempt to incorporate an understanding of the changed market, but still fall far short of success. Here are some examples, again from disguised, but real and current advertising.

> A disposable diaper commercial shows a man talking to his young daughter while he diapers the new baby. His daughter is giving him advice on child care and discussing the merits of the advertised product. As they leave the room. she tells him that he would make a 'good mom'. The commercial ends with a male voice-over.

On the surface, this advertisement depicts a warm and loving attempt at role reversal—a man diapers the baby. But there are serious problems. The most subtle is that a small child is giving child-care advice to a grown man. The girl is shown as a knowledgeable mother-in-training, her father as a surprisingly ignorant adult (presumably he has never changed a diaper before). The major problem is most important: the child's final comment, ''you'd make a good mom'', changes the entire trust of the advertisement. Dad makes a good mom by diapering the baby, because it isn't really dad's role to perform such tasks. The surface message, that it is acceptable for a father to care for a baby, seems to break from the traditional in a way women will approve. But the more subtle messages in the advertisement reinforce stereotypes and are offensive to both sexes. A male can be portrayed as a good father or a good parent (rather than a good mother); this will be acceptable to both males and females. The implication, that caring for a child is a woman's job and that a man needs to be taught by a girl child to do it correctly, demeans both parents.

> A commercial for a disinfectant shows a husband and wife with their new baby. While the wife takes the child to bathe it, the husband sprays the nursery with the advertised product. The advertisement concludes with a male voice-over.

Role reversals in commercials have a great deal of potential for helping advertisers to break out of stereotyped portrayals, but they can only work when they carry the reversal through in all aspects of the advertisement. This example utilizes role-sharing as a solution to the problem and does so quite effectively. The advertisement shows the division of work without self-consciousness and makes no patronizing or obvious comment about it. Only the concluding male voice-over in this advertisement detracts somewhat from its progressive portrayal of the sexes.

> In a commercial for a dessert topping, the man cannot figure out how to use the spray can. His wife, laughing gently at his problem, shows him how to use the product. The commercial ends with a male voice-over.

This example is least effective in its use of role reversal. Although a man is shown working at preparing a meal, he is depicted as silly, inept, and in need of help from his wife in performing a simple task. When advertisers treat housewives as intelligent but insult the intelligence of the husbands instead, communication failure results. Humor research indicates that neither men nor women find it acceptable to see a man denigrated. Role reversals of this kind will alienate both the men and the women in the audience.

> A woman is shown working in an office. She is portrayed as an intelligent, hard-working person who has a headache because of the pressures of work. The commercial ends with a male voice-over.

This is one of the still rare commercials to show a woman working outside the home and to make her job the central focus of the advertisement. It is a positive attempt because the woman is neither portrayed as a secretary nor as a high-powered executive. By showing her working, but avoiding explicit mention of her occupation, it avoids two common pitfalls: showing the woman in a pink-collar job or turning her into an unrealistic superwoman. In the late 1970s a common portrayal was the superwoman who was an executive, a sex symbol, a wonderful housewife, and supermom. These portrayals, reaching so far beyond most women's expectations for themselves, created a kind of offensive stereotyping. Women do like to see themselves portrayed as achievers and as capable of multiple roles, but exaggeration or tokenism create difficulties. The headache-remedy commercial avoids these problems. The advertisement shows her headache to be the result of work pressures, rather than as a symptom of some elusive female ailment. The commercial does a good job at eliminating stereotypes. Unfortunately, the male announcer's voice detracts from the success; apparently even the working woman requires the voice of male authority.

> A print advertisement for a station wagon shows a large picture of a beautiful woman; the car is shown in the background. The headline says that the woman bought the wagon "out of wedlock". The copy has the woman saying that it is not necessary to have a husband and children to get a station wagon. Although she is a single woman, she hopes someday to load it up with kids.

This advertisement illustrates some of the problems advertisers can create when they try to target the new woman consumer, but have not fully understood what she is like. On the positive side the advertisement recognizes that women do control money, that they buy cars, that they are concerned about more than color and upholstery, and that they can make intelligent decisions. On the other hand, the advertiser or agency obviously lost its nerve and reverted to insulting and traditional stereotypes. The headline is an unfunny and offensive double entendre, and the copy speaks only of the single woman's aspirations to marry and have children. Thus, the detail of the advertisement actually detracts from the intended strategy.

> The commercial opens with a beautiful young woman wearing a skimpy bikini, reclining on a beach. She tells the viewers that she bought what there is of this skimpy suit on the Riviera and used the advertised credit card to pay for it. The commercial ends with a male voice-over.

> In a commercial for an after-bath beauty product, both male and female nudity are discretely shown. The woman is heard saying she wants to 'do it' again and again.

The last two commercials show attempts to find new ways to represent female sexuality and women's acceptance of it. Like many such advertisements, however, these fail to do so acceptably. The credit card commercial, on the plus side, shows a woman in control of her own money and with access to commercial credit. It is unfortunate that the advertiser could think of nothing else for her to spend her money on than a skimpy bikini and that the advertisement uses an explicitly sexual picture more likely to appeal to male than to female viewers. The commercial might have been more effective had the bathing-suit purchase been shown among a series of other products and services obtained with the card and if the sexuality had been portrayed less explicitly.

The beauty product commercial touches on a similar problem. Of course, women do use perfume to enhance their attractiveness and sexuality. One important motivation for buying fashion, beauty, and cosmetic products is to be more sexually attractive. However, evidence shows that advertisements that play on this motivation in a vulgar and provocative way are likely to alienate the majority of female consumers. Few advertisers have been able to find ways to portray the sexually attractive woman without lapsing into a vulgarity that many women find offensive.

These seven advertisements are laudable in at least one sense—all of the advertisements are trying to respond positively to change. However, they ultimately fail to do so as effectively as they might. In most cases the problem is not strategic, but creative. While the advertising strategy recognizes the new consumer, the creative execution does not follow through with conviction. Thus, the diaper commercial gives a mixed message about the value of fatherhood; the car advertisement tries to appeal to the single woman, and then insults her; the credit card and beauty-product commercials use creative approaches that women find insulting. It is not the basic strategies that are at fault so much as it is a failure of agency creative groups to fully understand and internalize the changes going on around them. The result is advertising that is neither traditional nor progressive, advertising which is therefore less than fully effective in communicating with the target audience.

Progressive Portrayals

It is recognized that advertising messages must employ stereotypes because stereotypes are a shorthand which helps to convey ideas and images quickly and clearly. Within the constraints of an advertising message, particularly a television commerical, the images used must conform closely to what the viewer will quickly recognize and accept as true. When there is little new and important functional information to be conveyed about the product, those user images are particularly important. Finding an effective way to get attention and to show the psychological rewards of product usage often requires use of an easily recognized stereotype.

However, that stereotype need be neither old-fashioned nor offensive. It is possible to create advertising that accepts the changes in society without apologizing for them, without explaining them away, without denigrating them, and without manipulating them. Such advertising can be simultaneously progressive in its view of the consumer, creative in expression of that view, and effective in presentation of the product. Some current advertisements which accomplish this successfully are:

> An advertisement for a throat remedy shows a man with a sore throat and uses a female voice-over to explain how the advertised brand will help him. (The commercial does not apologize for, nor explain, the reason for using a female voice-over that is authoritative.)

> A commercial for a cookie dough shows boys and girls participating in preparation of the cookies. (It makes no self-conscious explanation for the presence and competent participation of the boys.)

> A print advertisement shows two young, attractive women sharing lunch and the advertised beer. (It portrays women who are attractive, but not seductive. It makes no patronizing reference either about women drinking nor about the obvious friendship shown.)

> A credit card commercial shows a young woman who has moved from one city to another. During the move, her car has given her trouble. She has coped effectively by using the card for car repairs and hotel accommodation. (She is shown as intelligent, independent, and capable. She is not portrayed as lost without her credit card or overly dependent on it.)

It is unfortunate that the good examples are outnumbered so dramatically by the bad. Nonetheless, they illustrate that effective, progressive advertising is possible—when it respects both men and women, accepts change in traditional male and female roles as a matter of course, and ensures that every creative detail reinforces that central message. What is required is a reeducation of advertisers and their agencies about the new consumer and their internalization of a good understanding of that consumer. Together with willingness to experiment with and test new strategies and new creative approaches, advertisers and their agencies will be able to create advertisements and commercials that are both progressive and communicate effectively. From the good examples of modern advertising, this book draws a set of general principles that could help attempts to create successful 'new' advertising:

> Successful new advertising, like successful old advertising, remembers and understands its audience. It speaks to a specific market segment and does not attempt to be all things to all people.

> Successful new advertising recognizes that women have changed in dramatic ways. All women like to see themselves as achievers, to see women in the work force, to view the housewife as an authority in her own right, to see women who are independent and intelligent about financial matters and product choice. But tokenism and the superwoman stereotype are both unacceptable.

Successful new advertising recognizes that overtly sexual or seductive portrayals are perceived as insulting, denigrating, and result in consumer turnoff. Portraying a woman as attractive and sexy, if done carefully and tested, can be acceptable.

Successful new advertising is produced by agencies and advertisers who are aware of, have accepted, and have internalized the research data about the changing consumer and his and her response to advertisements.

Successful new advertising denigrates neither men nor women. Both sexes are shown as intelligent and capable. Other approaches alienate both sexes.

Successful new advertising allows women to be portrayed in authoritative roles—as voice-overs, as manufacturers' representatives, and as product representatives.

Successful new advertising recognizes that every element in the execution of the advertisement must be consistent with the changed strategy. What is otherwise a good new advertisement can be undermined by the use of an inappropriate authority figure, by an improper voice-over, or by stereotyped acting, voice inflection, and body language.

If the new advertising is self-conscious, heavy handed, or patronizing, the consumer will be aware of this. For example, role reversals must be shown as natural. It is inappropriate to comment on them explicitly or to try to explain them away.

Finally, successful new advertising is advertising that is submitted to careful pretesting by the advertiser, using methods sensitive enough to elicit the target segment's perceptions of the role portrayals employed.

Notes

1. R.S. Alexander, "Some Aspects of Sex Differences in Relation to Marketing," *Journal of Marketing* (10 October 1947):166.

2. *Advertising and Women: A Report on Advertising Portraying or Directed to Women* (New York: National Advertising Review Board, 1975).

3. Gurprit S. Kindra, "Comparative Study of the Roles Portrayed by Women in Print Advertising," *Proceedings of the 1982 ASAC Conference* (Ottawa: Canadian Association for the Administrative Sciences, 1982), p. 115.

4. Rosemary Scott, *The Female Consumer* (New York: John Wiley, 1976), p. 265.

5. Maureen Callan, "Male Chauvinism in Ads Rolls On," *Advertising Age,* 4 October 1976, pp. 75–76.

6. Lorraine Baltera, "Sex Stereotyping Belongs in Ads, Retailers Advised," *Advertising Age,* 4 October 1976, p. 44.

7. John Fisher, "Despite What the CAAB Says About Women in Advertising, Those Rotten Sex-Stereotyped Ads Sell, Dammit!," *Marketing,* 6 March 1978, p. 17.

8. Rena Bartos, *The Moving Target: What Every Marketer Should Know about Women* (New York: The Free Press, 1982), p. 276.

9. Rosemary Scott, *The Female Consumer,* p. 314.

10. Cartoon, *Marketing,* 19 January 1981, p. 4.

Bibliography

Aaron, Dorothy. *About Face: Toward a Positive Image of Women in Advertising*. Toronto, Ontario: Ontario Status of Women Council, 1975.

Adler, Marilyn, and Brouder, Kathleen. "Real Market Muscle." *Advertising Age,* 28 April 1980, p. S-4.

"Ads Glorifying Career 'Superwomen' Can Alienate Full-Time Homemakers." *Marketing News,* 1 May 1981, pp. 1–2.

Advertising Advisory Board. Annual Meeting/Seminar news media briefing material, Toronto, 26 November 1980.

Advertising Advisory Board. *Canadian Code of Advertising Standards.* Toronto, 1980.

Advertising Standards Council. Interview with Evelyn Crandell, 13 January 1978.

"Adwomen See Gains in How Ads Portray Women." *Advertising Age,* 11 September 1978, p. 54.

Akamatsu, Muriel. *Liberating the Media: Advertising.* Freedom of Information Center Report. No. 290. School of Journalism. Columbia, Miss.: University of Missouri, 1972.

Alder, Richard P., et al. *The Effects of Television Advertising on Children.* Lexington, Mass.: Lexington Books, D.C. Heath and Company, 1980.

Alexander, R.S. "Some Aspects of Sex Differences in Relation to Marketing." *Journal of Marketing,* October 1947, pp. 158–169.

Alexander, M. Wayne and Judd, Ben. "Do Nudes in Ads Enhance Brand Recall?" *Journal of Advertising Research,* February 1978, pp. 47–50.

Allen, Donna. "Testimony Concerning the Socio-Economic Influence of Advertising." *The Corporate Influence on the Images of Women in Advertising.* Transcript of public hearings held by the Interfaith Center on Corporate Responsibility, New York, 7 and 8 October 1976.

Allen, M. "Appreciation of 'Male Derisive,' 'Female Derisive,' and 'Sexual' Cartoons in Frustrated and 'Fulfilled' Housewives—The Use of Humor as a Coping Mechanism." Paper delivered at the Western Psychological Association Meeting. Vancouver, B.C., 1969.

Alpert, Mark I. "Sex Roles, Sex and Stereotyping in Advertising; More Questions than Answers." In *Advances in Consumer Research,* ed. W. Wilkie, pp. 73–77. Ann Arbor: Association for Consumer Research, 1979.

Alter, Jennifer. *The Female Culture.* Toronto: Vickers & Benson Ltd., 1976.

Alter, Jennifer, "Working Women 'Neglected'—Study." *Advertising Age,* 4 May 1981, p. 50.

Alter, Jennifer. "Working Women Now More Attractive—Y&R." *Advertising Age,* 11 January 1982, p. 76.

Anderson, Beverlee B. "Working Women Versus Non-Working Women: A Comparison of Shopping Behaviors." In *1972 Combined Proceedings,* ed. B.W. Becker and H. Becker, pp. 355–359. Chicago: American Marketing Association, 1973.

Andrew, Gunner, et al. *Rhetoric and Ideology in Advertising.* Stockholm: Liber-Forlay, 1978.

Association of Canadian Advertisers. "Speech Notes." Notes for Seminar Presentation, Toronto, 1980.

Atkin, Charles K. *Effects of Television Advertising on Children: Second Year Experimental Evidence.* Report No. 2. East Lansing, Michigan: Michigan State University, 1975.

Atkin, Charles K., and Miller, M. Mark. "The Effects of Television on Children: Experimental Evidence." Paper presented to the Mass Communications Division of the International Communication Association, Chicago, April 1975.

"B & B Study Says Males Domestic." *Advertising Age,* 6 October 1980, p. 53.

"BBDO Discovers Women Have It Tougher." *Advertising Age,* 26 November 1979, p. 3.

"Backpage." *Ms,* October 1980, p. 108.

Bailyn, Lotte. "Mass Media and Children: A Study of Exposure Habits and Cognitive Effects." *Psychological Monographs* 73 (1959):1.

Baker, Michael J., and Churchill, Gilbert A., Jr. "The Impact of Physically Attractive Models on Advertising Evaluations." *Journal of Marketing Research,* November 1977, pp. 538–555.

Baltera, Lorraine. "Sex Stereotypes Belong in Ads, Retailers Advised." *Advertising Age,* 4 April 1976, p. 44.

Baltera, Lorraine. "The Working Woman's Come a Long Way, But Can Advertising Find Her?" *Advertising Age,* 22 July 1974, p. 2.

Banks, Sharon. "An Attributional Experiment on Sexual Biases Toward Salespeople." In *1979 Educators' Conference Proceedings,* ed. N. Beckwith et al., pp. 431–434. Chicago: American Marketing Association, 1979.

Barcus, F. Earle. "Saturday Children's Television: A Report of TV Programming and Advertising on Boston Commerical Television." Prepared for Action for Children's Television, 1971.

Barcus, F. Earle. "Television in the Afternoon Hours." Prepared for Action for Children's Television, 1975.

Barcus, F. Earle. "Weekend Commercial Children's Television." Prepared for Action for Children's Television, 1975.

Bardwick, Judith M., and Schumann, Suzanne I. "Portrait of American Men and Women in TV Commercials." *Psychology* 4 (1967):18–23.

Barron, Frank. *Creativity and Psychological Health*. New York: Van Nostrand, 1963.

Barry, Thomas E. "Children's Television Advertising: The Attitudes and Opinions of Elementary School Guidance Counselors." *Journal of Advertising,* Fall 1978, pp. 9–16.

Bartos, Rena. "The Moving Target: The Impact of Women's Employment on Consumer Behavior." *Journal of Marketing,* July 1977, pp. 31–37.

Bartos, Rena. *The Moving Target: What Every Marketer Should Know About Women*. New York: The Free Press, 1982.

Bartos, Rena. "What Every Marketer Should Know About Working Women." *Harvard Business Review,* May–June 1978, pp. 73–85.

Beasley, Maurine, and Silver, Sheila. *Women in Media: A Documentary Source Book*. Washington, D.C.: Women's Institute for Freedom of the Press, 1977.

Belkaoui, Ahmed, and Belkaoui, Janice J. "A Comparative Analysis of the Roles Portrayed by Women in Print Advertisements, 1958, 1970, 1972." *Journal of Marketing Research,* May 1976, pp. 168–172.

Bell, Howard H. "Self-Regulation by the Advertising Industry." *California Management Review,* Spring 1974, pp. 59–63.

Bennie, Fay. "Differences of Recall, Perceived Effectiveness, Invitation, and Behavioral Intention Measures of Radio Commercials with Respect to Male and Female Voices and Product Relatedness." Master's thesis, Guelph, Ontario: University of Guelph, 1979.

Berger, Emmanuel M. "The Relation Between Expressed Acceptance of Self and Expressed Acceptance of Others." *Journal of Abnormal and Social Psychology* 47 (1952):778–782.

Berger, John. *Ways of Seeing*. London: British Broadcasting Corporation and Baltimore: Penguin Books, 1972.

Berk, Richard, and Berk, Sarah F. "A Simultaneous Equation Model for the Division of Household Labor." Revision of paper presented at 1976 annual meeting of the American Academy for the Advancement of Science, 1976.

Bernstein, Sid. "How Research Finds the Obvious." *Advertising Age,* 22 August 1977, p. 16.

Berryman, Cynthia L., and Eman, Virginia A., eds. *Communications, Language and Sex*. Rowley, Mass.: Newbury House, 1980.

Bettinger, C.O., III, and Dawson, Lyndon. "Changing Perspectives in Advertising: The Use of 'Liberated' Feminine Life-Style Themes." In *Developments in Marketing Science,* ed. H.S. Gitlow and E.W. Wheatley, pp. 111–114. Coral Gables, Florida: Academy of Marketing Science, 1979.

Beuf, Ann H. "Doctor, Lawyer, Household Drudge." *Journal of Communication,* Spring 1974, pp. 142–145.

Beuf, Ann H. "Television Commercials as Socializing Agents." In *Advances in Consumer Research: Proceedings of the Annual Conference of the Association For Consumer Research,* 1976, pp. 3, 528–530.

Boddewyn, J.J. "Decency and Sexism in Advertising: An International Survey of their Regulation and Self-Regulation." Report prepared for the International Advertising Association, Inc., New York, 1979.

Bonoma, Thomas V., and Felder, Leonard C. "Nonverbal Communication in Marketing: Toward a Communication Analysis." *Journal of Marketing Research,* May 1977, pp. 169–180.

"Brief to the CRTC Task Force on Sex-Role Stereotyping." Toronto, 23 June 1980.

Britt, Steuart Henderson. "The Use and Misuse of Sex in Advertising." In *Sharing for Understanding,* ed. G.E. Miracle, pp. 163–165. East Lansing, Michigan: American Academy of Advertising, 1977.

Britton, Helen Ann. "The Role of Women in Television: Avenues for Change." Paper presented at the 4th Annual Telecommunication Policy Research Conference, Airlie, Virginia, April 21–24, 1976.

Bruce, Elaine. "To See Ourselves as Others See Us: Television and Its Portrayal of the Female." Montreal: Sir George Williams University, 1974.

Buchanan, Lauranne, and Reid, Leonard N. "Women Role Portrayals in Advertising Messages as Stimulus Cues: A Preliminary Investigation." In *Sharing for Understanding,* ed. G.E. Miracle, pp. 99–104. East Lansing, Michigan: American Academy of Advertising, 1977.

Burns, William J., and Tyler, John D. "Appreciation of Risqué Humor in Male and Female Repressors and Sensitizers." *Journal of Clinical Psychology* 32 (1976):315–321.

Busby, Linda Jean. "Mass Media Research Needs: A Media Target for Feminists." *The University of Michigan Papers in Women's Studies,* June 1974, pp. 9–29.

Busby, Linda Jean. "Sex-Role Research on the Mass Media." *Journal of Communication,* Autumn 1975, pp. 107–131.

Busch, Paul, and Bush, Ronald F. "Women Contrasted to Men in the Industrial Salesforce: Job Satisfaction, Values, Role Clarity, Performance, and Propensity to Leave." *Journal of Marketing Research,* August 1978, pp. 438–447.

Butler-Paisley, Matilda, et al. *Image of Women in Advertisements: A Preliminary Study of Avenues for Change.* Stanford, California: Stanford University Institute of Communication Research, 1975.

"C & W Discovers a 'New Breed' of Husband." *Advertising Age,* 10 November 1980, p. 84.

Callan, Maureen. "Male Chauvinism in Ads Roles On." *Advertising Age,* 4 October 1976, pp. 75–76.

Canadian Radio-Television and Telecommunications Commission, *Attitudes of Canadians Toward Advertising on Television*. Hull, Quebec: Supply and Services Canada, 1978.

Canadian Radio-Television and Telecommunications Commission. *Sex-Role Stereotyping in Advertising: A Summary of Concerns*. Toronto, 1980.

Cantor, Joanne R. "What is Funny to Whom? The Role of Gender." *Journal of Communication,* Summer 1976, pp. 164–172.

Cantor, Muriel G. "Women and Public Broadcasting." *Journal of Communication,* Winter 1977, pp. 14–19.

Carney, Landis, and Ross, John W.H. "Humor and Its Relation to Other Personality Traits." *The Journal of Social Psychology* 4 (1933): 156–175.

Carruthers, Margaret. "Women Who Complain About the Portrayal of Women in Advertising." Unpublished research paper, College of Family and Consumer Studies. Guelph, Ontario: University of Guelph, 1977.

Cartoon. *Marketing,* 19 January 1981, p. 4.

Cattin, Philippe, and Jain, Subhash C. "Content Analysis of Children's Commercials." In *Educators' Conference Proceedings,* ed. N. Beckwith et al., pp. 639–644. Chicago: American Marketing Association, 1979.

Chapman, Anthony J., and Gadfield, Nicholas J. "Is Sexual Humor Sexist?" *Journal of Communication,* Summer 1976, pp. 141–153.

Cheles-Miller, Pamela. "Reaction to Marital Roles in Commercials." *Journal of Advertising Research,* August 1975, pp. 45–49.

Chestnut, Robert W.; Lachance, Charles C.; and Lubitz, Amy. "The 'Decorative' Female Model: Sexual Stimuli and the Recognition of Advertisements." *Journal of Advertising,* Fall 1977, pp. 11–14.

"Children on the Block." *The Globe and Mail,* 9 March 1981 p. 6.

Christenson, Susan, and Swanson, Alice. "Women and Drug Use: An Annotated Bibliography." *Journal of Psychedelic Drugs,* October-December 1974, pp. 371–414.

Chulay, Cornell, and Francis, Sara. "The Image of the Female Child on Saturday Morning Television Commercials." Paper presented at the annual meeting of the International Communication Association, 17–20 April 1974, New Orleans, Louisiana.

Churchill, Gilbert A., Jr.; and Moschis, George P. "Television and Interpersonal Influences on Adolescent Consumer Learning." *Journal of Consumer Research,* June 1979, pp. 23–35.

Clearinghouse for Research on Children's Advertising, *Children and Advertising: A Bibliography*. New York: Council of Better Business Bureaus, June 1978.

Coates, Colby. "Growth of Working Women a Boon to NBC Radio." *Advertising Age,* 7 August 1978, p. 32.

Code Authority of the National Association of Advertisers. "The Code and Personal Products Advertising: A Chronology." *Code News,* April 1977.

Comstock, George, et al. *Television and Human Behavior.* New York: Columbia University Press, 1978.

Courtney, Alice E., and Lockeretz, Sarah W. "Woman's Place: An Analysis of the Roles Portrayed by Women in Magazine Advertisements." *Journal of Marketing Research,* February 1971, pp. 92–95.

Courtney, Alice E., and Whipple, Thomas W. "Advertising Implications of Gender Differences in the Appreciation of Humor." In *Advances in Advertising Research and Management,* ed. S.E. Permut, pp. 103–106. East Lansing, Michigan: American Academy of Advertising, 1979.

Courtney, Alice E., and Whipple, Thomas W. *Canadian Perspectives On Sex Stereotyping in Advertising.* Ottawa: Advisory Council on the Status of Women, June 1978.

Courtney, Alice E., and Whipple, Thomas W. *Reaction to Traditional Versus Liberated Portrayals of Women in TV Advertising.* Toronto, Ontario: Canadian Advertising Advisory Board, 1976.

Courtney, Alice E., and Whipple, Thomas W. *Sex Stereotyping in Advertising: An Annotated Bibliography.* Cambridge, Mass.: Marketing Science Institute, 1980.

Courtney, Alice E., and Whipple, Thomas W. "Strategies for Self-Regulation of Sex Stereotyping in Advertising: The Canadian Experience." In *Advances in Advertising Research and Management,* ed. S.E. Permut, pp. 146–149. East Lansing, Michigan: American Academy of Advertising, 1978.

Courtney, Alice E., and Whipple, Thomas W. "Women in T.V. Commercials." *Journal of Communication,* Spring 1974, pp. 110–118.

Cowan, Ruth Schwartz. "Two Washes in the Morning and a Bridge Party at Night: The American Housewife Between the Wars." *Women's Studies* 3 (1976):147–171.

Cragi, Sheri. "TV Day: Just One Thing Missing." *Marketing,* 10 November 1980, pp. 3, 57.

Cross, Larry, and Jeffries-Fox, Suzanne. "What Do You Want to be When You Grow Up, Little Girl?" In *Home and Hearth: Images of Women in the Mass Media,* ed. G. Tuchman et al., pp. 240–265. New York: Oxford University Press, 1978.

Culley, James D., and Bennett, Rex. "Selling Women, Selling Blacks." *Journal of Communication,* Autumn 1976, pp. 160–174.

Cunningham, Isabella C.M., and Cunningham, William H. "Standards for Advertising Regulation." *Journal of Marketing,* October 1977, pp. 92–97.

Curley, Bill. "Fight for the 'Right' to Stereotype." *Marketing,* 4 August 1980.

Dabney, Dick. "Wimps?" *The Toronto Star,* 18 January 1982, p. A 10.

Danielenko, R. "Do Sexy Ads Sell Products?" *Product Management,* February 1974, pp. 21–26.

Davis, Harry L. "Decision Making Within the Household." *Journal of Consumer Research,* March 1976, pp. 241–260.

Davis, Harry L. "Dimensions of Marital Roles in Consumer Decision Making." *Journal of Marketing Research,* May 1970, pp. 168–177.

Decision Marketing Research Limited. *Women in Canada.* 2d ed. Ottawa, Ontario: Office of Co-Ordinator, International Women's Year Secretariat, 1976.

Defleur, Melvin L. "Children's Knowledge of Occupational Roles and Prestige: Preliminary Report." *Psychological Reports,* December 1963, pp. 57–74.

Defleur, Melvin. "Occupational Roles as Portrayed on Television." *Public Opinion Quarterly,* Spring 1964, pp. 57–74.

Defleur, Melvin L., and Defleur, Lois B. "The Relative Contribution of Television as a Learning Source for Children's Occupational Knowledge." *American Sociological Review,* October 1967, pp. 777–789.

Derrick, Frederick W., and Wolken, John D. "Comment on 'The Decorative Female Model: Sexual Stimuli and the Recognition of Advertisements', by Chestnut, Lachance and Lubitz, *Journal of Advertising,* 6, no. 4, Fall, 1977, pp. 11–14," *Journal of Advertising,* Spring 1978, pp. 57–60.

Dispenza, Joseph E. *Advertising the American Woman.* Cincinnati, Ohio: Cebco/Standard Publishing, 1975.

Dominick, Joseph R., and Rauch, Gail. "The Image of Women in Network TV Commercials." *Journal of Broadcasting,* Summer 1972, pp. 259–265.

Doolittle, John, and Pepper, Robert. "Children's TV Ad Content: 1974." *Journal of Broadcasting,* Spring 1975, pp. 131–142.

Douglas, Susan P. "Cross National Comparisons and Consumer Stereotypes: A Case Study of Working and Non-Working Wives in the U.S. and France." *Journal of Consumer Research,* June 1976, pp. 12–20.

Douglas, Susan P. "Do Working Wives Read Different Magazines from Non-Working Wives?" *Journal of Advertising,* Winter 1977, pp. 40–43.

Douglas, Susan P. "Working Wife and Non-Working Wife as a Basis for Market Segmentation." Report Number 75–114. Cambridge, Mass.: Marketing Science Institute, 1975.

Douglas, Susan, and Urban, Christine D. "Life-Style Analysis to Profile Women in International Markets." *Journal of Marketing,* July 1977, pp. 46–54.

DuBrin, Andrew J., and Fram, Eugene H. "Coping With Women's Lib." *Sales Management,* June 1971, pp. 20–21.

Duker, Jacob M., and Tucker, Lewis, R., Jr. "'Women's Lib-ers' Versus Independent Women: A Study of Preferences for Women's Roles in Advertisements." *Journal of Marketing Research,* November 1977, pp. 469–475.

Embree, Alice. "Media Images 1: Madison Avenue Brainwashing—the Facts." In *Sisterhood is Powerful,* ed. R. Morgan, pp. 175–191. New York: Vintage Books, 1970.

Equal Opportunities Commission and Marketing Consultancy and Research Services. *Adam and Eve: A Study of the Portrayal of Women in Advertising.* Manchester: University of Lancaster, April, 1982.

"European Women Hit Mass Media Image of Being Robots, Sex Objects." *Advertising Age,* 9 August 1971, p. 26.

Faber, Ronald, and Ward, Scott. *Consumer Socialization of Young Children: A Bibliography.* Cambridge, Mass.: Marketing Science Institute, June 1976.

Farrell, Warren. "Masculine Images in Advertising." In *The Liberated Man, Beyond Masculinity: Freeing Men and Their Relationships with Women,* ed. W. Farrell. N.Y.: Random House, 1974.

Ferber, Marianne A., and Birnbaum, Bonnie G. "Rejoiner." *Journal of Consumer Research,* December 1977, pp. 183–184.

Ferber, Marianne A., and Birnbaum, Bonnie G. "The 'New Home Economics': Retrospects and Prospects." *Journal of Consumer Research,* June 1977, pp. 19–28.

Ferber, Marianne A., and Lowry, Helen M. "Women's Place: National Differences in the Occupational Mosaic." *Journal of Marketing,* July 1977, pp. 23–30.

Ferber, Robert, and Lee, Lucy Chao. "Husband-Wife Influence in Family Purchasing Behavior." *Journal of Consumer Research* 1 (1974):43–56.

Feshbach, Seymour. "Mixing Sex With Violence—A Dangerous Alchemy." *New York Times,* 3 August 1980, p. D 29.

Fisher, John. "Despite What the CAAB Says About Women in Advertising, Those Rotten Sex-Stereotyped Ads Sell, Dammit!" *Marketing,* 6 March 1978, p. 17.

Fisk, George, and Venkatesh, Allad. "Marketing Implications of the Women's Movement." Paper presented at the Macromarketing Services Seminar, August 1977, at University of Colorado.

Fox, Harold W., and Renas, Stanley R. "Stereotypes of Women in the Media and Their Impact on Women's Careers." *Human Resource Management,* Spring 1977, pp. 28–31.

Francher, J. Scott. "It's the Pepsi Generation . . . , Accelerated Aging and the Television Commercial." *International Journal of Aging and Human Development,* Summer 1973, pp. 245–255.

Franzwa, Helen H. "Working Women in Fact and Fiction." *Journal of Communication,* Spring 1974, pp. 104–109.

Friedan, Betty. *The Feminine Mystique.* New York: W.W. Norton and Company, 1963.

Friedman, Leslie J. *Sex Role Stereotyping in the Mass Media: An Annotated Bibliography.* New York and London: Garland Publishing, Inc., 1977.

Fruch, Terry, and McGhee, Paul E. "Traditional Sex-Role Development and Amount of Time Spent Watching Television." *Developmental Psychology* 11 (1975):109.

Garbarino, James, and Turner, Susan. "Television and Vocational Socialization." Cambridge, Mass.: Marketing Science Institute, 1975.

Gentry, James W., and Doering, Mildred. "Masculinity-Femininity Related to Consumer Choice." In *Contemporary Marketing Thought,* ed. B.A. Greenburg and D.N. Bellenger, pp. 423–427. Chicago: American Marketing Association, 1978.

Gerbner, George, and Signorielli, Nancy. "Women and Minorities in Television Drama, 1969–1978." Research Report, Annenberg School of Communications. Philadelphia: University of Pennsylvania, 1979.

Gerponer, George. "The Dynamics of Cultural Resistance." In *Home and Hearth: Images of Women in the Mass Media,* ed. G. Tuchman et al., pp. 46–50. New York: Oxford University Press, 1978.

"'GH' Readers Say Ads Turning Them Away From TV." *Advertising Age,* 29 January 1979, p. 65.

Gillespie, Karen R. "The Status of Women in the Department and Specialty Stores: A Survey." *Journal of Retailing,* Winter 1977–1978, pp. 17–32.

Gitter, George A., and Coburn, B. Casey. "Trustworthiness: The Effect of Respondent's Sex, and Communicator's Occupational Title, Organizational Affiliation, and Sex." *CRC Report No. 82.* Boston: Boston University, 1981.

Goffman, Erving. *Gender Advertisements.* Cambridge, Mass.: Harvard University Press, 1979.

Goldberg, P.A. "Are Women Prejudiced Against Women?" *Trans-Action* 5 (1968):28–30.

Grant, Don. "Women's Lib Dialogue Tells Adfolk: Mend Ad Implications." *Advertising Age,* 25 January 1977, p. 3.

Green, Robert, and Cunningham, Isabelle. "Feminine Role Perception and Family Purchasing Decisions." *Journal of Marketing Research,* August 1975, pp. 325–332.

Greenberg, Bradley S., et al. *Life on Television—Content Analysis of U.S. TV Drama.* Norwood, N.J.: Albex, 1980.

Groch, Alice S. "Generality of Response to Humor and Wit in Cartoons, Jokes, Stories and Photographs." *Psychological Reports,* October 1974, pp. 835–838.

Groch, Alice S. "Joking and Appreciation of Humor in Nursery School Children." *Child Development* 45 (1974):1098–1102.

Grote, Barbara, and Cvetkovich, George. "Humor Appreciation and Issue Involvement." *Psychoanalytic Science* 39 (1972):199–200.

Hansen, L. Sunny. "We Are Furious (Female) But We Can Shape Our Own Development." *Personnel and Guidance Journal,* October 1972, pp. 87–93.

Henneke, B.G., and Dummit, E.S. *The Announcers Handbook.* New York: Holt, Rinehart and Winston, 1959.

Hennessee, Judith Adler, and Nicholson, Joan. "NOW Says: Commercials Insult Women." *New York Times Magazine,* 28 May 1972, p. 12.

Herold, Don. *Humor in Advertising and How to Make it Pay.* New York: McGraw-Hill, 1963.

Heslop, Louise A., and Courtney, Alice E. "Advertising and Women." In *Marketplace Canada: Some Controversial Dimensions,* ed. S.J. Shapiro and L.A. Heslop. Toronto: McGraw-Hill Ryerson, 1982.

Holbrook, Morris B. "More on Content Analysis in Consumer Research." *Journal of Consumer Research,* December 1977, pp. 176–177.

Holtzman, Eleanor. "New Generation's Advent Means Marketing Change." *Marketing News,* 19 May 1978, p. 8.

Honey, Maureen. "Images of Women in the *Saturday Evening Post* 1931-1936." *Journal of Popular Culture,* Fall 1976, pp. 352–358.

Howard, John A., and Tinkahm, Spencer F. "A Framework for Understanding Social Criticism of Advertising." *Journal of Marketing,* October 1971, pp. 2–7.

Ingrassia, Barbara Combes, and Matlin, Margaret W. "An Analysis of the Roles of Women and Men in Television Commercials." Geneseo: State University of New York, 1976.

Jennings-Walstedt, Joyce; Geis, Florence L.; and Brown, Virginia. "Influence of Television Commercials on Women's Self-Confidence and Independent Judgment." *Journal of Personality and Social Psychology* 38 (1980):203–210.

Joesph, W. Benoy. "The Credibility of Physically Attractive Communicators: A Review." *Journal of Advertising,* Summer 1982, pp. 15–24.

Johnson, Barbara, P. "Women Marketers, Their Aspirations and Frustrations." *Product Marketing,* January 1977, pp. 17–22.

Johnson, D.K., and Satow, K. "Consumers Reactions to Sex in TV Commercials." In *Advances in Consumer Research,* ed. H.K. Hunt, pp. 411–414. Chicago: Association for Consumer Research, 1978.

Joyce, Mary, and Guilitnan, Joseph. "The Professional Woman: A Potential Market Segment for Retailer." *Journal of Retailing,* Summer 1978, pp. 57–70.

Jones, Norma, et al. *The Media in Montana: Its Effects on Minorities and*

Women. Report to the U.S. Commission on Civil Rights. Helena, Montana: Montana Advisory Committee, 1976.

"Judge Not." *Globe and Mail,* 11 August 1980, p. 6.

Kambouropoulou, P. "Individual Differences in the Sense of Humor." *American Journal of Psychology* 37 (1926):268-278.

Kanner, Bernice. "BBDO Finds What Women Think of Men—Wow!" *Advertising Age,* 4 June 1979, p. 3.

Kanner, Bernice. "C & W Finds Males Doing More at Home." *Advertising Age,* 14 July 1980, p. 84.

Kanter, Donald L. "Psychological Considerations in Advertising Regulation." *California Management Review,* Spring 1974, pp. 73-79.

Kanuk, Leslie. "Women in Industrial Selling: How Great Are the Career Opportunities? How Well Are They Performing?" *Journal of Marketing,* January 1978, pp. 87-91.

Kanungo, Rabindra N., and Johar, Jotindar S. "Effects of Slogans and Human Model Characteristics in Product Advertisements." *Canadian Journal of Behavioural Science,* April 1975, pp. 127-138.

Kanungo, Rabindra N., and Pang, Sam. "Effects of Human Models on Perceived Product Quality." *Journal of Applied Psychology* 57 (1973): 172-178.

Kaplan, Harriet E. "Ratings of Television Commercials in Saskatoon." 1975." Report for the University Women's Club, Saskatoon, Saskatchewan, 1975.

Kassarjian, Harold H. "Content Analysis in Consumer Research." *Journal of Consumer Research,* June 1977, pp. 8-18.

Katz, Bill. "The Influence of Lifestyle on Women's Media Habits." *Marketing,* 21 April 1980, pp. 20-28.

Kelly, Patrick J., and Solomon, Paul J. "Humor in Television Advertising." *Journal of Advertising,* Summer 1975, pp. 31-35.

Kelly, Patrick J.; Solomon, Paul J.; and Burke, Marion. "Male and Female Responses to Women's Roles in Advertising." In *Sharing for Understanding,* ed. G.E. Miracle, pp. 94-98. East Lansing, Michigan: American Academy of Advertising, 1975.

Kerin, Roger A.; Lundstrom, William J.; and Sciglimpaglia, Donald. "Women in Advertisements: Retrospect and Prospect." *Journal of Advertising,* Summer 1979, pp. 37-42.

Key, Mary Ritchie. "Linguistic Behavior of Male and Female." *Linguistics* 88 (1972):15-31.

Kilbourne, Jean. *Killing Us Softly: Advertising Images of Women.* Film. Available from Jean Kilbourne, P.O. Box 385, Cambridge, Mass.

Kindra, Gurprit, S. "Comparative Study of the Roles Portrayed by Women in Print Advertising." *Proceedings of the 1982 ASAC Conference,* p. 115. Ottawa: Canadian Association for the Administrative Sciences, 1982.

Klassen, Rita. "A Content Analysis of Women's Roles in TV Ads in Ontario." Undergraduate thesis, Department of Consumer Studies, Guelph, Ontario: University of Guelph, 1977.

Klemesrud, J. "On Madison Avenue, Women Take Stand in Middle of the Road." *New York Times,* 3 July 1973, p. 28.

Komisar, Lucy. "The Image of Women in Advertising." In *Women in Sexist Society,* ed. V. Gornick and B. Moran, pp. 207–217. New York: Basic Books, 1972.

Kovacs, Midge. "New Magazines (and ads) Show New Attitude Toward Women." *Advertising Age,* 13 March 1972, pp. 41–42.

Kovacs, Midge. "Women Simply Don't Recognize Themselves in Many Ads Today." *Advertising Age,* 12 June 1972, p. 48.

Kramer, Cheris. "Women's Speech: Separate But Unequal?" *Quarterly Journal of Speech* 60 (1974):14–20.

Kunnes, Richard. "Poly-drug Abuse: Drug Companies and Doctors." *American Journal of Orthopsychiatry,* July 1973, pp. 530–532.

LaLonde, Marc. "Stereotypes Changing the Image of Women." In *Toward Equality for Women,* pp. 28–29. Toronto: Status of Women Canada, 1979.

Lazer, William, and Smallwood, John E. "The Changing Demographics of Women." *Journal of Marketing,* July 1977, pp. 14–22.

Leavitt, Clark. "Even Housewives Prefer Working Women in TV Ads." *Marketing News,* 19 May 1978, p. 10.

Leff, Laurel. "TV Ads Reflect Power of Working Women." *Wall Street Journal,* 30 October 1980, p. 25.

Leiss, W.; Kline, S.; Hachman, A.; and Wright, J. *Advertising, Human Needs, and Resource Conservation.* Ottawa: Department of Consumer and Corporate Affairs, September, 1976.

Levenson, H. et al. "Are Women Still Prejudiced Against Women?" *Journal of Psychology* 89 (1975):67–71.

Levere, Jane. "Portrayal of Women in Ads Defended by Top Ad Women." *Editor and Publisher,* June 1974, p. 11.

Levinson, D., and Huffman, P. "Traditional Family Ideology and Its Relation to Personality." *Journal of Personality,* 23 (1955):251–273.

Levinson, Richard M. "From Olive Oyl to Sweet Poly Purebread: Sex Role Stereotypes and Televised Cartoons." *Journal of Popular Culture,* Winter 1975, pp. 561–572.

Liebert, Robert M., and Poulos, Roberta Wicks. "Television and Personality Development: The Socializing Effects of an Entertainment Medium." In *Child Personality and Psychopathology: Current Topics,* vol. 2. New York: John Wiley, 1975.

Liebert, Robert M., and Poulos, Roberta Wicks. "TV for Kiddies: Truth, Goodness and Beauty and a Little Bit of Brainwash." *Psychology Today,* November 1972, p. 123.

Linden, Fabian. "Woman, Worker." *Across the Board,* March 1977, pp. 25–27.

Lorenzo, Benet. "Sex: An Effective Sales Pitch or a Sellout in Women's Golf?" *The Plain Dealer,* 19 August 1982, p. 2-E.

Losco, Jean, and Epstein, Seymour. "Humor Preferences as a Subtle Measure of Attitudes Toward the Same and Opposite Sex." *Journal of Personality* 43 (1975):321–334.

Lovenheim, Barbara. "Voiceovers: They are Invisible Salesmen." *Advertising Age,* 23 July 1979, pp. 21–22.

Lull, James T.; Hanson, Catherine A.; and Marx, Michael J. "Recognition of Female Stereotypes in TV Commercials." *Journalism Quarterly,* Spring 1977, pp. 153–157.

Lundstrom, William J., and Sciglimpaglia, Donald. "Sex Role Portrayals in Advertising." *Journal of Marketing,* July 1977, pp. 72–79.

Lynch, Merrin D., and Hartman, Richard C. "Dimensions of Humor in Advertising." *Journal of Advertising Research,* August 1968, pp. 39–45.

MacCoby, Eleanor E., and Wilson, William C. "Identification and Observational Learning from Films." *Journal of Abnormal and Social Psychology,* July 1957, pp. 76–78.

Madden, Thomas J., and Weinberger, Marc G. "The Effects of Humor on Attentions in Magazine Advertising." Working paper WP 89–19. Amherst, Mass.: University of Massachusetts, 1981.

"Males Don't Like New Women: DDB." *Advertising Age,* 20 October 1980, p. 60.

Manes, Audrey L., and Melnyk, Paula. "Televised Models of Female Achievement." *Journal of Applied Social Psychology,* October 1974, pp. 365–374.

Mankiewicz, Frank, and Swerdlow, Joel. *Remote Control: Television and the American Life.* New York: New York Times Books, Inc., 1978.

Mannes, M. "Television: The Splitting Image." *Saturday Review,* 14 November 1970, p. 668.

Mannes, M. "Women are Equal, But . . ." In *Current Thinking and Writing,* ed. J. Bachelor, R. Henry and R. Salisburg. New York: Appleton-Century-Crofts, 1969.

Mant, Andrea, and Darroch, Dorothy Broom. "Media Images and Medical Images." *Social Science Medicine,* November–December 1975, pp. 613–618.

Marecek, Jeanne, et al. "Women as TV Experts: The Voice of Authority?" *Journal of Communication,* Winter 1978, pp. 159–168.

Markiewicz, Dorothy. "Effects of Humor on Persuasion." *Sociometry* 37 (1974):407–422.

Marschalk, Co., Inc. *A Study to Evaluate Consumer Attitudes Towards Television Commercials.* New York, 1980.

Mason, Ken O.; Cxajka, John L.; and Aber, Sara. "Change in U.S. Womens' Sex-Role Attitudes 1964–1974." *American Sociological Review,* August 1976, pp. 573–596.

Mazis, Michael B., and Beuttenmuller, Marilyn. "Attitudes Toward Women's Liberation and Perception of Advertisements." In *Advances in Consumer Research,* pp. 428–434. Chicago: Association for Consumer Research, 1973.

McArthur, Leslie Zebrowitz, and Resko, Beth Gabrielle. "The Portrayal of Men and Women in American TV Commercials." *Journal of Social Psychology,* December 1975, pp. 209–220.

McCall, Suzanne H. "Meet the Workwife." *Journal of Marketing,* July 1977, pp. 55–65.

McCarthy, E. Jerome, and Shapiro, Stanley J. *Basic Marketing,* 2nd ed. Georgetown, Ontario: Irwin-Dorsey Ltd., 1979.

McGhee, Paul E. "Sex Differences in Children's Humor." *Journal of Communication,* Summer 1976, pp. 176–189.

McGhee, Paul E. "Television As A Source of Learning Sex Role Stereotypes." Paper presented at the Biennial Meeting of the Society for Research in Child Development, 10 April 1975, Denver, Colorado.

McKee, Christine; Corder, Billie F.; and Haizlip, Thomas. "Psychiatrists Response to Sexual Bias in Pharmaceutical Advertising." *American Journal of Psychiatry,* November 1974, pp. 1273–1275.

McKnight, Diane. "Sexism in Advertising: What's a Nice Girl Like You . . ." *Technology Review,* May 1974, pp. 20–21.

McMahan, Harry W. "No Joking; Humor Sells!" *Advertising Age,* 29 December 1950, p. 19.

Meringoff, Laurene, ed. *Children and Advertising: An Annotated Bibliography.* New York: Advertising Review Unit, Council of Better Business Bureaus, 1980.

"Miami Poster Fires Up Locals." *Advertising Age,* 3 December 1979, p. 44.

Miles, Betty. *Channeling Children: Sex Stereotyping in Prime-Time TV.* Princeton, N.J.: Women on Words and Images, 1975.

Miles V. "The New Woman: Her Importance to Marketing." *International Advertiser,* Fall 1971, pp. 13–16.

Miller, G.R., and McReynolds, M. "Male Chauvinism and Source Competence: A Research Note." *Speech Monographs* 40 (1973):154–155.

Miller, Judith, and Margulies, Leah. "The Media: New Images of Women In Contemporary Society." In *The American Woman: Who Will She Be?,* ed. M. McBee and K.A. Blade, pp. 95–105. Beverly Hills, California: Glencoe Press, 1974.

Miller, M. Mark, and Reeves, Byron. "Dramatic TV Content and Children's Sex-Role Stereotypes." *Journal of Broadcasting,* Winter 1976, pp. 35–49.

Mills, J. "Fighting Sexism on the Airwaves." *Journal of Communication,* Spring 1974, pp. 150–155.

Millum, Trevor. *Images of Women: Advertising in Women's Magazines.* Totowa: N.J.: Rowman and Littlefield, 1975.

Morrison, B.J., and Sherman, R.C. "Who Responds to Sex in Advertising." *Journal of Advertising Research,* April 1972, pp. 15–19.

Mosher, Elissa Henderson. "Portrayal of Women in Drug Advertising: A Medical Betrayal." *Journal of Drug Issues,* Winter 1976, pp. 72–78.

Moyer, Mel S., and Banks, John C. "Industry Self-Regulation: Some Lessons from the Canadian Advertising Industry." In *Problems in Canadian Marketing,* ed. D.N. Thompson. Chicago: American Marketing Association, 1977.

"NARB Polls Public on Ad Gripes." *Advertising Age,* 23 March 1981, p. 42.

National Advertising Review Board. *Advertising and Women; A Report on Advertising Portraying or Directed to Women,* New York, N.Y., 1975.

National Commission on the Observance of International Women's Year. "To Form a More Perfect Union." *Justice for American Women.* Washington, D.C.: U.S. Government Printing Office, 1976.

"New Breed' Husbands are Happy Cookers: New Research Identifies Five Subsegments of Married Men." *Marketing News,* 14 November 1980, p. 7.

Niffenger, Philip B., and Wise, Rose N. "Female Use of Cosmetics: Is Feminist Orientation Important in the Decision to Purchase?" In *Developments in Marketing Science,* ed. H.S. Gitlow and E.W. Wheatley, pp. 20–24. Coral Gables, Florida: Academy of Marketing Science, 1979.

O'Bryant, Shirley L., and Corder-Bolz, Charles R. "The Effects of Television on Children's Steretyping of Women's Work Roles." *Journal of Vocational Behavior,* April 1978, pp. 233–243.

O'Connor, John J. "Sex Roles in Advertising Draw Hisses and Boos." *Advertising Age,* 12 March 1979, p. 48.

O'Donnell, William J., and O'Donnell, Karen J. "Update: Sex-role Messages in TV Commercials." *Journal of Communication,* Winter 1978, pp. 156–158.

Ogilvy, David. *Confessions of an Advertising Man.* New York: Dell, 1963.

O'Kelly, Charlotte G. "Sexism in Children's Television." *Journalism Quarterly,* Winter 1974, pp. 722–723.

O'Kelly, Charlotte C., and Bloomquist, Linda Edwards. "Women and Blacks on T.V." *Journal of Communication,* Autumn 1976, pp. 179–184.

O'Neil, Nora; Schoonover, Sandra; and Adelstein, Lisa. "The Effect of TV Advertising on Children's Perceptions of Roles." Summarized in "Children and Television: A Report to Montessori Parents," ed.

Thomas W. Whipple. Mimeographed. Cleveland, Ohio: Cleveland State University, 1980.

Ontario Ministry of Transportation and Communication. "Communications in Ontario," Toronto, 1973.

Orkin, Dick, and Berdis, Bert. "The Funny Thing About Some Commercials." *Broadcasting,* 20 June 1977, p. 16.

Patzer, Gordon L. "A Comparison of Advertising Effects: Sexy Female Communicator vs. Non-Sexy Female Communicator." In *Advances in Consumer Research,* ed. J.C. Olson, pp. 359–364. Ann Arbor: Association for Consumer Research, 1980.

Peck, Ellen. "Advertising Unite! Strike a Blow Against Motherhood." *Advertising Age,* 24 January 1972, p. 33.

Perloff, Richard M.; Brown, Jane Delano; and Miller, M. Mark. "Mass-Media and Sex-Typing: Research Perspectives and Policy Implications," *International Journal of Women's Studies* 5 (1982):265–273.

Pesch, Marina, et al. "Sex Role Stereotypes on the Airwaves of the Eighties." Paper delivered at the Annual Convention of the Eastern Communication Association, Pittsburgh, 23–25 April 1981.

Peterson, Robert A., and Kerin, Roger A. "The Female Role in Advertisements: Some Experimental Evidence." *Journal of Marketing,* October 1977, pp. 59–63.

Pheterson, G.I.; Kiesler, S.R.; and Goldberg, P.A. "Evaluation of the Performance of Women as a Function of Sex, Achievement and Personal History." *Journal of Personality and Social Psychology* 19 (1971): 114–118.

Pingree, Suzanne. "The Effects of Nonsexist Television Commercials and Perceptions of Reality on Children's Attitudes about Women." *Psychology of Women Quarterly,* Spring 1978, pp. 262–276.

Pingree, Suzanne; Hawkins, Robert Parker; Butler, Matilda; and Paisley, William. "A Scale for Sexism." *Journal of Communication,* Autumn 1976, pp. 193–200.

Poe, Alison. "Active Women in Ads." *Journal of Communication,* Autumn 1976, pp. 185–192.

"Portrayal of Women in TV Commercials: Has the Controversy had any Real Impact?" *Listening Post,* February 1978, p. 8.

Pralle, Michael E. "Survey Dispels Myths About Growing Dual-Earner Market." *Marketing News,* 16 May 1980, p. 17.

Prather, Jane, and Fidell, Linda S. "Sex Differences in the Content and Style of Medical Advertisements." *Social Science and Medicine,* January 1975, pp. 23–26.

Priest, Robert F., and Wilhelm, Paul G. "Sex, Marital Status and Self-Actualization as Factors in Appreciation of Sexist Jokes." *The Journal of Social Psychology* 92 (1974):245–249.

Pyke, S.W., and Stewart, J.D. "This Column is About Women: Women and Television." *Ontario Psychologist,* December 1974, pp. 66–69.

Ravinal, Rosemary. "Study of Sex-Roles Portrayals Shows that Viewers Are Likely to Turn Off to Stereotypes in TV Commercials." In *Newsrelease,* pp. 1–2. New York: Advertising Research Foundation 28 February 1979.

Reeves, Byron, and Greenburg, Bradley S. "Children's Perceptions of Television Characters." Paper presented at the 50th Annual Meeting of the Association for Education in Journalism, p. 30. College Park, Maryland, July 31–August 4, 1976.

Reid, Leonard N., and Soley, Lawrence C. "Another Look at the "Decorative" Female Model: The. Recognition of Visual and Verbal Ad Components." In *Current Issues and Research in Advertising,* ed. J.H. Leigh and C.R. Martin, Jr., pp. 123–133. Ann Arbor: The University of Michigan, 1981.

Resjskend, G., and Moss, B. "Image of Women in Television Commercials." Brief presented to The Advertising Standards Council, Toronto, 1974.

Reynolds, Fred D.; Crasky, Melvin R.; and Wells, William D. "The Modern Feminine Life-Style." *Journal of Marketing,* July 1977, pp. 38–45.

Roberts, Mary Lou, and Wortzel, Lawrence H. "New Life-Style Determinants of Women's Food Shopping Behavior." *Journal of Marketing,* Summer 1979, pp. 28–39.

Roberts, Mary Lou, and Wortzel, Lawrence H. "Wives' Employment and Shopping Goals as Determinants of Information Gathering Strategies for Food Purchasing and Preparation." In 1979 Educators' Conference Proceedings, ed. N. Beckwith et al., pp. 220–225. Chicago: American Marketing Association, 1979.

Roberts, Mary Lou, and Koggan, Perri B. "How Should Women Be Portrayed in Advertisement?—A Call for Research." In *Advances in Consumer Research,* ed. W. Wilkie, pp. 66–72. Ann Arbor: Association for Consumer Research, 1979.

Robinson, John P. "The 'New Home Economics': Sexist, Unrealistic, or Simply Irrelevant?" *Journal of Consumer Research,* December 1977, pp. 178–181.

Rozhon, Tracie. "Racy Ads Do An End Run Around Network Censors." *The Plain Dealer,* 7 December 1980, p. 16–17.

Scanzoni, John. "Changing Sex Roles and Emerging Directions in Family Decision Making." *Journal of Consumer Research,* December 1977, pp. 185–188.

Scheibe, Cyndy. "Sex Roles in Television Commercials." *Journal of Advertising Research,* February 1979, pp. 23–27.

Schneider, Kenneth C. "Sex Roles in Television Commercials: New Dimensions for Comparison." *Akron Business and Economic Review,* Fall 1979, pp. 20–24.

Schneider, Kenneth C., and Schneider, Sharon Barich. "Trends in Sex Roles in Television Commercials." *Journal of Marketing,* Summer 1979, pp. 79–84.

Schoonover, Sandra L. "Voice-Over Effectiveness: An Examination of Gender Differences." Master's thesis, Cleveland State University, 1979.

Schuetz, Stephen, and Sprafkin, Joyce N. "Spot Messages Appearing Within Saturday Television Programs." In *Home and Hearth: Images of Women in the Mass Media,* ed. G. Tuchman et al., pp. 69–77. New York: Oxford University Press, 1978.

Sciglimpaglia, Donald; Belch, Michael A.; and Cain, Richard F., Jr. "Demographic and Cognitive Factors Influencing Viewers Evaluations of 'Sexy' Advertisements." In *Advances in Consumer Research,* ed. W. Wilkie, pp. 62–65. Ann Arbor: Association for Consumer Research, 1979.

Scott, Rosemary. *The Female Consumer.* New York: John Wiley, 1976.

Seaman, Debbie. "Spokesmen Spread the Retailers' Word." *Advertising Age,* 27 April 1981, pp. S–34—S–35.

Seidenberg, Robert. "Advertising and Abuse of Drugs." *New England Journal of Medicine* 28 (1972):789–790.

Seidenberg, Robert. "Drug Advertising and Perception of Mental Illness." *Mental Hygiene,* January 1971, pp. 21–31.

Seidenberg, Robert. "Images of Health, Illness and Women in Drug Advertising." *Journal of Drug Issues,* Summer 1974, pp. 226–267.

Sexton, Donald F., and Haberman, Phyllis. "Women in Magazine Advertisements." *Journal of Advertising Research,* August 1974, pp. 41–46.

"Sexy Alaskan Tour Ad Draws Heated Reaction." *Advertising Age,* 12 March 1979, p. 48.

Shama, Avraham, and Coughlin, Maureen. "An Experimental Study of the Effectiveness of Humor in Advertising." In *1979 Educators' Conference Proceedings,* ed. N. Beckwith et al., pp. 249–252. Chicago: American Marketing Association, 1979.

Sharits, Dean, and Lammers H. Bruce. "Men Fill More TV Sex Roles." *Marketing News,* 3 September 1982, p. 1.

Silverstein, Arthur, and Silverstein, Rebecca. "The Portrayal of Women in Television Advertising." *Federal Communications Bar Journal* 27 (1974):71–98.

Slatton, Yvonne L. "The Role of Women in Sport as Depicted in Advertising in Selected Magazines, 1900–1968." Ph.D. dissertation, University of Iowa, 1971.

Sloan, Pat. "Women WAP Wanton Ads." *Advertising Age,* 15 February 1982, p. 3.

Smith, George Horsley, and Engel, Rayme. "Influence of a Female Model on Perceived Characteristics of an Automobile." *Proceedings of the 76th Annual Convention of the American Psychological Association,* 1968, pp. 681–682.

Sosanie, Arlene K., and Szybillo, George J. "Working Wives: Their General Television Viewing and Magazine Readership Behavior." *Journal of Advertising,* Spring 1978, pp. 5–13.

Sprafkin, Joyce M., and Liebert, Robert M. "Sex-typing and Children's Television Preferences." In *Home and Hearth: Images of Women in the Mass Media,* ed. G. Tuchman et al., pp. 228–239. New York: Oxford University Press, 1978.

Stanley, Nancy E. "Federal Communications Law and Women's Rights: Women in the Wasteland Fight Back." *Hastings Law Journal* 23 (1971):15–53.

Steadman, Major. "How Sexy Illustrations Affect Brand Recall." *Journal of Advertising Research,* March 1969, pp. 15–19.

Stemple, Diane, and Tyler, Jane E. "Sexism in Advertising." *American Journal of Psychoanalysis,* Fall 1974, pp. 271–273.

Sternglanz, Sarah H., and Serbin, Lisa A. "Sex Role Stereotyping in Children's Television Programs." *Development Psychology* 10 (1974): 710–715.

Sternthal, Brian, and Craig, Samuel C. "Humor in Advertising." *Journal of Marketing,* October 1973, pp. 12–18.

Stewart, Jennifer. "Functions of Women in Ads Is to Sell the Product." *Marketing News,* 21 April 1978, p. 13.

Stimson, Gerry V. "The Message of Psychotropic Ads." *Journal of Communication,* Summer 1975, pp. 153–160.

Stimson, Gerry. "Women in a Doctored World." *New Society,* May 1975, pp. 265–267.

Stone, Vernon A. "Attitudes Toward Television Newswomen." *Journal of Broadcasting,* Winter 1973–1974, pp. 49–61.

Streicher, Helen White. "The Girls in the Cartoons." *Journal of Communication,* Spring 1974, pp. 125–129.

Strober, Myra H. "Wives' Labor Force Behavior and Family Consumption Patterns." *American Economic Review, Papers and Proceedings of the 89th Annual Meeting of the American Economic Association,* February 1977, pp. 410–417.

Strober, Myra H., and Weinberg, Charles B. "Working Wives and Major Family Expenditures." *Journal of Consumer Research,* December 1977, pp. 141–147.

Strong, Edward C. "Prisoner of Sex in Advertising." In *Advances in Con-*

sumer Research, ed. W. Wilkie, pp. 78–81. Ann Arbor: Association for Consumer Research, 1979.

Stuteville, John R. "Sexually Polarized Products and Advertising Strategy." *Journal of Retailing,* Summer 1971, pp. 3–13.

Surlin, Stuart H. "Differences in Socially Responsible Behavior by Male and Female Advertising Executives." In *Sharing for Understanding,* ed. G.E. Miracle, pp. 77–80. East Lansing, Michigan: American Academy of Advertising, 1977.

Surlin, Stuart H. "Sex Differences in Socially Responsible Advertising Decisions." *Journal of Advertising,* Summer 1978, pp. 36–39.

Swan, John E.; Futrell, Charles M.; and Todd, John T. "Same Job—Different Views: Women and Men in Industrial Sales." *Journal of Marketing,* January 1978, pp. 92–98.

Task Force on Women and Advertising. *Women and Advertising: Today's Messages—Yesterday's Images?* Toronto: Canadian Advertising Advisory Board, 1977.

Tavris, Carol, and Jayaratue, Toby. "How do You Feel About Being A Woman: The Results of a *Redbook* Questionnaire." Reprint McCall Publishing Co., 1972.

Terry, Roger L., and Ertel, Sarah L. "Exploration of Individual Differences in Preference for Humor." *Psychological Reports,* June 1974, pp. 1030–1037.

The Advertising Standards Authority. *Annual Report, 1974–1975.* London, 1975.

The Advertising Standards Authority. *ASA Case Report 77.* London, 1981.

The Advertising Standards Authority. *"Herself Appraised", The Treatment of Women in Advertisements.* London: 1982.

The Advertising Standards Authority. *Women in Advertisements, ASA Case Report 38.* London, 1978.

"The Bum's Rush in Advertising." *Time,* 1 December 1980, p. 75.

"The Image of Women in Television: An Annotated Bibliography." In *Home and Hearth: Images of Women in the Mass Media,* ed. G. Tuchman et al., pp. 273–299. New York: Oxford University Press, 1978.

Thomas, Barbara. "Ad Needn't Tell What She's Like (She Knows)." *Marketing News,* 21 April 1978, p. 13.

Toronto Women's Media Committee. "Study of the Image of Women in Toronto Area Television Commercials." Toronto, 1973.

Tucher, W.T. "A Long Day of Discrepant Behavior." In *Marketing: 1776–1976 and Beyond,* ed. K.L. Bernhardt, pp. 351–353. Chicago: American Marketing Association, 1976.

"TV Ads Sexual Offensiveness Depends on Appropriateness, Audience, Other Factors." *Marketing News,* 24 March 1978, p. 7.

"TV Commercials Dominated by Men, S&G Study Shows." *Advertising Age,* 11 November 1974, p. 22.

UNESCO. *Women in the Media.* Paris, 1980.

Venkatesan, M., and Losco, Jean. "Women in Magazine Ads: 1959–1971." *Journal of Advertising Research,* October 1975, 49–54.

Venkatesh, Alladi. "Changing Roles of Women—A Life Style Analysis." *Journal of Consumer Research,* September 1980, pp. 189–197.

Venkatesh, Alladi. "Changing Roles of Women—Some Empirical Findings with Marketing Implications." In *Contemporary Marketing Thought,* ed. B.A. Greenburg and D.N. Bellenger, pp. 417–422. Chicago: American Marketing Association, 1971.

Ventura, Charlene. "Ad Liberation: The Feminist Impact." *Sybil-Child* 1 (1975):37–54.

Verna, Mary Ellen. "The Female Image in Children's TV Commercials." *Journal of Broadcasting,* Summer 1975, pp. 301–309.

Wagner, Louis C., and Banos, Janis D. "A Woman's Place: A Follow-up Analysis of the Roles Portrayed by Women in Magazine Advertisements." *Journal of Marketing Research,* May 1973, pp. 213–214.

Ward, Scott. *Consumer Socialization.* Cambridge, Mass.: Marketing Science Institute, January 1974.

"Warn Australia Shops About Sex in Ads." *Advertising Age,* 1 August 1977, p. 55.

Warren, Denise. "Commercial Liberation." *Journal of Communication,* Winter 1978, pp. 169–173.

Warwick, Welsh & Miller, Inc. *Study of Consumer Attitudes Toward TV Programming and Advertising.* New York, 1981.

Weinberger, Marc G.; Petroshius, Susan M.; and Westin, Stuart A. "Twenty Years of Women in Magazine Advertising: An Update." In *1979 Educators' Conference Proceedings,* ed. N. Beckwith et al., pp. 373–377. Chicago: American Marketing Association, 1979.

Wells, William D.; Leavitt, Clark; and McConville, Maureen. "A Reaction Profile for TV Commercials." *Journal of Advertising Research,* December 1971, pp. 11–18.

"While Marketers Strive to Pinpoint the New Woman, Enterprising Women are Finding their Way in Marketing Field, AMA Session Learns." *Marketing News,* 25 February 1977, p. 1.

Whipple, Thomas W., and Courtney, Alice E. "How Men and Women Judge Humor: Advertising Guidelines for Action and Research." In *Current Issues and Research in Advertising,* ed. J.H. Leigh and C.R. Martin, Jr., pp. 43–56. Ann Arbor: The University of Michigan, 1981.

Whipple, Thomas W., and Courtney, Alice A. "How to Portray Women in TV Commercials, *Journal of Advertising Research,* April 1980, pp. 53–59.

Whipple, Thomas W., and Courtney, Alice E. "Male and Female Differences in Response to Nonsensical Humor in Advertising." In *Adver-*

tising 1980: Voice of a Nation at Work, ed. S.E. Permut, pp. 71–74. East Lansing, Michigan: American Academy of Advertising, 1980.

Whipple, Thomas W., and Courtney, Alice A. "Social Consequences of Sex Stereotyping in Advertising." In *Future Directions for Marketing,* ed. G. Fisk et al., pp. 332–350. Cambridge, Mass.: Marketing Science Institute, 1978.

Whittaker, J. "Sex Differences and Susceptibility to Interpersonal Persuasion." *Journal of Social Psychology* 66 (1965):91–94.

Whittaker, Susan, and Whittaker, Ron. "Relative Effectiveness of Male and Female Newscasters." *Journal of Broadcasting,* Spring, 1976, pp. 177–183.

Wight, Robin. *The Day the Pigs Refused to be Driven to Market.* London: Hart-Davis, MacGibbon, 1972.

Willett, Roslyn. "Do Not Stereotype Women—An Appeal to Advertisers." *Journal of Home Economics,* October 1971, pp. 549–551.

Wilson, R. Dale, and Moore, Noreen K. "The Role of Sexually-Oriented Stimuli in Advertising: Theory and Literature Review." In *Advances in Consumer Research,* ed. W. Wilkie, pp. 55–61. Ann Arbor: Association for Consumer Research, 1979.

Window Dressing on the Set: Women and Minorities in Television. Washington, D.C.: United States Commission on Civil Rights, 1977.

Wise, Gordon L.; King, Allan L.; and Merenski, J. Paul. "Reactions to Sexy Ads Vary With Age." *Journal of Advertising Research,* August 1974, pp. 11–16.

Witkowski, Terrence H. "An Experimental Comparison of Women's Self Image." In *New Marketing for Social and Economic Progress,* ed. R.C. Curhan, pp. 431–434. Chicago: American Marketing Association, 1975.

Wolheter, Maralinda, and Lammers, H. Bruce. "An Analysis of Roles in Print Advertisements Over a 20-year Span: 1958–1978." In *Advances in Consumer Research,* ed. J.C. Olson, pp. 760–761. Ann Arbor: Association for Consumer Research.

"Women, Kids Vulnerable to TV Ads, Adams Says." *Advertising Age,* 22 November 1971, pp. 61–62.

"Women in Advertising." *Marketing Research Society Newsletter,* April 1980.

Women in the Wasteland Fight Back; a Report on the Image of Women Portrayed in TV Programming. Washington, D.C.: National Organization for Women, National Capital Area Chapter, 1972.

Woodside, Arch G., and Motes, William H. "Husband and Wife Perceptions of Marital Roles in Consumer Decision Processes for Six Products." In *1979 Educators' Conference Proceedings,* ed. N. Beckwith et al., pp. 214–219. Chicago: American Marketing Association, 1979.

"Working Wives Become Major Marketing Force." *Advertising Age,* 5
    April 1976, p. 34.
"Working Women Reject Stereotyped Ad Roles." *Advertising Age,* 14
    February 1977, p. 62.
Wormley, Wallace. "Images of Women in Media Advertising." *Cable-
    lines,* 11 November 1974, pp. 4–5.
Wortzel, Lawrence H. *The Young Adult Consumer: An Introduction and
    Overview.* Report No. 77–118. Cambridge, Mass.: Marketing Science
    Institute, 1977.
Wortzel, Lawrence H., and Frisbie, John M. "Women's Role Portrayal
    Preferences in Advertisements: An Empirical Study." *Journal of Mar-
    keting,* October 1974, pp. 41–46.
Yalch, Richard, and Elmore-Yalch, Rebecca. "Segmentation and Stereo-
    types: An Investigation of Sex Differences in Response to Advertising
    Messages." In *1979 Educators' Conference Proceedings,* ed. N. Beck-
    with et al., pp. 253–257. Chicago: American Marketing Association,
    1979.
Zillman, Dolf, and Stocking, S. Holly. "Putdown Humor." *Journal of
    Communication,* Summer 1976, pp. 154–163.

Index

About the Authors

Alice E. Courtney is associate professor of marketing in the Faculty of Administrative Studies, York University, Toronto. She received the D.B.A. from the Harvard Business School. Her articles on sex stereotyping in advertising have appeared in several books and professional journals, including the *Journal of Marketing Research, Journal of Advertising Research,* and *Journal of Communication.* Dr. Courtney is a leading expert in Canada on how to improve advertising's portrayal of women.

Thomas W. Whipple is professor of marketing at the James J. Nance College of Business Administration, Cleveland State University. He received the Ph.D. from the State University of New York at Buffalo. His work on the effectiveness and social consequences of advertising, product planning, and marketing research has appeared in a number of books and journals, including the *Journal of Marketing, Journal of Marketing Research, Journal of Advertising Research, Journal of Retailing,* and *Journal of Communication.*